Working with Students with Disabilities

D0841440

Like no other book available, *Working with Students with Disabilities: A Guide for School Counselors* provides comprehensive coverage of school counselors' roles in special education and working with students with disabilities, and connects that coverage to both the ASCA National Model and CACREP standards.

In *Working with Students with Disabilities*, school counselors will find thoughtful analyses of the legal and regulatory basis for many of the practices in special education, including an overview of pertinent laws including the Individuals with Disabilities Education Improvement Act and Section 504 of the Rehabilitation Act. They'll gain an in-depth understanding of the leadership role that school counselors should play in supporting students, teachers, and families, and they'll also come away with an understanding of the common challenges—such as bullying, cyberbullying, and successful transitioning from high school to adult life—to which students with disabilities may be more vulnerable, as well as less common challenges such as behavioral difficulties, autism spectrum disorders, and many more.

Theresa A. Quigney, PhD, is an associate professor of special education at Merrimack College in North Andover, Massachusetts. Prior to moving into higher education, she had been both a teacher and supervisor of special education. She has written professional publications, made professional presentations, completed research investigations, and been involved in service activities and grant-related pursuits.

Jeannine R. Studer, EdD, is professor emerita at the University of Tennessee. Dr. Studer was previously a high school counselor in Sandusky, Ohio, and an assistant/associate professor at Heidelberg University in Tiffin, Ohio, and California State University–Stanislaus.

Working with Students with Disabilities

A Guide for School Counselors

Theresa A. Quigney
Jeannine R. Studer

Routledge
Taylor & Francis Group

NEW YORK AND LONDON

First published 2016
by Routledge
711 Third Avenue, New York, NY 10017

and by Routledge
2 Park Square, Milton Park, Abingdon, Oxon, OX14 4RN

Routledge is an imprint of the Taylor & Francis Group, an informa business

Library of Congress Cataloging in Publication Data
Quigney, Theresa A.
    Working with students with disabilities : a guide for school counselors;
    Theresa A. Quigney, Jeannine R. Studer.
        pages   cm
    Includes bibliographical references and index.
    1. Students with disabilities–Counseling of–United States.   2. Educational
    counseling–United States.   I. Studer, Jeannine R.   II. Title.
    LC4031.Q54   2016
    371.910973–dc23   2015027348

ISBN: 978-0-415-74318-1 (hbk)
ISBN: 978-0-415-74319-8 (pbk)
ISBN: 978-1-315-81382-0 (ebk)

Typeset in Minion
by Out of House Publishing

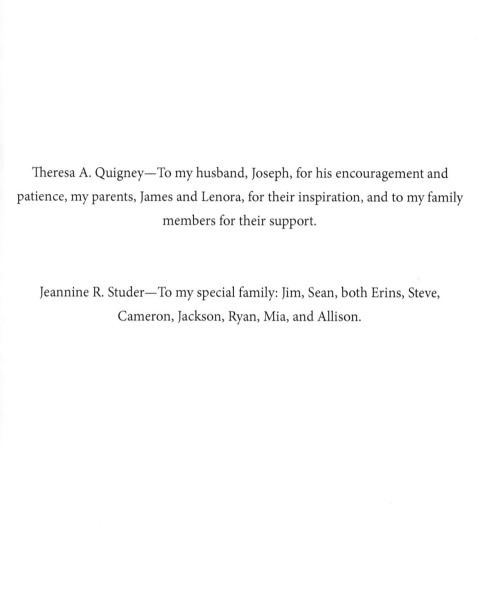

Theresa A. Quigney—To my husband, Joseph, for his encouragement and patience, my parents, James and Lenora, for their inspiration, and to my family members for their support.

Jeannine R. Studer—To my special family: Jim, Sean, both Erins, Steve, Cameron, Jackson, Ryan, Mia, and Allison.

Contents

Preface   ix
Acknowledgments   xii

PART I
Issues Related to Legislation and Regulations   1

1   The Role of the School Counselor in Working with Students
    with Disabilities   3

2   Laws and Regulations Related to Students with Disabilities   19

3   Areas of Disability   36

4   Identification Process for Students with Disabilities   64

5   Individualized Education Programs (IEPs) and Educational
    Placement Issues   77

PART II
Issues for Involvement of School Counselors Specific to Working
with Students with Disabilities, Educators, and Family/Community   101

6   Individual Counseling for Students with Disabilities   103

7   Creative Counseling Strategies for Students with Disabilities   126

8   Group Counseling Options for Students with Disabilities   137

9   The School Counselor's Role in Transition and Career
    Development   155

10 Support for Teachers and Educational Personnel Working
    with Students with Disabilities   179

11 Collaboration and Consultation with Parents/Families of
    Students with Disabilities and Members of the Community   196

PART III
Issues of an Ever-Evolving Field   209

12 Current and Evolving Issues in Regard to Students
    with Disabilities   211

    Appendix: Resources for Working with Students with Disabilities 230
    Index   236

Preface

School counselors have an obligation to work with all students, including those with special needs. The American School Counselor Association (ASCA) specifically recognizes the importance of professional school counselors' involvement in special education-related issues, as conveyed in their position statement, "professional school counselors are committed to helping all students realize their potential, and meet or exceed academic standards yearly progress regardless of challenges resulting from disabilities or other special needs" (ASCA, 2013, para. 1). Furthermore, this responsibility is recognized by agencies such as the Council for Accreditation of Counseling and Related Educational Programs (CACREP). This council highlights the importance of understanding and assessing barriers that impede the growth of school-aged youth, comprehending exceptional abilities and strategies for differentiated interventions, and recognizing the school counselor's role in the individualized education plan (IEP) process (CACREP, 2009).

Although school counselors do have formal preparation in such critical areas as counseling dynamics, interpersonal skills training, collaborative practice, advocacy, and consultation, many have not had adequate exposure or practice regarding the specific application of such areas to the needs of students with disabilities. Moreover, some school counselors had not had ample opportunity in their training to gain a strong knowledge base and practical experience with issues unique to students with special needs. For example, school counselors often have little training in the process involved with the identification of a disability, IEP development and implementation, formal transitional planning for post-secondary issues, and the legislative basis for many aspects of the field of special education.

There is obviously a strong disconnect between the mandate, recommendation, and expectation that school counselors will work effectively with students with special needs and their formal preparation to fulfill this responsibility. We have written this book to close the gap between training, expectations, and professional responsibilities.

This book is divided into three sections. Part I focuses on the legal and regulatory basis for many of the practices in special education, including an overview of many of the pertinent laws. Part I will not only provide critical information for a strong knowledge base in special education, but we make specific application to the roles of the school counselor related to the content.

While Part I will expose school counselors to a special education framework and enable them to ascertain how their roles correspond to this context, Part II focuses on areas more traditionally associated with school counselor preparation, specifically with students with disabilities. The major theme of this section emphasizes the leadership role that school counselors should play in supporting students with disabilities, teachers and educational personnel who work with the students, families/parents of the students, and pertinent members of the community.

Part III of the book provides a discussion of current issues of particular importance to school counselors as they work with students with disabilities and their families. Special education is a field that is continually evolving, which makes it imperative that school counselors keep informed regarding pertinent issues. Some of the issues to be discussed are ones that other students without disabilities face, such as bullying, cyberbullying, and graduation from high school, but to which students with disabilities may be more vulnerable.

Through the discussion of themes, the overall objective is to provide comprehensive coverage of special education-related topics. This framework also promotes the specific objectives for school counselors to: (a) attain a working legislative knowledge of the field of special education and how their roles relate to this context; (b) understand how traditional areas associated with their formal preparation can and should be adapted to students with disabilities as well as in collaboration with educational personnel and families; (c) gain a working knowledge of issues specific to students with disabilities, such as the transition process and specific social and emotional concerns, as well as their roles in addressing such areas; and (d) become informed consumers of current information of particular importance in special education and how it affects their role. CACREP-related standards are also addressed in each chapter.

For School Counselors-in-Training

As you learn about the school counselor's role in a comprehensive, developmental school counseling (CDSC) program, you have an obligation to learn how the ASCA National Model is designed to promote the growth and achievement of pre-K-12 students, including those with disabilities. In this text you will read about the various disabilities commonly found among school-aged youth, the laws and procedures that protect and support these students, and how to apply developmental and learning theories as you work with students with disabilities. Furthermore, common individual and group counseling theories and techniques that are successful with students with disabilities, and specific strategies that assist in collaboration with stakeholders are additional topics discussed in this text.

For Professional School Counselors

This text provides you with current trends, laws, and strategies that are designed to facilitate your work with students with disabilities and their families. The information in the chapters is designed to supplement your work in the school with students enrolled in special programs. Counseling theories and techniques, collaborative approaches, and transition strategies that can be adapted for students with various disabilities are introduced, and information that will aid in your understanding of how the ASCA National Model can be used to reach students with different abilities and needs is provided.

For Counselor Educators

Students who are training for the school counseling profession often receive inconsistent knowledge regarding their work with students with disabilities. Although the ASCA and CACREP mandate that we work with all students in the educational environment, school counselors often feel ill-prepared to work effectively with students with disabilities and their families. The information in this text is designed to prepare school counseling students as they work with students with disabilities. Case studies, conceptual application activities designed for self-reflection and application, and student activities that can be adapted for school-aged youth are included for concept relevance.

References

ASCA (2013). *The Professional School Counselor and Students with Disabilities*. Retrieved from www.schoolcounselor.org/files/PS_SpecialNeeds.pdf.
CACREP (2009). www.cacrep.org/wp-content/uploads/2013/12/2009-Standards.pdf.

Acknowledgments

We want to acknowledge the many individuals who have assisted with this book.

Many thanks to the practicing school counselors who have contributed their stories to this book. These experiences have made the concepts "come to life" and have painted a picture of various incidents in which school counselors are involved as they actively perform tasks on behalf of students with disabilities and their families.

With much appreciation to:

Beverly Anderson
Kat Coy
April Baer
Meghan Bechtle
Tracy Cagle
Amy Kroninger
Joseph Lang

In addition, we are grateful to the many people at Routledge for their expertise in making this book come to fruition.

Many special thanks to Anna Moore.

Part I

Issues Related to Legislation and Regulations

1 The Role of the School Counselor in Working with Students with Disabilities

The following CACREP standards are addressed in this chapter:

PROFESSIONAL COUNSELING ORIENTATION AND ETHICAL PRACTICE
a. history and philosophy of the counseling profession and its specialty areas

SOCIAL AND CULTURAL DIVERSITY
c. multicultural counseling competencies
d. the impact of heritage, attitudes beliefs, understandings, and acculturative experiences on an individual's views of others
h. strategies for identifying and eliminating barriers, prejudices, and processes of intentional and unintentional oppression and discrimination

ENTRY-LEVEL SPECIALTY AREAS: SCHOOL COUNSELING CONTEXTUAL DIMENSIONS
g. characteristics, risk factors, and warning signs of students at risk for mental health and behavioral disorders

PRACTICE
i. approaches to increase promotion and graduation rates

Chapter Objectives

After you have completed this chapter, you should be able to:

• Describe historical trends that have influenced the school counselor's role with students with disabilities.
• Recognize the ASCA National Model components and their relationship to students with disabilities.
• Self-reflect on attitudes toward students with disabilities.

So there I was, sitting across from mom, who—within seconds—lurched across the room stating firmly, "and it's all because of *you!*" I wasn't quite sure how to respond. However, as I listened further, mom went on to explain that it was after my explanation of Joey's EXPLORE [test to assist students plan their high school courses and choose a career path] scores and the discrepancy of not being within reasonable reach of his post-secondary goals that mom realized something had to be done. Sadly, it was the spring of his sophomore year when this pursuit of further testing began; however, mom had been persistent for years in making several requests for parent/teacher conferences due to her instinct that "something wasn't quite right" with Joey, but because he was "managing his bipolar without significant negative educational impact," he was never tested outside of his outside, independent evaluation. Joey was finally able to be identified as a student needing special assistance and an IEP was created.

As a school counselor, I find it difficult to walk the balance of protecting school protocols and advocating for students. As a parent of a child with special needs, I know that the families who are persistent are the ones who eventually get the system to "oil their squeaky wheels." I feel my job is to extend the voice of the parent, bring it to notice of administration, and then leave it to the administration to determine the next step.

As it turned out, Joey's mom was actually grateful for the EXPLORE results as it gave her the concrete evidence to refute the decisions school personnel had determined. Thus, the lunge across the room was really an expression of gratitude for simply doing my job as a professional school counselor.

Secondary-level school counselor

As indicated in the scenario above, the school counselor is instrumental in facilitating the academic, vocational, and social/emotional growth of all students, particularly those with disabilities. Legislative mandates such as Title 1 of the Elementary and Secondary Education Act (ESEA) and No Child Left Behind (NCLB) have provided the catalyst to encourage schools to pay greater attention to certain groups of students and to maximize educational achievement for *all* students (McDonnell, 2005). These legislative directives have changed the system's approach to at-risk students—such as those with disabilities—and in response to these mandates, the training and education of school counselors has also changed. Although school counselors have a responsibility to work with all students in pre-K-12 educational settings, unfortunately students with disabilities have not always received the school counseling benefits that their non-disabled peers have enjoyed (Bergin & Bergin, 2004; Milsom, 2002, 2006).

The American School Counselor Association (ASCA) sets the guidelines for the practice and role of school counselors in all school settings. As stated in the ASCA position statement on students with disabilities, school counselors "advocate for students with special needs, encourage family involvement in their child's education and collaborate with other educational professionals to promote academic achievement for all" (ASCA, 2013, para. 6).

Despite this directive, there is a wide variation in the types of assistance school counselors provide to students with disabilities. Milsom (2002) investigated the critical role that school counselors play in regard to students with disabilities to determine: (a) school counselor activities in relation to students with disabilities; (b) school counselor preparation to engage in these activities; and (c) the amount of education school counselors receive to effectively work with these youth. The results of this study indicated that school counselor participants at all levels felt "somewhat prepared" to work with students with disabilities, but less prepared for transition planning. In another study (Milsom & Akos, 2003), school counselors indicated that they felt inadequately trained for working with students with disabilities, and that school counselor preparation programs varied in the training provided to pre-service school counselors regarding special education issues, which suggests inconsistent skills and knowledge among school counselors.

With the critical obligation to work with students with disabilities, it is perplexing as to the reason why more school counselors are not adequately prepared for this challenge. The history of the school counseling profession, special education legislation, and professional attitudes toward students with differences provide partial answers to this dilemma.

History of School Counseling and Students with Disabilities

The Industrial Revolution is credited as ushering in "guidance counselors," and what today are known as *professional school counselors*. At the turn of the 20th century, the United States shifted from a rural to an urban society, and—with mandatory education laws—youth from all socioeconomic groups entered schools in unprecedented numbers. Teachers were unprepared for the diverse youth in need of guidance to prepare for careers that were unprecedented before this time. To address this problem, teachers assumed the role of "guidance worker" in which there was no relief from regular teaching duties, no training, and no additional pay (Gysbers, 2001). There was also a need to provide assistance to alleviate the social and emotional concerns that youth brought into the educational setting; an objective that was added to the already demanding workload.

For numerous years, school personnel ignored the needs of students with disabilities due to the belief that they were inferior, and not educable (DeLambo et al., 2007). As a result, these youth were confined to education at home, placed in expensive private schools, or enrolled in institutions with classes segregated from the general education classes. With legislation, the testing movement, the development of psychological theories, and the mental hygiene movements, views regarding students with disabilities changed. In the decade of the 1930s, 16 states in America created laws that authorized special education instruction, and in the following decade, additional laws were created that stipulated an additional focus on the education of students with disabilities. In the 1960s, funding was provided for training personnel in relation to students with disabilities, but it wasn't until 1975, when the Education of All Handicapped Children Act (Public Law 94–142) became law, that free and appropriate public education (FAPE) was legislated for all children with disabilities. In the 1990s, the Americans with Disabilities Act (ADA) was passed to prevent discrimination against individuals with disabilities (Marshak et al., 2010), and in 2002, NCLB mandated that students with disabilities were to be included in annual assessments to demonstrate adequate yearly progress (AYP). School counselors were expected to assist with the increasing numbers of students with disabilities who were entering general education classrooms (Greer & Greer, 1995). Unfortunately, despite legal mandates and the passage of many years since this original legislation, few school counselor training programs offer courses in issues surrounding students with disabilities.

To rectify this curricular training omission, the Council for Accreditation of Counseling and Related Educational Programs (CACREP) identified standards to address all student needs, including those with disabilities. Likewise, the ASCA School Counselor Competencies acknowledged the knowledge, skills, and attitudes school counselors needed to work effectively in a comprehensive, developmental school counseling (CDSC) program. Yet, despite these directives, effective working relationships require attention to personal attitudes, beliefs, and behaviors, particularly in regard to those who may be perceived as different.

Attitudes Influencing Students with Disabilities

Unfortunately, negative attitudes toward individuals with disabilities have been pervasive throughout the ages (DeLambo et al., 2007), which impair productive working relationships.

Conceptual Application Activity 1.1

Interview a school counselor in a school setting of your choice. What training has this school counselor received in working with students with disabilities? What are the most frequent tasks in which he/she engages with this population of students? Compare your answers with those of your peers.

When there is a lack of adequate training and preparation for assistive services, negative attitudes are often an outcome (Praisner, 2003), which may contribute to lowered academic expectations for students with disabilities (Bowen & Glenn, 1998, as cited in Milsom, 2006). There is also the continual assumption that the teacher of special education would take care of all the needs of students with disabilities (Bergin & Bergin, 2004); a belief that has contributed to educators' reservations to reach out to these students. Furthermore, school counselors who adhere to these negative attitudes may dissuade students from taking rigorous courses or discourage them from attending post-secondary education.

The perception of the cause of the disability often contributes to negative attitudes and social distancing (DeLambo et al., 2007). Although these attitudes are difficult to change, education makes a difference in changing stigmas associated with persons with disabilities. School counselors are instrumental personnel in promoting positive school experiences and modifying attitudes through educational programming. For instance, bringing in speakers from the National Alliance for the Mentally Ill (NAMI) to discuss causes of mental illness and methods for assisting those with mental illness could provide helpful knowledge and lead to a change in beliefs. Or, exposing students to media presentations that negatively represent those with disabilities could provide them with opportunities to reflect on and analyze these portrayals to discredit these depictions (DeLambo et al., 2007).

Obviously, self-reflection and training under supervision to attain the necessary skills and knowledge to successfully assist students is essential. Conceptual Application Activities 1.2 and 1.3 are designed to begin evaluating personal beliefs, knowledge, and skills to effectually assist students with disabilities.

Conceptual Application Activity 1.2

Self-Assessment for Students with Disabilities

I. Self-Awareness of values and biases

A. Attitudes and Beliefs

I believe that…
1. awareness of personal beliefs regarding individuals with disabilities is vital.
2. my own background and experiences play a role in my attitudes, values, and biases.
3. I am able to recognize the limits of my competence and knowledge in working with students with disabilities.
4. I am able to recognize sources of discomfort that exist between students with disabilities and myself.

B. Knowledge

I am knowledgeable of…
1. my own background and how it personally and professionally influences my view of students with differences.
2. my impact on others including my communication style, and counseling techniques and theory.
3. the influences of parental beliefs and parenting styles on the educational goals of students with special needs.
4. legal mandates that influence academic, vocational, and personal/social growth (e.g., transition, IEP, 504 Plans).

C. Skills

I am able to…
1. seek out educational experiences to improve my understanding and effectiveness in working with students with disabilities.
2. seek out opportunities to better understand myself (e.g., personal counseling).

II. Counselor Awareness of Student's Worldview

A. Attitudes and Beliefs

I believe that…
1. I am aware of my negative and positive emotions toward students with disabilities that may prove detrimental to the counseling relationship.
2. I am aware of my biases and preconceived notions that I may hold toward students with special needs.

B. Knowledge

I am knowledgeable of...
1. specific information about the particular group with whom I am working. I am aware of how the life experiences, biological, sociological, psychological, educational factors of students with disabilities.
2. how disabilities may influence personality formation, vocational choices, help seeking behaviors, and the appropriateness or inappropriateness of counseling approaches.
3. how disabilities are associated with at-risk behaviors.

C. Skills

I am able to...
1. familiarize myself with current research regarding disorders that affect students with disabilities. I actively seek out educational experiences to enrich my knowledge, understanding, and cross-cultural skills for more effective counseling strategies.
2. become actively involved with individuals outside of the counseling setting to acquire available resources to assist students with disabilities.

III. Counseling Intervention Strategies

A. Beliefs and Attitudes

I believe that...
1. all students, regardless of abilities, have a right to achieve.
2. I believe that not all students are able to benefit from "talk therapy" and that alternative counseling strategies may be better able to reach students.

B. Knowledge

I am knowledgeable of...
1. institutional barriers that prevent students with disabilities from achieving.
2. the potential bias in assessment instruments and use procedures that are appropriate to the needs of the student.
3. family issues that could influence youth welfare.
4. discriminatory attitudes held by general education teachers that could impair student growth.

C. Skills

I am able to...
1. engage in a variety of verbal and non-verbal helping responses that are appropriate to each individual student, regardless of special needs. When I sense my helping style is unsuitable for the student, I am able to modify it.
2. advocate on behalf of students, or teach advocacy skills to students to promote themselves.

3. seek consultation when appropriate.
4. seek supervision when necessary.
5. receive training in my role as a school counselor for all students.
6. take responsibility for educating students, teachers, and parents about the special needs of students with disabilities.

Conceptual Application Activity 1.3

After you have completed Conceptual Application Activity 1.2, self-reflect on how these characteristics will assist you in effectively working with students with special needs and their parents/guardians. What areas do you wish to improve? Next, identify the areas that you would like to improve and strategies for acquiring these attributes and complete the chart below.

Competency to attain	Strategies for acquiring this competency	Benchmark for reaching goal	Evaluation to assess competency

Studies reveal that when counselors have an opportunity to evaluate their own counseling performances, an increased confidence in counseling abilities occurs (Little et al., 2005). Assessment of beliefs in regard to students with special needs is a primary step for effectively working with this population, but it is not enough; self-reflecting on how beliefs are congruent with the goals of the ASCA National Model is an additional step.

The ASCA National Model and Students with Disabilities

As mentioned previously, when "guidance workers" initiated vocational guidance for students in schools, there was primarily no training for the additional duties that teachers assumed. Furthermore, variations in school counselor roles from school to school, district to district, and state to state resulted due to a lack of a structured organization to standardize the role of these professionals. In the 1930s and 1940s, a service-oriented pupil personnel model was proposed to organize the educational professionals who did not fit into any other structure, with the intention of maximizing resources without service duplication (Gysbers, 2001). This configuration included such individuals as attendance officers, school nurses, visiting teachers, school psychologists, and "guidance workers." This reactionary model, also known as "student services," continued to be the organizational structure that focused on responsibilities of the "guidance counselor" rather than the needs of students. Despite this structure, confusion regarding the tasks and responsibilities of school counselors continued.

Figure 1.1 High school students exploring vocational post-secondary options.
Source: ©iStockphoto.com, www.istockphoto.com/photo/diverse-young-adults-8359714.

A competency-based guidance program was proposed and developed by Gysbers and Moore (Gysbers, 2001) as an alternative guidance structure during the 1970s and 1980s. Despite proven student benefits of this model in enhancing academic achievement, career development, and social/emotional growth (Lee et al., 2008) "guidance counselors" continued to work in a traditional program that varied depending on the school culture.

With legislation that mandated accountability efforts to demonstrate program effectiveness, and requirements designed to address the opportunity gap among marginalized students, the American School Counselor Association developed the ASCA National Standards for School Counseling Programs in 1997 (later renamed the ASCA National Standards for Students) (ACSA, 2012). Nine standards are identified in academic, career, and personal/social (now retitled social/emotional) domains, with identified competencies and indicators to determine and assess student acquisition of knowledge, behavior, and attitudes as a result of participating in a school counseling program. In 2014, the ASCA once again revised these standards to align with the Common Core State Standards in a document entitled *Mindsets and Behaviors for Student Success* (ASCA, 2014).

Although the original standards provided direction for school counseling programs, more focus and structure was needed, and six years later the ASCA National Model was created as a framework for building CDSC programs that are connected to the school mission and integral to the total educational program (ASCA, 2005). The National Model provides a map for school counselors to transform their school counseling program from one that is ancillary and service-oriented to one that addresses social justice and educational gaps for marginalized students, such as those with disabilities (Lee & Goodnough, 2007; Ratts et al., 2007). In 2012, the ASCA National Model was revised to

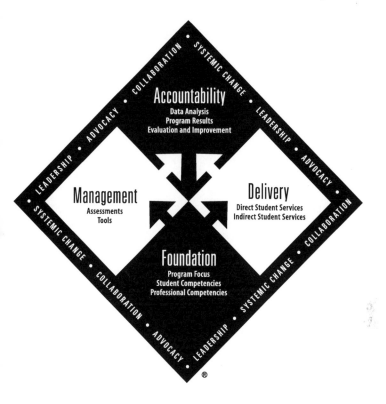

Figure 1.2 The ASCA National Model.

Source: Reprinted with permission American School Counselor Association. The ASCA National Model diamond graphic is a registered trademark of the American School Counselor association and may not be reprinted or modified without permission.

clarify language, to promote opportunities for all students, and to ease implementation (ASCA, 2012). Figure 1.2 is an illustration of the ASCA National Model.

The ASCA Model Components and Themes

The ASCA National Model incorporates the four components of foundation, management, delivery, and accountability, with themes of leadership, systemic change, collaboration, and advocacy interwoven throughout the components (ASCA, 2012).

The Foundation Component

Program focus, student competencies, and professional competencies are three subsections within the foundation component. The *program focus* ensures that the school counseling program is built upon a well-defined and understood set of beliefs that are aligned with the school's mission, and guided by well-defined program goals. School counselors have a responsibility to use inclusive language that emphasizes the school counseling program commitment to social justice when writing mission, vision, and belief statements.

Beliefs are formulated around personal experiences and backgrounds (ASCA, 2012) with attention to self-perceptions, views of others, and school counselor programming. Integral to educational beliefs is the view that *all* students are valued, and that opportunities provided to students in the general education curriculum are also provided to students with disabilities. The school counselor vision statement is shaped by how the school counseling program is envisioned for the future, whereas the mission statement provides structure for reaching the vision, and program goals are created after the school counselor examines data to address any groups of students whose needs are not being addressed (ASCA, 2012).

The ASCA Student Standards (formerly the ASCA National Standards), renamed ASCA Mindsets and Behaviors for Student Success, and other educational standards such as those identified by individual states, identify the knowledge, skills, and attitudes students should be able to display due to their participation in a school counseling program. Attention is given to ensuring that students with disabilities have the same opportunities to acquire the standards selected for the general student body.

Finally, the ASCA School Counselor Competencies serve as a self-assessment or as a guide for administrators to understand the essential role of the school counselor, and can be accessed at www.schoolcounselor.org/files/SCCompetencies.pdf.

With social justice as a critical concept within the counseling profession and a foundation for developing and implementing strategies that support egalitarian practice (Locke & Bailey, 2014), the ASCA Ethical Standards provide guidance in making decisions for all stakeholders (ASCA, 2010).

Conceptual Application Activity 1.4

Select a school and look at the school counseling vision and mission statements. Do these assertions have references to diversity and students with disabilities? Rewrite the statements with attention to these issues.

The Management Component

The management component includes assessments and tools. *Assessments* include the school counselor competencies, school counseling program assessment, and use of time assessment. Attention is given to ensure that the school counselor has the indispensable competencies to understand students and their families with disabilities, and the necessary skills and attitudes to work effectively with these individuals.

Conceptual Application Activity 1.5

Interview a school counselor and talk with this individual about the time he/she spends performing direct services to students enrolled in the general curriculum. How does this time compare with the time spent with students with disabilities?

Tools include such areas as annual agreement, advisory council, data, curriculum, lesson plans, and calendars that provide structure to the program and attention to students with disabilities. With the post-secondary focus that was traditionally the purview of our school counselor predecessors, stakeholders often have difficulty understanding the multiple responsibilities that school counselors assume, with little comprehension of how the school counselor assists students with disabilities. Therefore, the school counselor has a responsibility to teach these stakeholders and others about the ASCA National Model, how school counselors serve as leaders of this program, and the needs of *all* students within the educational setting.

Conceptual Application Activity 1.6

Take a look at the school counselor's calendar of events and discuss the various activities that address students with disabilities.

The Delivery Component

The delivery component includes *direct* and *indirect* services. Direct activities include the school counseling core curriculum, individual student planning, and responsive services. Indirect activities comprise referrals, consultation, and collaboration.

The *school counseling core curriculum* is delivered either through classroom instruction or group activities, and conveyed to every student when appropriate. According to the ASCA position statement *The Professional School Counselor and Students with Disabilities*, school counselors have a responsibility to provide curriculum lessons "to students with special needs within the scope of the comprehensive school counseling program" (ASCA, 2013, para. 4). As a result, school counselors are able to work collaboratively with the special educator by team-teaching on topics such as assertiveness, bullying, or social skill development.

Individual student planning assists with individual goal-setting and is implemented through appraisal and advisement strategies. Students with disabilities are not to be overlooked, and their personal and career goals and strategies for reaching these desires are to be addressed. The ASCA, in its position statement, maintains that school counselors provide "assistance with academic and transition plans for students in the IEP when appropriate" (ASCA, 2013, para. 4). *Responsive services* in the form of individual and group counseling and crisis response facilitate problem resolution. Counselors are able to use such concrete strategies such as social stories, comic strip conversations, mirror or imitative exercises, and videotaping (Marshak et al., 2010) to reach students who rely on concrete strategies in individual or group counseling. Counselors are reminded that the provision of long-term therapy is an inappropriate activity in the school setting (ASCA, 2013, para. 5).

Case Study 1.1

I have found that teachers are perplexed by students diagnosed with ADD or ADHD, and I have been delighted to work with some amazing teachers who go out of their way to accommodate the needs of these students. One of the eighth-grade students had a difficult time sitting through an entire class period and remain on-task. Although he was very intelligent, his off-task behaviors drove his teachers crazy. His teachers decided to outline perimeters around his desk that gave him a space to pace, stand, stretch, and do whatever he needed to do. The teachers went out of their way to meet his need to move while he learned.

The more effort I put into making the teachers in the special education department familiar with the skills and topics that I can provide, the more they see me as an addition to the faculty who can help them meet the goals of the students. I take as many opportunities as I can to speak with the classes about study skills, test-taking techniques, and learning styles.

Middle school counselor

In the indirect student services area, school counselors engage in making *referrals* when they are unable to effectively provide services to students. Students with disabilities often have needs that the school is not able to accommodate, and in these instances students benefit when the school counselor is able to connect them to school-based programming or community resources. Furthermore, *collaboration* and *consultation* support student achievement as school counselors work with others through partnerships that enhance the learning environment. The need for collaboration on behalf of students with disabilities has never been greater. When the Individuals with Disabilities Education Improvement Act (IDEIA) was authorized, students with disabilities were given access to the general curriculum in the least restrictive environment (LRE), which established a belief that collaboration would occur among educational professionals (Cook & Friend, 2010). The unfortunate reality is that inconsistent attention is given to collaborative practices within teacher and counselor preparation programs (Cook & Friend, 2010), leading to little knowledge as to how to prepare, participate, and evaluate this partnership. Strategies for creating a collaborative relationship are found in Chapter 10.

Conceptual Application Activity 1.7

Read the literature surrounding students with special needs. What are some of the workshop topics that could be addressed for teachers or parents regarding students with special needs?

The Accountability Component

Data analysis, program results, and evaluation and improvement are the elements integral to this component. *Data* is examined to see whether or not the school counseling program is reaching all students to determine if achievement gaps exist. An analysis of data reveals program effectiveness (ASCA, 2012), and includes school counselor performance, school counseling program effectiveness and assessment, and serves as a compass for personnel and/or program improvement.

Conceptual Application Activity 1.8

Identify a school and locate the school report card. Analyze the report card and the achievement data. Determine the numbers of students with disabilities who are proficient in designated academic areas and compare their scores with their non-disabled peers. What conclusions are you able to make regarding this population? How can the school counselor assist in closing any achievement gap that may be apparent?

The themes of leadership, advocacy, collaboration, and systemic change (Education Trust, 1997) are integrated within each of the components of the ASCA National Model, and serve as reminders of how the school counselor serves as a moderator while negotiating their way between the various stakeholders.

Leadership

Leadership involves more than developing and implementing a vision for comprehensive school counseling programs. Although leadership is viewed as the purview of the school administrator, school counselors are leaders of a CDSC program, and have a responsibility to support underserved students. This support includes identifying and removing barriers that prevent students from accessing opportunities and achieving academic success (Campbell & Dahir, 1997; Dollarhide, 2003).

Advocacy

Advocacy promotes school achievement for all students. School counselors advocate in a variety of forms, such as empowering students to take constructive action on their own behalf, intervening in support of students, organizing community support to address a concern, and initiating school-wide or district-wide changes (ASCA, 2012). The ASCA position statement is clear that "advocating for students with special needs in the school and in the community" (ASCA, 2012, para. 4) is a professional responsibility. Case Study 1.2 provides an example of the importance of advocacy.

Case Study 1.2

When making a suspected child abuse/neglect report in our state, we are asked whether or not the child receives special education services. The question did not faze me until the first time I answered "yes." I worked with a student who made a report about the sexual abuse she had been experiencing in her home. After a social worker from the Department of Children Services (DCS) interviewed the student, I was told that she was not a "credible source" and that the situation would not be further investigated. It took an entire year, several additional reports, and multiple phone calls to DCS supervisors to get someone to actually open the case and work with this family.

The student's report turned out to be factual, and the perpetrator was removed from the home. It was a very disheartening situation, but also proof of the importance of advocacy in the role of the school counselor.

Elementary school counselor

Collaboration

The more success counselors have in building working partnerships with others both in and outside of the school setting, the more impact they will have in promoting student achievement (Balfanz & Byrnes, 2012) and addressing critical issues that impede academic success (Epstein & Van Voorhis, 2010). Collaboration is critical in supporting the needs of students with disabilities, particularly when general education teachers who are unfamiliar with the instructional needs of these students in their classrooms are resistant to accommodations or assistance these students may need (Romano et al., 2009). Additional information regarding collaboration is found in Chapters 10 and 11.

Case Study 1.3

At times it is helpful to see a situation from a different perspective. I once worked with a young male student with a hearing impairment who needed a sign language interpreter in his classes. This student came to see me about his poor grades in one of his classes. I came to observe him in the classroom in which he was struggling and realized that the teacher habitually stood between the student and his sign language interpreter, which resulted in the young man not able to see what was being communicated.

Middle school counselor

Systemic Change

Systemic change represents the significant efforts of school counselors to address gaps in educational access, opportunity, and aspiration from a systems perspective (ASCA, 2012). Counselors generally focus on helping students deal with their issues, either individually or in groups, but it is also possible that student problems may be the result of systems or people functioning inappropriately or insensitively toward subgroups of students.

Conceptual Application Activity 1.9

Interview a school counselor and discuss his/her role in regard to students with disabilities. In what ways has he/she utilized the skills of leadership, advocacy, collaboration, and systemic change in his/her work with these students? Discuss your interview with your classmates.

Conclusion

School counselors have been remiss in their work with students with disabilities due to reasons such as the history of the school counseling profession, omissions in training programs, and negative attitudes toward students with disabilities. With educational reform, the American School Counselor Association developed the ASCA Student Standards (now Mindsets and Behaviors for Student Success), and later the ASCA National Model to provide direction for school counselors to work in a comprehensive, developmental school counseling program to address standards for *all* students. It is no longer feasible for school counselors to ignore the needs of students with special needs. Greater opportunities for school counselor involvement with this group of students have been created through legislation, enhanced attention to student needs, and issues of social justice. No longer can counselor training programs exclude curricula, knowledge, or skills that emphasize the academic, vocational, and social/emotional needs of exceptional students. School counselors have a responsibility to assist all students to promote growth and well-being.

References

ASCA (2005). *The ASCA National Model: A Framework for School Counseling Programs*, 2nd edn. Alexandria, VA: American School Counselor Association.

ASCA (2010). *Ethical Standards for School Counselors*. Retrieved from www.schoolcounselor.org/files/EthicalStandards2010.pdf.

ASCA (2012). *The ASCA National Model: A Framework for School Counseling Programs*, 3rd edn. Alexandria, VA: American School Counselor Association.

ASCA (2013). *The Professional School Counselor and Students with Disabilities*. Retrieved from www.schoolcounselor.org/files/PS_SpecialNeeds.pdf.

ASCA (2014). *Mindsets and Behaviors for Student Success*. Retrieved from www.schoolcounselor.org/studentcompetencies.

Balfanz, R. & Byrnes, V. (2012). *Chronic Absenteeism: Summarizing What We Know from Nationally Available Data*. Baltimore: Johns Hopkins University Center for Social Organization of Schools.

Bergin, J. W. & Bergin, J. J. (2004). The forgotten student. In *ASCA School Counselor*, Alexandria, VA: American School Counselor Association.

Campbell, C. A. & Dahir, C. A. (1997). *The National Standards for School Counseling Programs*. Alexandria, VA: American School Counselor Association.

Cook, L. & Friend, M. (2010). The state of the art of collaboration on behalf of students with disabilities. *Journal of Educational and Psychological Consultation*, 20, 1–8.

DeLambo, D. A., Chandras, K. V., Homa, D., & Chandras, S. V. (2007). Adolescent attitudes toward disabilities: what every school counselor needs to know. *Georgia School Counselors Association Journal*, 14, 30–38.

Dollarhide, C. T. (2003). School counselors as program leaders: applying leadership contexts to school counseling. *Professional School Counseling*, 6, 304–308.

Education Trust (1997). *The National Guidance and Counseling Reform Program*. Washington, DC: Education Trust.

Epstein, J. L. & Van Voorhis, F. L. (2010). School counselors' roles in developing partnerships with families and communities for student success. *Professional School Counseling*, 14, 1–14.

Greer, B. B. & Greer, J. G. (1995). The inclusion movement and its impact on counselors. *School Counselor*, 43, 124–132.

Gysbers, N. C. (2001). School guidance and counseling in the 21st century: remember the past into the future. *Professional School Counseling*, 5, 96–105.

Lee, S. M., Daniels, M. H., Puig, A., Newgent, R. A., & Nam, S. K. (2008). A data-based model to predict postsecondary educational attainment of low-socioeconomic-status students. *Professional School Counseling*, 11, 306–316.

Lee, V. V. & Goodnough, G. E. (2007). Creating a systemic, data-driven school counseling program. In B. Erford (ed.), *Transforming the School Counseling Profession* (pp. 121–141). Upper Saddle River, NJ: Pearson.

Little, C., Packman, J., Smaby, M. H., & Maddux, C. D. (2005). The skilled counselor training model: skills acquisition, self-assessment, and cognitive complexity. *Counselor Education and Supervision*, 44, 189–200.

Locke, D. C. & Bailey, D. C. (2014). *Increasing Multicultural Understanding*, 3rd edn. Los Angeles, CA: Sage.

McDonnell, L. M. (2005). The federal role in education: evolution or revolution? *Peabody Journal of Education*, 80, 19–38.

Marshak, E., Dandeneau, C. J., Prezant, F. P., & L'Amoreaux, N. A. (2010). *The School Counselor's Guide to Helping Students with Disabilities*. San Francisco, CA: Jossey-Bass.

Milsom, A. (2002). Students with disabilities: school counselor involvement and preparation. *Professional School Counseling*, 5, 331–338.

Milsom, A. (2006). Creating positive school experiences for students with disabilities. *Professional School Counseling*, 10, 66–72.

Milsom, A. & Akos, P. (2003). Students with disabilities: school counselor involvement and preparation. *Professional School Counseling*, 5, 331–338.

Praisner, C. L. (2003). Attitudes of elementary school principals toward inclusion of students with disabilities. *Exceptional Children*, 69, 135–145.

Ratts, M. J., DeKruyf, L., & Chen-Hayes, S. C. (2007). The ACA Advocacy Competencies: a social justice advocacy framework for professional school counselors. *Professional School Counseling*, 11, 90–97.

Romano, D. M., Paradise, L. V., & Green, E. J. (2009). School counselors' attitudes towards providing services to students receiving Section 504 classroom accommodations: Implications for school counselor educators. *Journal of School Counselor*, November 20. Retrieved from www.jsc.montana.edu/articles/v7n37.pdf.

United States Department of Education (2012). *National Center for Education Statistics*. Retrieved from http://nces.ed.gov/fastfacts/display.asp?id=64.

2 Laws and Regulations Related to Students with Disabilities

The following CACREP standards are addressed in this chapter:

PROFESSIONAL COUNSELING ORIENTATION AND ETHICAL PRACTICE
i. ethical standards of professional counseling organizations and credentialing bodies, and applications of ethical and legal considerations in professional counseling

ENTRY-LEVEL SPECIALTY AREAS: SCHOOL COUNSELING CONTEXTUAL DIMENSIONS
m. legislation and government policy relevant to school counseling
n. legal and ethical considerations specific to school counseling

Chapter Objectives

After you have completed this chapter, you should be able to:

- Describe the major laws and legal tenets in regard to the provision of services to students with disabilities.
- Self-reflect on the importance of school counselors being knowledgeable of these laws and regulations as they work with students with disabilities.

The evolution of the policies and practices associated with working with students with disabilities is not only based on such models as those involved with medical research, behavioral inquiry, and pedagogical methodology. While clearly critical perspectives, the field of special education also has a rich history in both legislation and litigation, which has had and continues to have a fundamental influence on both the content and provision of services to students with disabilities.

This chapter will provide a legislative foundation of the field of special education from which can emanate a greater understanding of the evolution of the provision of educational, counseling, and other appropriate services to individuals with disabilities, as well as a working knowledge of required legal aspects of the implementation of such activities. It is imperative that school counselors have a strong knowledge base in laws and regulations related to special education, as they are involved as participants in various activities for which standards are set. Moreover, school counselors are resources not only for students with disabilities, but for a number of individuals associated with the field of special education, including families of the students with disabilities, teachers, administrators, and other school personnel who work with students with disabilities, and pertinent community and agency resources.

Individuals with Disabilities Education Improvement Act (IDEIA), 2004

While this chapter will provide an overview of five major laws that focus on individuals with disabilities and related issues, this discussion will center initially on the law that appears to have had the greatest impact on the provision of individualized specialized services to students with disabilities. The Individuals with Disabilities Education Improvement Act of 2004 (Public Law 108–446) (Jones & Apling, n.d.) is the current name of the law, which was originally passed in 1975 and was a landmark piece of legislation regarding educational services for students with disabilities.

This law has been revised and reauthorized since it was first passed in 1975 as the Education for All Handicapped Children Act (Public Law 94–142). While the law has always had its focus on the provision of appropriate individualized services for students with disabilities, it has continually evolved in its various reauthorizations/revisions. To appreciate the impact of this law on the provision of services to students with disabilities, this discussion will highlight some of its major revisions/reauthorizations and provide examples of some of its most critical components.

Education for All Handicapped Children Act (Public Law 94–142), 1975

This historical legislation, the Individuals with Disabilities Education Improvement Act of 2004, with its initiation in 1975, as the Education for All Handicapped Children Act, has at times been summarized according to several key principles that typify its focus of providing an appropriate education to students with disabilities. These guiding principles refer to the practices associated with: (a) zero rejection of students; (b) non-discriminatory evaluation; (c) free appropriate education; (d) least restrictive environment; (e) due process and procedural safeguards; (f) parental participation; and (g) the individualized education program (IEP) (Heward, 2013; Rosenberg et al., 2011; Turnbull et al., 2013; Werts et al., 2007). As these major guiding principles are still areas of focus in the most recent version of the law (2004), a more in-depth discussion of each of the topics will be covered in the section of this chapter that relates specifically to the 2004 reauthorization, rather than in this section. It is important, however, to recognize that the Education for All Handicapped Children Act (Public Law 94–142) provided a foundation for much of the legal tenets in effect today for the field of special education.

To avoid redundancy, two additional legislatively based topics will be discussed later in the book: categories of disabilities (Chapter 3) and related services (Chapter 5). The categories of disabilities that could possibly enable students to receive specialized services will be listed in the section of this chapter relating specifically to the 2004 reauthorization. In addition, each of these disability areas will be discussed extensively in Chapter 3. Further, the topic of related services, which may accompany the provision of special education programming, will be discussed in Chapter 5.

Education of the Handicapped Amendments (Public Law 99–457), 1986

As was mentioned previously, this law has evolved over the years as a result of reauthorizations and/or revisions. A major aspect of this piece of legislation from 1986 was that it lowered the age of eligibility for specialized services and established early intervention infants and toddlers programming (Werts et al., 2007). Infants and toddlers who were experiencing developmental delays, as designated by the state, were a focus for multidisciplinary evaluations and individualized service plans, referred to as Individualized Family Service Plans (IFSPs) (Hardman et al., 2008).

Education of the Handicapped Amendments (Public Law 101–476), 1990

In 1990, in addition to changing the name of the law to the Individuals with Disabilities Education Act (IDEA), the Education of the Handicapped Amendments (Public Law 101–476) expanded the listing of disabilities covered by the law to include individuals with autism and traumatic brain injury (Quigney, 2005). There was also the inclusion of social work services, rehabilitation, and counseling as related services. Moreover, assistive technology services and transition services were noted as options available for consideration for an IEP (Werts et al., 2007). Both assistive technologies (e.g., enlarged computer key boards, amplification aids) and transition services (activities to assist the student to make the transition from school to post-school life) will be discussed in depth in later chapters of the book.

Individuals with Disabilities Education Act (IDEA) Amendments of 1997 (Public Law 105–17)

The reauthorization of the law in 1997, the Individuals with Disabilities Education Act (IDEA) Amendments of 1997 (Public Law 105–17), continued in its support of the tenets of previous versions of the law as well as reviewing other issues, some of which will be discussed herein as they are of particular interest to school counselors. One of the major topics addressed in Public Law 105–17 was related to ensuring that students with disabilities would have access to the general education curriculum (Wehmeyer et al., 2002). The IEP is a major avenue through which this assurance is to be enacted, in that there are provisions on the IEP that relate to the student's participation in the general education curriculum. For example, if the students with disabilities are not receiving all of their special education services with their peers who are non-disabled, a justification for this situation is to be provided (Ohio Department of Education, 2012).

The 1997 Amendments also required the participation of a general education teacher as a member of the IEP team if the student was currently participating or may later be participating in the general education setting (US Department of Education, Office of Special Education and Rehabilitative Services, n.d., 34 CFR, S 300.344). The transition process was also addressed, as well as the students' participation in state- and district-wide assessments. Transition will be covered in depth in a later chapter, specifically Chapter 9. In regard to general state- and district-wide assessments, students must be included in these types of evaluations with the availability of appropriate accommodations and adaptations. If the student with a disability is unable to participate in these assessments, alternate assessments must be available to him/her. These decisions are made on an individual basis and managed by the IEP team.

Individuals with Disabilities Education Improvement Act of 2004 (Public Law 108–446)

The most recent reauthorization of this law is called the Individuals with Disabilities Education Improvement Act of 2004 (Public Law 108–446) (Heward, 2013). This law is "commonly referred to as IDEA 2004" (Gargiulo, 2015, p. 50), and consequently from this point, throughout this book, this 2004 reauthorization of this law will be referred to in that manner.

"The IDEA's primary directive is the same now as when the Education for All Handicapped Children Act was passed in 1975: all children with disabilities must be provided a free appropriate public education" (Chapman, 2008, p. 3). As previously noted, there are several guiding principles associated with IDEA 2004, which will be discussed individually:

- **Zero rejection:** No child with a disability may be excluded from receiving a free and appropriate public education (Werts et al., 2007). Further, states are required to employ a system of locating and evaluating children from birth to age 21, who are suspected of having disabilities. This mandate is referred to as the Child Find System (Heward, 2013).
- **Non-discriminatory evaluation:** The purposes of the non-discriminatory assessment process is to first determine whether or not the student has a disability and, second, if a disability is revealed, to establish the specialized services the student will be receiving (Turnbull et al., 2013). To this end, schools are required to employ nonbiased and multi-factored evaluation methods. The assessment must not be discriminatory based on the student's racial, linguistic, and/or cultural background. Testing must be accomplished in the student's native language, and the identification of a disability and placement determinations cannot be based on a single test result/score (Heward, 2013).
- **Free appropriate public education:** Simply put, a free appropriate public education (FAPE) is the practice where "every student with a disability has an appropriate public education at no cost to the parents or guardian" (Hallahan et al., 2012, p. 17). A complete array of appropriate options must be provided in regard to direct and related services (Rosenberg et al., 2011, p. 34). Additional information about services and their provision, including IEPs, will be addressed in later chapters.
- **Least restrictive environment (LRE):** Students with disabilities must be provided an educational program that "facilitates progress in the general education curriculum in a setting with peers who are not disabled to the maximum extent appropriate" (McLaughlin & Ruedel, 2012, p. 77). Removal of students from the general education setting should be considered only when the nature of the disabilities prevents the students from receiving an appropriate education in that environment, even with supplemental aids and/or services (Werts et al., 2007).

- **The individualized education program (IEP):** If a student is identified as having a disability with the stipulations of IDEA 2004, an IEP must be designed. An IEP is a written document that records and guides the educational programming and related services for the students (Rosenberg et al., 2011). There are several specific requirements surrounding the design and implementation of the IEP, which will be discussed in depth in Chapter 5.

- **Procedural safeguards and due process:** To ensure that the rights of students with disabilities and their parents are protected, schools must ensure the provision of a set of procedural safeguards. A few examples of these procedures relate to: (a) the requirement of parental consent for evaluations and placement decisions; (b) the mandate for schools to maintain the confidentiality of the student's records and making these records available for the parents; and (c) the right to request a due process hearing if there is disagreement about the student's evaluation, placement, or services (Heward, 2013).

- **Parental participation:** This component is obviously related to the previous one, but again emphasizes the importance of the parental role in special education. In addition to the aforementioned rights, another example of the vital importance and encouragement of parental participation includes their "right to participate in and agree to all decisions regarding their child's identification, evaluation, educational placement, and the provision of free appropriate public education" (McLaughlin & Ruedel, 2012, p. 8).

As well as these guidelines, IDEA 2004 specifically denotes the areas of disability that it addresses. The law describes a "child with a disability" as one:

> with mental retardation, hearing impairments (including deafness), speech or language impairments, visual impairments (including blindness), serious emotional disturbance (referred to in this title as "emotional disturbance"), orthopedic impairments, autism, traumatic brain injury, other health impairments, or specific learning disabilities; and … who, by reason thereof, needs special education and related services.
>
> (Individuals with Disabilities Education Improvement Act of 2004, Public Law 108–446, Part A, Sec. 602 [3] [A] [i] [ii])

Chapter 3 will provide in-depth information about each of these disability areas.

The law provides additional information in regard to a "child with a disability," for ages three to nine, who may be experiencing developmental delays and consequently requires specialized and related services (IDEA 2004, Part A, Sec. 602 [3] [B] [i] [ii]). This stipulation will also be discussed more in Chapter 3.

IDEA 2004 also addresses other major practices, three of which will be highlighted, as they have particular relevance to the role of the school counselor when working with students with disabilities. "IDEA 2004 included a new provision requiring the special education and related services, supplemental aids and services outlined on a student's IEP need to be based on 'peer-reviewed research'" (National Center for Learning Disabilities, n.d., p. 2). The implementation of evidence-based practice is a major emphasis in special education and there is an expectation that teachers should implement interventions and techniques that have been validated through research (Smith et al., 2014).

A second major practice is related to the fact that a state/local education agency has the option of considering a student's response to scientific and research-based interventions as part of the eligibility determination of specific learning disabilities (SLD), and must not require the employment of a formula to determine the discrepancy between ability and achievement for SLD eligibility (McLaughlin & Ruedel, 2012; National Council for Learning Disabilities, n.d.). Consequently, the practice of Response to Intervention (RTI) was related to the reauthorization of the law in 2004 (Marshak et al., 2010), in regard to it being acceptable for implementation as part of the eligibility procedures for SLD. Briefly, RTI is a process whereby a "student is exposed to increasing levels of validated instructional intervention; responsiveness to the instruction is assessed; a lack of adequate progress typically leads to a referral for possible special education services" (Gargiulo, 2015, p. 608). The RTI process will be explained in much more depth in Chapter 4 and Chapter 10.

A third example of a major issue related to IDEA 2004 which is pertinent to school counselors is the requirement of a "Summary of Performance" for each "student who exits special education by graduating with a regular diploma or exceeding the age for special education under state law" (National Center for Learning Disabilities, n.d., p. 2). This "Summary of Performance" is to include a synopsis of the student's functional and academic performance, and may prove to be beneficial for students with disabilities in their post-secondary experiences as they pursue the accessing of accommodations or services (National Center for Learning Disabilities, n.d.). The "Summary of Performance" stipulation will be discussed further in Chapter 9.

The Rehabilitation Act of 1973, Section 504 (Public Law 93–112)

Although IDEA 2004 may be regarded as the most pertinent piece of legislation related to students with disabilities obtaining services in school-age educational environments, a second law has also had a major impact on the field of special education. The Rehabilitation Act of 1973 (Public Law 93–112) is "civil rights legislation" (Gargiulo, 2012, p. 59), and was legislated to generally safeguard the legal entitlements of individuals with disabilities (Jasper, 2004). While this law impacts various facets of rehabilitative practices, the component of the law that is particularly relevant to the promotion of non-discriminatory activities toward students with disabilities is Section 504 of the Rehabilitation Act of 1973 (Smith & Patton, 1998). The goal of Section 504 "is to prevent any form of discrimination against individuals with disabilities who are *otherwise qualified*. Section 504 applies to entities that receive federal funds" (Smith, 2001, p. 335, emphasis in original). Since some sort of federal assistance is generally provided to public schools, Section 504 is applicable to such public educational environments (Jasper, 2004).

Eligibility for Services

Clearly, Section 504 is a statute that emphasizes anti-discrimination in regard to individuals with disabilities (Russo & Osborne, 2008). For a student to be eligible for Section 504 protections, he or she "must be determined to: (1) have a physical or mental impairment that substantially limits one or more major life activities; or (2) have a record of such an impairment; or (3) be regarded as having such an impairment"

Figure 2.1 Legislative mandates provide support for all students to have equal access to a free appropriate public education in the least restrictive environment.
Source: ©*iStockphoto.com, www.istockphoto.com/photo/group-of-school-children-focus-on-girl-and -boy-15370486.*

(US Department of Education, Office for Civil Rights, 2013, para. 21). Section 504 also requires that a free appropriate public education be provided to eligible students (Giuliani, 2012). The previous two statements, although relatively brief in length and straightforward in language, are essential to a basic appreciation of Section 504's influence on the education of students with disabilities, and consequently require clarification of essential concepts.

WHAT CONSTITUTES AN ELIGIBLE PHYSICAL OR MENTAL IMPAIRMENT?

The Section 504 regulatory provision at 34 C.F.R. 104.3(j)(2)(i) defines a physical or mental impairment as any physiological disorder or condition, cosmetic disfigurement, or anatomical loss affecting one or more of the following body systems: neurological; musculoskeletal; special sense organs; respiratory, including speech organs; cardiovascular; reproductive; digestive; genito-urinary; hemic and lymphatic; skin; and endocrine; or any mental or psychological disorder, such as mental retardation, organic brain syndrome, emotional or mental illness, and specific learning disabilities. The regulatory provision does not set forth an exhaustive list of specific diseases and conditions that may constitute physical or mental impairments because of the difficulty of ensuring the comprehensiveness of such a list.

(US Department of Education, Office for
Civil Rights, 2013, para. 22)

WHAT IS CONSIDERED A MAJOR LIFE ACTIVITY? WHAT CONSTITUTES SUBSTANTIAL LIMITATION OF SUCH AN ACTIVITY?

"Major life activities means functions such as caring for one's self, performing manual tasks, walking, seeing, hearing, speaking, breathing, learning, and working" (US Department of Education, n.d., 34 CFR Part 104.3 (j) (2) (ii), emphasis in original). While all of these activities are of foremost importance, the function of particular applicability to educational personnel is *learning*.

In 2008, the Americans with Disabilities Act Amendments (ADAA) were passed with January 1, 2009 being its effective date (Zirkel, 2012). Although the ADAA will be discussed later in this chapter, it is important to note that these amendments resulted in corresponding modifications to Section 504 (Bowman, 2011).

While the ADAA did not alter the legal description of a disability, it changed the method for its interpretation (Cortiella & Kaloi, 2010). The ADAA essentially had an expanding effect in regard to the two aspects of the definition of disability, which relate to *major life activities* and their level of *substantial* limitation. As an example in regard to *major life activities*, there have been expanded interpretations for students with learning issues, by including such alternatives as related to thought processes, reading, and concentration (Zirkel, 2009).

Moreover, the impact of ADAA on Section 504 is also evident in its expanding criterion regarding the definition of disability, specifically the aspect which relates to *substantial* limitation of a major life activity (Zirkel, 2009). As Kaloi and Stanberry (n.d., para. 6) note: "ADAA requires that the limitation on a 'major' life activity be broadly, rather than narrowly, interpreted," as well as "without regard to the ameliorative effects of mitigating measures like medication or medical equipment. (The only stated exception is eyeglasses or contact lenses)" (Gargiulo, 2012, p. 62).

The potential consequence of such changes is the expansion of the number and scope of students with disabilities meeting eligibility requirements according to Section 504 (Zirkel, 2009). There may be some students who had previously not met qualification requirements who may now be eligible for the protections and services afforded by Section 504, such as accommodations and auxiliary supports (Kaloi & Stanberry, n.d.). The identification process in relation to students' eligibility for Section 504 protections will be addressed in Chapter 4.

WHAT IS A FREE APPROPRIATE PUBLIC EDUCATION ACCORDING TO SECTION 504?

According to the US Department of Education, an *appropriate education* involves "the provision of regular or special education and related aids and services that … are designed to meet individual educational needs of handicapped persons as adequately as the needs of nonhandicapped persons are met" (US Department of Education, n.d., 34 CFR Part 104.33 [b]). (Please note that although some quotes/references employ the term "handicap" due to the age of the legal reference, the accepted term is "disability.") Therefore, because of Section 504, equal access to educational aids and services is assured for students with disabilities (Chapman, 2008).

Section 504 Plans

After it has been determined that a student is eligible for Section 504 protections, an individualized plan must be derived. Although an IEP is not a requirement as it is with IDEA 2004, a written plan is mandatory, and is often referred to as a Section 504 Plan. These plans must include information relevant to ensuring that appropriate accommodations are made for the student and he/she is provided a free appropriate public education (Smith, 2001).

Being knowledgeable about Section 504 and its legal requirements and implementation is vital to the role of the school counselor. In a study of practices in the implementation of Section 504 requirements, Madaus and Shaw (2008) found that school counselors were second only to school administrators in being responsible for running meetings focused on Section 504 issues, and the "responsibility for managing completed Section 504 Plans most often fell to school counselors" (Madaus & Shaw, 2008, p. 371), followed by other school personnel. Additional information on Section 504 meetings and plans may be found in Chapter 5.

The Relationship between Section 504 and Non-Academic Activities

It is important to appreciate that Section 504 is a statute related to civil rights (deBettencourt, 2002; Gargiulo, 2012) and as such, is focused on non-discrimination. While school personnel are often focused on the academic and/or behavioral needs of a student who meets the eligibility requirements for Section 504 protections, it is important to also recognize that non-academic and extracurricular options are also considerations. Section 504 requires that students with disabilities are afforded equal opportunities for participation in such activities. For example, educational personnel must consider what accommodations and/or supports may be required for students with disabilities in regard to such activities as field trips and school-sponsored activities, such as dances and other functions (*Special Education Report*, 2014).

Conceptual Application Activity 2.1

Application of Section 504 to Non-Academic School Activity

As Section 504 is focused on various aspects of non-discrimination of students with disabilities, including non-academic and extracurricular activities, the school counselor may be called upon as an advocate for the students to ensure that equal opportunities for participation are provided. Read the description that follows and reflect on your role as an advocate for the student.

Donald is a tenth-grader who has recently transferred to the high school at which you are one of the school counselors. Donald has been diagnosed with an intellectual disability and has been receiving specialized services through special education at his former school district for many years. He also played soccer at his former school as a freshman and would like to continue being on the soccer team at your school. Donald is a talented soccer player, but can have difficulty with explanations of plays and play sequences. Consequently, he will require extra time, individualized coaching, and much repetition to be prepared for a match. Donald's parents have come to you seeking assistance. They have already spoken with the soccer coach, who was pleasant but firm in his response, that he could not provide Donald with that type of instruction and coaching, as he had many other players taking his coaching time. Donald's parents are upset as this is an area in which Donald could excel.

Based on what you have learned about Section 504, in particular:

1. Clarify the issue(s) of concern, particularly from a legal perspective.
2. How would you address this situation with the parents? Consider the roles of the school, coach, and other invested personnel as to how this situation should be resolved.
3. How would you address the situation with the soccer coach if he comes to you and asks for advice and information?
4. What steps could you initiate to see that a fair, ethical, and legal conclusion is met?

This activity may be completed individually, in small groups, or as a large group discussion.

A Comparison of IDEA 2004 and Section 504

While both IDEA 2004 and Section 504 have considerable influence on the education of students with disabilities, it is interesting to compare them to determine how they differ. Both laws clearly emphasize the importance of educating students with disabilities with their peers who are non-disabled, while still meeting the areas of need for the students with disabilities (Smith, 2002). Yet there are differences between them worth discussing.

One of these areas is that of the identification of disabilities. As we have seen from the previous discussion, IDEA 2004 notes specific categories of disability. With IDEA 2004, eligibility requirements are associated with these particular categories of disabilities and their criteria as specified within its tenets, as well as the existence of a detrimental effect on the student's educational performance. However, as we have seen with Section 504, the criteria for meeting eligibility requirements are much broader in scope. As such, students who may not meet the eligibility requirements for services through IDEA 2004 may in fact be eligible for services through the stipulations of Section 504.

There are also factors that are different between the two laws in regard to the evaluation procedures, with IDEA 2004 at times being more specific in its stipulations. For example, while Section 504 requires that decisions be made by a "knowledgeable group" (deBettencourt, 2002, p. 20), IDEA 2004 is more specific about the conditions of the evaluation process, that is, that a comprehensive evaluation be completed by a multidisciplinary team of individuals (deBettencourt, 2002).

While both laws involve a documented written educational plan (Hardman et al., 2008), IDEA 2004 requires the design of an IEP with specific requirements as to its components and to the team membership involved with this activity, again being more explicit in its mandates. Moreover, there is a difference in the age limitations covered in both laws. For example, while there is a focus on the age of 21 regarding the age limitation for coverage for IDEA 2004, there is no restriction on age in Section 504 for termination of coverage (Baditoi & Brott, 2011). Many of these issues (e.g., descriptions of disabilities, evaluation procedures, IEPs, 504 Plans) will be addressed in later chapters.

The Americans with Disabilities Act (ADA) and the ADA Amendments Act of 2008 (ADAA) (Public Law 110–325)

In 1990, the Americans with Disabilities Act (ADA) was signed into law. Like the Rehabilitation Act of 1973, the ADA provided civil rights and protections to people with disabilities. The definition of a person with a disability within the ADA is generally equivalent to that found within Section 504 (Chapman, 2008). The ADA addressed such matters as public services, employment, public accommodations, transportation, and telecommunications (Culatta et al., 2003; Hardman et al., 2008; Hunt & Marshall, 2002).

Although the ADA is not as educationally specific as IDEA 2004, it does have an influence on specialized services. Students in the public school system are protected by Title II of this law (Mead & Risch, 2008). Because Title II of the ADA prohibits discrimination of individuals with disabilities by government programs on the local and state levels, this would include public school systems (Culatta et al., 2003). In addition, the ADA ensures the accessibility of school facilities to individuals with disabilities (Baumberger & Harper, 2007; Salend, 2001).

As noted previously, this law was revised and the ADA Amendments Act of 2008 (ADAA) went into effect in 2009 (Zirkel, 2009). This piece of legislation, also referred to as Public Law 110–325 (Gargiulo, 2012), was discussed earlier in this chapter as it is specifically associated with Section 504. Both the ADAA and Section 504 have a focus of anti-discrimination, and their commonality is providing protections from bias and unfairness in public school environments (Kaloi & Stanberry, n.d.).

Although ADAA is much broader in scope than specific *educational* mandates for individuals with disabilities (e.g., IDEA 2004), the fact that it is related to Section 504 and it provides corresponding modifications to Section 504 (Bowman, 2011) causes it to exert important influence on school-related options, in particular. Being aware of the interrelatedness of the ADAA with Section 504 is of importance to professional school counselors, because as we have seen in the previous section of this chapter, Section 504 is a piece of legislation that has a considerable impact on the identification of some students with disabilities and the provision of various specialized services in educational environments. (Please refer to the previous topic of Section 504 in this chapter for a review of the changes in ADAA and their corresponding effect on Section 504.)

Every Student Succeeds Act

The Elementary and Secondary Education Act (ESEA) was first passed by Congress in 1965 (Cortiella, 2007). In 2001, ESEA was reauthorized by Congress and became more commonly known as the No Child Left Behind Act (NCLB) (Public Law 107–110) (Gargiulo, 2012). NCLB's influence had been far-reaching and sometimes controversial, in that it had been both lauded by some and criticized by others (Quigney, 2008).

The most recent reauthorization of the Elementary and Secondary Education Act is referred to as the Every Student Succeeds Act (ESSA). President Obama signed this Act on December 10, 2015. While student testing and accountability for the schools are still points of focus in the ESSA as with the previous re-authorization, the importance of state involvement in the implementation of this law is noted. A focus is now on "the states to work with local stakeholders and districts to design, for example, new and better assessments and accountability systems and follow through on identifying and filling opportunity gaps" (Walker, 2015, para. 10).

Although this law has broader implications than the education of students with disabilities, it has direct implications for this population. In the *CEC's Summary of Selected Provisions in Every Student Succeeds Act (ESSA)*, the Council for Exceptional Children (n.d.) notes that for children who have disabilities, the ESSA:

- Ensures access to the general education curriculum.
- Ensures access to accommodations on assessments.
- Ensures concepts of Universal Design for Learning.
- Includes provisions that require local education agencies to provide evidence – based interventions in schools with consistently underperforming subgroups.
- Requires states in Title I plans to address how they will improve conditions for learning including reducing incidents of bullying and harassment in schools, overuse of discipline practices and reduce the use of aversive behavioral interventions (such as restraints and seclusion) (para. 14).

As with other laws and regulations discussed thus far, school counselors should have a knowledge base in The Elementary and Secondary Education Act, its reauthorizations and revisions, and its implementation in general, and in particular as to its effect on the education of students with disabilities, as their job functions may be directly or indirectly affected by such legal mandates and practices. As school counselors are cooperative partners with teachers, administrators, and other pertinent professionals, it is imperative for them to appreciate these legislative requirements, to be effective in their roles as collaborative and supportive resources and school leaders. School counselors are also often involved with student assessment practices, including the interpretation of evaluation results and the preparation of students for completing the assessments through instruction in testing and study skills (Baumberger & Harper, 2007).

Family Educational Rights and Privacy Act (FERPA)

Although knowledge of the content and implementation of the four previously discussed laws are vital to practicing school counselors, especially as they work with students with disabilities and other invested parties, a co-existing legal tenet also has relevance for the particular practice of confidentiality by the school counselor. The importance of confidentiality has already been discussed in reference to IDEA 2004 in this chapter as well as in Chapter 1. In Chapter 1, the *Ethical Standards for School Counselors* (ASCA, 2010) were introduced and discussed as a major component of the role of an effective school counselor. Two of these ethical standards, in particular, are directly related to a major law. Standard A2, *Confidentiality*, and Standard A8, *Student Records*, may be associated with aspects of the Family Educational Rights and Privacy Act (FERPA).

"The Family Educational Rights and Privacy Act (FERPA) (20 U.S.C. § 1232g; 34 CFR Part 99) is a Federal law that protects the privacy of student education records" (US Department of Education, Family Policy Compliance Office, n.d., para. 1). This law notes that parents have the right to review the educational records of their child and to challenge the exactness of their contents. In addition, written parental consent is required for release of the educational records to others, except for specific classifications of individuals, such as officials from the school (Bateman et al., 2007; Latham et al., 2008). FERPA also institutes a system for parental concerns regarding related legal issues, and districts are required to have a written policy focused on the individuals who will be having access to the students' records (Bateman et al., 2007). The rights afforded parents with FERPA are transferred to students at age 18 or when they attend post-secondary educational institutions (Latham et al., 2008).

Clearly, certain aspects of the role of the school counselor relate to confidentiality and school records, as was evidenced in the discussion from Chapter 1 and in reference to IDEA 2004. It is vital for school counselors to be aware that critical information such as that resulting from the assessment procedures to ascertain whether or not a student has a disability will be placed into the student's file, along with such information as IEPs and IEP goal achievement reports. Consequently counselors should work to ensure that these files are appropriately safeguarded (Bateman et al., 2007). Protecting records such as these speaks to the importance of school counselors being aware of the legal basis for confidentiality as well as the ethical foundation of their role in its regard.

Conceptual Application Activity 2.2

Reflection on the Impact of Special Education Law on the Role of a School Counselor when Working with Students with Disabilities and Pertinent Stakeholders

Directions: Early in this chapter, this assertion was made:

School counselors are resources not only for students with disabilities, but for a number of individuals associated with the field of special education, including families of the students with disabilities, teachers, administrators, and other school personnel who work with students with disabilities, and pertinent community and agency resources.

As school counselors are clearly key players in the educational lives of students with disabilities, and there is such a clear influence of legal tenets and mandates on various aspects of the provision of specialized services to students with disabilities, it is vital that school counselors are aware of the laws and their requirements.

Now that you have been exposed to an overview of five of the most pertinent laws related to special education, reflect on how this knowledge can be beneficial to your role as a school counselor when working with the key stakeholders in the process of providing specialized services. Specifically reflect on how this knowledge will be advantageous to you as you work with the following groups: (a) students with disabilities; (b) parents and families of students with disabilities; (c) teachers and other educational personnel who work with students with disabilities; (d) school administrators; and (e) community and agency personnel who may be involved with the students with disabilities. In the table that follows, for each of the five groups of stakeholders, note three to five items you have learned about from this chapter's discussion on the law that could have direct applicability to your role as school counselor as you work with each of these groups.

This activity may be completed individually, in small groups, or as a large group discussion.

The Law, Special Education, and the Role of School Counselors

Students with disabilities	Parents/families of students with disabilities	Teachers and other educational personnel who work with students with disabilities	School administrators	Community and agency personnel

Conclusion

School counselors are committed to working with *all* students, with and without special needs:

> The professional school counselor takes an active role in student achievement by providing a comprehensive school counseling program for all students. As a part of this program, professional school counselors advocate for students with special needs, encourage family involvement in their child's education and collaborate with other educational professionals to promote academic achievement for all.
>
> (ASCA, 2013, para. 6)

Special education continues to have a strong foundation in legislative tenets and findings based in litigation. Therefore, it is critical that school counselors are aware of the legal foundation for many of the aspects of their role, particularly as they relate to students with disabilities. This chapter has emphasized five of the most relevant laws in which school counselors should have a sound working knowledge as they work with students with disabilities. A foundation in such laws should assist school counselors as they work to effectively meet the needs of students with disabilities and to successfully interact with others associated with the field of special education, while functioning within the legal standards and regulations that are required.

References

ASCA (2010). *Ethical Standards for School Counselors.* Retrieved from www.schoolcounselor. org/asca/media/asca/Resource%20Center/Legal%20and%20Ethical%20Issues/Sample%20 Documents/EthicalStandards2010.pdf.

ASCA (2013). *The Professional School Counselor and Students with Disabilities.* Retrieved from www.schoolcounselor.org/asca/media/asca/PositionStatements/PS_Disabilities.pdf.

Baditoi, B. E. & Brott, P. E. (2011). *What School Counselors Need to Know about Special Education and Students with Disabilities.* Arlington, VA: Council for Exceptional Children.

Bateman, D. F., Bright, K. L., O'Shea, D. J., O'Shea, L. J., & Algozzine, B. (2007). *The Special Education Program Administrator's Handbook.* Boston, MA: Pearson Education, Inc.

Baumberger, J. P. & Harper, R. E. (2007). *Assisting Students with Disabilities: A Handbook for School Counselors,* 2nd edn. Thousand Oaks, CA: Corwin Press, Inc.

Bowman, L. (2011). Americans with Disabilities Act as amended: principles and practice. *New Directions for Adult and Continuing Education,* 132, 85–95.

Chapman, R. (2008). *The Everyday Guide to Special Education Law: A Handbook for Parents, Teachers, and Other Professionals,* 2nd edn. Denver, CO: Legal Center for People with Disabilities and Older People.

Cortiella, C. (2007). No Child Left Behind and students with disabilities. *Exceptional Parent,* 37(9), 70–73.

Cortiella, C. & Kaloi, L. (2010). Meet the new and improved Section 504. *Exceptional Parent,* 40(2), 14–15.

Council for Exceptional Children (n.d.). *CEC's Summary of Selected Provisions in Every Student Succeeds Act (ESSA).* Retrieved from http://cecblog.typepad.com/files/cecs-summary-of-selected-issues-in-every-student-succeeds-act-essa-1.pdf.

Culatta, R. A., Tompkins, J. R., & Werts, M. G. (2003). *Fundamentals of Special Education: What Every Teacher Needs to Know,* 2nd edn. Upper Saddle River, NJ: Merrill Prentice-Hall.

deBettencourt, L. U. (2002). Understanding the differences between IDEA and Section 504. *Teaching Exceptional Children,* 34(3), 16–23.

Gargiulo, R. M. (2012). *Special Education in Contemporary Society, an Introduction to Exceptionality.* Thousand Oaks, CA: Sage.

Gargiulo, R. M. (2015). *Special Education in Contemporary Society: An Introduction to Exceptionality,* 5th edn. Thousand Oaks, CA: Sage.

Giuliani, G. A. (2012). *The Comprehensive Guide to Special Education Law.* London and Philadelphia, PA: Jessica Kingsley.

Hallahan, D. P., Kauffman, J. M., & Pullen, P. C. (2012). *Exceptional Learners: An Introduction to Special Education,* 12th edn. Upper Saddle River, NJ: Pearson Education, Inc.

Hardman, M. L., Drew, C. J., & Egan, M. W. (2008). *Human Exceptionality, School, Community, and Family,* 9th edn. Boston, MA: Houghton Mifflin Company.

Heward, W. M. (2013). *Exceptional Children: An Introduction to Special Education,* 10th edn. Upper Saddle River, NJ: Pearson Education, Inc.

Hunt, N. & Marshall, K. (2002). *Exceptional Children and Youth: An Introduction to Special Education,* 3rd edn. Boston, MA: Houghton Mifflin Company.

Individuals with Disabilities Education Improvement Act, Public Law 108–446 (2004). *An Act to reauthorize the Individuals with Disabilities Education Act, and for Other Purposes. Title I-Amendments to the Individuals with Disabilities Education Act.* Retrieved from www.copyright.gov/legislation/pl108446.pdf.

Jasper, M. C. (2004). *The Law of Special Education,* 2nd edn. Dobbs Ferry, NY: Oceana Publications, Inc.

Jones, N. L. & Apling, R. N. (n.d.). *CRS Report for Congress, the Individuals with Disabilities Education Act (IDEA): Overview of P.L. 108–446*. Retrieved from http://congressionalresearch .com/RS22138/document.php.

Kaloi, L. & Stanberry, K. (n.d.). *Section 504 in 2009: Broader Eligibility, More Accommodations*. Retrieved from www.ncld.org/disability-advocacy/learn-ld-laws/adaaa-section-504/section-504-2009-broader-eligibility-more-accommodations.

Latham, P. S., Latham, P. H., & Mandlawitz, M. R. (2008). *Special Education Law*. Boston, MA: Pearson Education, Inc.

McLaughlin, M. M. J. & Ruedel, K. (2012). *The School Leader's Guide to Special Education*, 3rd edn. Bloomington, IN: Solution Tree Press.

Madaus, J. W. & Shaw, S. F. (2008). The role of school professionals in implementing Section 504 for students with disabilities. *Educational Policy*, 22(3), 363–378.

Marshak, L. E., Dandeneau, C. J., Prezant, F. P., & L'Amoreaux. N. A. (2010). *The School Counselor's Guide to Helping Students with Disabilities*. San Francisco, CA: Jossey-Bass, John Wiley & Sons, Inc.

Mead, J. F. & Risch, J. (2008). Fundamentals of federal disability law. In K. E. Lane, M. A. Gooden, J. F. Mead, P. Pauken, & S. Eckes (eds.), *The Principal's Legal Handbook*, 4th edn. (pp. 207–217). Dayton, OH: Education Law Association.

National Center for Learning Disabilities (n.d.). *IDEA 2004 Final Regulations Update*. Retrieved from www.ncld.org/disability-advocacy/learn-ld-laws/idea/idea-2004-final-regulations-update.

Ohio Department of Education (2012). *IEP Individualized Education Program, PR-07 IEP FORM*. Retrieved from http://education.ohio.gov/getattachment/Topics/Special-Education/Federal-and-State-Requirements/Procedures-and-Guidance/Individualized-Education-Program-IEP/Development-of-IEP/iep_form_09_static.pdf.aspx.

Quigney, T. A. (2005). Students with special needs. In J. R. Studer (ed.), *The Professional School Counselor: An Advocate for Students* (pp.82–106). Belmont, CA: Thomson Brooks/Cole.

Quigney, T. A. (2008). The reauthorization of the No Child Left Behind Act: recommended practices regarding teaching students with disabilities. *Planning and Changing*, 39(3–4), 146–157.

Rosenberg M. S., Westling, D. L., & McLeskey, J. (2011). *Special Education for Today's Teachers: An Introduction*, 2nd edn. Upper Saddle River, NJ: Pearson Education, Inc.

Russo, C. J. & Osborne, A.G. (2008). *Essential Concepts and School-Based Cases in Special Education Law*. Thousand Oaks, CA: Corwin Press.

Salend, S. J. (2001). *Creating Inclusive Classrooms: Effective and Reflective Practices*, 4th edn. Upper Saddle River, NJ: Merrill Prentice-Hall.

Smith, D. D., Tyler, N. C. and Smith, S. (2014). *Introduction to Contemporary Special Education: New Horizons*. Upper Saddle River, NJ: Pearson Education, Inc.

Smith, T. E. C. (2001). Section 504, the ADA, and public schools, what educators need to know. *Remedial and Special Education*, 22(6), 335–343.

Smith, T. E. C. (2002). Section 504: what teachers need to know. *Intervention in School and Clinic*, 37(5), 259–266.

Smith, T. E. C. & Patton, J. R. (1998). *Section 504 and Public Schools, a Practical Guide for Determining Eligibility, Developing Accommodation Plans, and Documenting Compliance*. Austin, TX: Pro-Ed.

Special Education Report (2014).Train staff on Section 504's relationship to nonacademic activities. *Special Education Report*, 40(2), 6.

Turnbull, A., Turnbull, R., Wehmeyer, M. L., & Shogren, K. A. (2013). *Exceptional Lives: Special Education in Today's Schools*, 7th edn. Upper Saddle River, NJ: Pearson Education, Inc.

US Department of Education (n.d.). *Title 34 Education, Subtitle B Regulations of the Offices of the Department of Education, Chapter1-Office for Civil Rights, Department of Education, Part 104: Nondiscrimination on the Basis of Handicap in Programs or Activities Receiving Federal Financial Assistance*. Retrieved from www2.ed.gov/policy/rights/reg/ocr/edlite-34cfr104 .html#S34.

US Department of Education, Family Policy Compliance Office (n.d.). *Family Educational Rights and Privacy Act (FERPA)*. Retrieved from www.ed.gov/policy/gen/guid/fpco/ferpa/index.html.

US Department of Education, Office for Civil Rights (2013). *Protecting Students with Disabilities: Frequently Asked Questions about Section 504 and the Education of Children with Disabilities*. Retrieved from www2.ed.gov/about/offices/list/ocr/504faq.html.

US Department of Education, Office of Special Education and Rehabilitative Services (n.d.). *IDEA '97 Final Regulations*. Retrieved from www.ideapractices.org/law/regulations/index .php.

Walker, T. (2015, December 9). With passage of Every Student Succeeds Act, life after NCLB begins. *NEA Today*. Retrieved from http://neatoday.org/2015/12/09/every-student-succeeds-act/.

Wehmeyer, M. L., Lance, G. D., & Bashinski, S. (2002). Promoting access to the general curriculum for students with mental retardation: a multilevel model. *Education and Training in Mental Retardation and Developmental Disabilities*, 37(3), 223–234.

Werts, M. G., Culatta, R. A., & Tompkins, J. R. (2007). *Fundamentals of Special Education: What Every Teacher Needs to Know*, 3rd edn. Upper Saddle River, NJ: Pearson Education, Inc.

Zirkel, P. A. (2009).The ADAA and its effect on Section 504 students. *Journal of Special Education Leadership*, 22(1), 3–8.

Zirkel. P. A. (2012). Section 504 for special education leaders: persisting and emerging issues. *Journal of Special Education Leadership*, 25(2), 99–105.

3 Areas of Disability

The following CACREP standards are addressed in this chapter:

HUMAN GROWTH AND DEVELOPMENT
  f. systemic and environmental factors that affect human development, functioning and behavior
  h. a general framework for understanding differing abilities and strategies for differentiated interventions

SECTION 5: ENTRY-LEVEL SPECIALTY AREAS
  G. SCHOOL COUNSELING
  2. CONTEXTUAL DIMENSIONS
  g. characteristics, risk factors, and warning signs of students at risk for mental health and behavioral disorders

Chapter Objectives

After you have completed this chapter, you should be able to:

- Describe the areas of disability discussed in the chapter according to their definition and characteristics.
- Discuss a sampling of educational approaches and supports for each area of disability.
- Discuss special considerations for the transition to post-secondary life for each area of disability.
- Self-reflect on the role of the school counselor in relation to the provision of educational approaches, supports, and assistance related to the transition to post-secondary life, for each area of disability.

Areas of Disability

Based on the legal and regulatory foundation that has been established in the preceding chapter, an overview of the specific areas of disability will now be discussed. It is critical that school counselors have an informed knowledge base of the students with whom they will be working in special education. Consequently, the various areas of disability will be discussed in regard to their definition, characteristics, and a sampling of applicable educational approaches and supports.

It is important to note that the specific areas of disability that will be discussed in this chapter are those that are listed as disabilities according to IDEA 2004. As you have learned from the discussion in Chapter 2, the regulations for the designation of a disability is much broader in regard to Section 504 than that of the tenets associated with IDEA 2004. As such, a discussion of all potential areas of disability that could fall within the parameters of Section 504 guidelines is beyond the scope of this book. Moreover, because IDEA 2004 is specifically an educational piece of legislation, it is appropriate that this chapter will address the specific areas of disability listed therein. It is important to note, however, that students who may not be eligible for services within IDEA 2004 stipulations may still be covered within the regulations of Section 504.

Areas of Disability According to the Individuals with Disabilities Education Improvement Act (IDEA 2004)

As we have previously discussed in Chapter 2, the Individuals with Disabilities Education Improvement Act, 2004 (Public Law 108–446) notes specific areas of disability as being eligible for services according to its stipulations.

> (3) CHILD WITH A DISABILITY—
>   (A) IN GENERAL—The term "child with a disability" means a child—
>   (i) with mental retardation, hearing impairments (including deafness), speech or language impairments, visual impairments (including blindness), serious emotional disturbance (referred to in this title as "emotional disturbance"), orthopedic impairments, autism, traumatic brain injury, other health impairments, or specific learning disabilities; and
>   (ii) who, by reason thereof, needs special education and related services.
>   (Individuals with Disabilities Education Improvement
>   Act of 2004, Public Law 108–446, Part A,
>   Sec. 602 [3] [A] [i] [ii])

This law further adds additional information in regard to students aged three to nine.

> (B) CHILD AGED 3 THROUGH 9—The term "child with a disability" for a child aged 3 through 9 (or any subset of that age range, including ages 3 through 5), may, at the discretion of the State and the local educational agency, include a child—
>   (i) experiencing developmental delays, as defined by the State and as measured by appropriate diagnostic instruments and procedures, in 1 or more of the following areas: physical development; cognitive development; communication development; social or emotional development; or adaptive development; and
>   (ii) who, by reason thereof, needs special education and related services (Individuals with Disabilities Education Improvement Act of 2004, Public Law 108–446, Part A, Sec. 602 [3] [B] [i] [ii].

A specific listing of the areas of disability and their definitions may be found in Table 3.1. Again, the focus of this text is on students with disabilities on the K-12 levels. Thus, the discussion will not include information on infants and toddlers with disabilities or at-risk infants and toddlers. Nor will there be further discussion of children with developmental delays, as this topic has already been addressed. The information in Table 3.1 is retrieved from the Council for Exceptional Children (n.d.) website and focuses on the special education topic of *Who Are Exceptional Learners?* As explained on the site: "The disability terms and definitions are taken from the Individuals with Disabilities Education Act" (Council for Exceptional Children, n.d., para. 1).

Autism Spectrum Disorder

BACKGROUND INFORMATION AND CHARACTERISTICS

Although the reasons for the diagnosis are not conclusive, there has been a striking increase in the incidence of autism spectrum disorder (ASD) (Heward, 2013). ASD is described as "a developmental disorder characterized by abnormal or impaired development in social interaction and communication and a markedly restricted repertoire of activity and interests" (Gargiulo, 2015, p. 329) The level of severity varies among students with ASD, with some being seriously influenced in many or all areas of functioning, while its effect on other students may be less (Heward, 2013).

Although Table 3.1 provides a legally based and educational definition of autism, according to IDEA 2004, another frequently cited description of this disability area is from the American Psychiatric Association (APA, 2013b) in the *Diagnostic and Statistical Manual of Mental Disorders, fifth edition* (DSM-5). Upon review of its criteria, it is clear that an emphasis is being placed on socialization issues, specifically social communication and social interaction, including a lack of social-emotional reciprocity. There is also a focus on non-verbal communicative characteristics associated with socialization activities and the building, understanding, and maintenance of interpersonal relationships. In addition to an emphasis on social behaviors, the DSM-5 diagnostic criteria also delineate the problem of exhibiting patterns of restricted and repetitive behaviors, pursuits, or actions, including stereotypical movements or speech, adherence to routine and consistency, abnormally intense and restricted interests, and atypical reactions to sensory input (APA, 2013b). It is important to note that the most recent edition of the APA's *Diagnostic and Statistical Manual of Mental Disorders* (DSM-5) (APA, 2013b) combines autistic disorder and Asperger's disorder, as well as pervasive developmental disorder, within the same heading of "autism spectrum disorder" (Gargiulo, 2015). For in-depth information on DSM-5 criteria for ASD, please refer to *Autism Spectrum Disorder: Diagnostic Criteria*, from the Division of Human Development, National Center on Birth Defects and Developmental Disabilities, Centers for Disease Control and Prevention (2014a and 2014b) at www.cdc.gov/ncbddd/autism/hcp-dsm.html.

Other characteristics that have been associated with some individuals with ASD are self-injurious behavior, aggression (Boutot & Myles, 2011), deficits with figurative language, repetitive language as in echolalia (Rosenberg et al., 2011), over-selectivity, problems with joint attention (Heward, 2013), and behaviors associated with perseveration (activities repeated for a long time) (Heflin & Alaimo, 2007). This discussion of characteristics of ASD is by no means exhaustive and should only be interpreted as an overview of this topic.

Table 3.1 Disability Terms and Definitions

The disability terms and definitions are taken from the Individuals with Disabilities Education Act.

Disability terms	Definitions
Autism	**Autism** means a developmental disability significantly affecting verbal and non-verbal communication and social interaction, generally evident before age three, that adversely affects a child's educational performance. Other characteristics often associated with autism are engagement in repetitive activities and stereotyped movements, resistance to environmental change or change in daily routines, and unusual responses to sensory experience. Autism does not apply if a child's education performance is adversely affected primarily because the child has an emotional disturbance.
Deaf-blindness	**Deaf-blindness** means concomitant hearing and visual impairments, the combination of which causes such severe communication and other developmental and educational needs that they cannot be accommodated in special education programs solely for children with deafness or children with blindness.
Deafness	**Deafness** means a hearing impairment that is so severe that the child is impaired in processing linguistic information through hearing, with or without amplification that adversely affects a child's educational performance.
Emotional disturbance	**Emotional disturbance** means a condition exhibiting one or more of the following characteristics over a long period of time and to a marked degree that adversely affects a child's educational performance: • An inability to learn that cannot be explained by intellectual, sensory, or health factors. • An inability to build or maintain satisfactory interpersonal relationships with peers and teachers. • Inappropriate types of behavior or feelings under normal circumstances. • A general pervasive mood of unhappiness or depression. • A tendency to develop physical symptoms or fears associated with personal or school problems. Emotional disturbance includes schizophrenia. The term does not apply to children who are socially maladjusted, unless it is determined that they have an emotional disturbance.
Intellectual disability	**Intellectual disability** means significantly sub-average general intellectual functioning, existing concurrently with deficits in adaptive behavior and manifested during the developmental period, that adversely affects a child's educational performance.
Hearing impairment	**Hearing impairment** means an impairment in hearing, whether permanent or fluctuating, that adversely affects a child's educational performance but that is not included under the definition of deafness in this section.
Multiple disabilities	**Multiple disabilities** means concomitant impairments (such as mental retardation–blindness or mental retardation–orthopedic impairment), the combination of which causes such severe educational needs that they cannot be accommodated in special education programs solely for one of the impairments. Multiple disabilities do not include deaf-blindness.

Table 3.1 *(cont.)*

Disability terms	Definitions
Orthopedic impairment	**Orthopedic impairment** means a severe orthopedic impairment that adversely affects a child's education performance. The term includes impairments caused by a congenital anomaly, impairments caused by disease (e.g., poliomyelitis, bone tuberculosis), and impairments from other causes (e.g., cerebral palsy, amputations, and fractures or burns that cause contractures).
Other health impairment	**Other health impairment** means having limited strength, vitality, or alertness, including a heightened alertness to environmental stimuli; that results in limited alertness with respect to the education environment, that is due to chronic or acute health problems such as asthma, attention deficit disorder or attention deficit hyperactivity disorder, diabetes, epilepsy, a heart condition, hemophilia, led poisoning, leukemia, nephritis, rheumatic fever, sickle cell anemia, and Tourette syndrome; and adversely affects a child's educational performance.
Specific learning disability	**Specific learning disability** means a disorder in one or more of the basic psychological processes involved in understanding or in using language, spoken or written, that may manifest itself in the imperfect ability to listen, think, speak, read, write, spell, or to do mathematical calculations, including conditions such as perceptual disabilities, brain injury, minimal brain dysfunction, dyslexia, and developmental aphasia. Specific learning disability does not include learning problems that are primarily the result of visual, hearing, or motor disabilities, of mental retardation, of emotional disturbance, or of environmental, cultural, or economic disadvantage.
Speech or language impairment	**Speech or language impairment** means a communication disorder such as stuttering, impaired articulation, a language impairment, or a voice impairment, that adversely affects a child's educational performance.
Traumatic brain injury	**Traumatic brain injury** means an acquired injury to the brain caused by an external physical force, resulting in total or partial functional disability or psychosocial impairment, or both, that adversely affects a child's educational performance. Traumatic brain injury applies to open or closed head injuries resulting in impairment in one or more areas, such as cognition; language; memory; attention; reasoning; abstract thinking; judgment; problem-solving; sensory, perceptual, and motor abilities; psychosocial behavior; physical functions; information processing; and speech. Traumatic brain injury does not apply to brain injuries that are congenital or degenerative, or to brain injuries induced by birth trauma.
Visual impairments including blindness	**Visual impairments including blindness** means an impairment in vision that, even with correction, adversely affects a child's educational performance. The term includes both partial sight and blindness.

Source: Council for Exceptional Children (n.d.).

EXAMPLES OF POSSIBLE APPROACHES AND SUPPORTS

As ASD is considered to be heterogeneous, interventions may vary, and consequently, "must be tailored for each individual and evaluated objectively to determine the level of effectiveness for a particular individual" (Haney, 2013, p. 195). As such, this section will provide a brief overview of a few of the major approaches and recommendations that have been discussed as intervention techniques for students with ASD.

Environmental Supports
Some recommendations relate to the educational environment, in that a highly structured setting with appropriate accommodations and environmental supports may be beneficial to students with ASD, including visual classroom routines (IDEA Partnership @ NASDSE, 2012), and supports related to communication, social interaction, and sensory issues (Haney, 2013). An example of this type of support is a schedule with picture activities (Heward, 2013).

Applied Behavior Analysis
A widely cited and implemented approach for students with ASD is referred to as applied behavior analysis (ABA). ABA "is the application of behavior change procedures involving functional relationships among antecedent events, specific behaviors, and actions that occur after behaviors of interest" (Rosenberg et al., 2011, p. 275). It can involve a Functional Behavioral Assessment (FBA) and the designing of a Behavioral Intervention Plan (Rosenberg et al., 2011), two procedures that are discussed in more depth in Chapter 5, which relates to the development of the individualized education program (IEP).

   Entire books and courses have been centered on the technique of ABA and its implementation. An in-depth discussion of ABA is beyond the scope of this book. A description provided by Haney (2013) may provide adequate background for an initial foundation in this practice, in her discussion of discrete trial instruction (DTI), which is noted as:

> the foundation of all ABA-based programming. The approach is built around educational trials always containing three elements:
>
> *   a prompt from the teacher
> *   a response by the child
> *   a consequence delivered by the teacher
>
> Teaching using DTI involves presenting the child with a series of opportunities (discrete trials) to make a response and then delivering consequences for each response.
>
> (Haney, 2013, p. 204)

Essentially the same theoretical foundation of behavioral analysis is implemented whether the goal is to increase or decrease behaviors: the selection of target behaviors, provision of reinforcement, and procedures for observation and assessment (Hall, 2013). Many research investigations have found that interventions implementing ABA principles lead to notable results for students who have been diagnosed with autism (Boutot & Myles, 2011).

Communication Techniques

Because of student needs, there is also often a focus on the development of functional communication (Gargiulo, 2015). An example of an approach that may be implemented relates to augmentative/alternative communication (AAC) strategies.

> Augmentative and alternative communication (AAC) includes all forms of communication (other than oral speech) that are used to express thoughts, needs, wants, and ideas. We all use AAC when we make facial expressions or gestures, use symbols or pictures, or write.
>
> (ASHA, n.d.a, para. 1)

The American Speech-Language-Hearing Association (ASHA) further notes that a major purpose of AAC is to supplement current speech or replace dysfunctional speech. ASHA also denotes that there are two types of communication systems. The focus of unaided communication is on the speaker's body as the main means of sending information, through gestures, body language, etc. Aided communication involves the implementation of some kind of equipment in addition to the speaker's body, and can range from pen and paper to various types of electronic communication devices.

One example of an AAC approach is related to the exchange of pictures in communication, and can be very beneficial for students who are non-verbal. Through the exchange of a picture, photograph, or a tiny component of an item, "Frost and Bondy (2002) have put together a method based on applied behavior analysis to teach children with developmental disabilities to begin to communicate" (cited in Hall, 2013, p. 184) or implement communication purposefully (Hall, 2013). This system is referred to as the Picture Exchange Communication System (PECS). This is only one example of an increasing availability of technologically based communication devices and applications (apps) that may assist a student with ASD with communication issues.

Interventions for Social Behaviors

As far as approaches to assist the student with social issues, again there are a number of possible techniques. One representative example is instruction in social skills. ABA techniques are often implemented, particularly with students who exhibit serious deficits in this area. With higher functioning students, the focus of social skills instruction is on interpreting social situations and engaging appropriately in social functioning (Rosenberg et al., 2011). Interventions based in stories and peer mediation are techniques that may be implemented in this regard (Haney, 2013).

Emotional Disturbance

BACKGROUND INFORMATION AND CHARACTERISTICS

Because there are several variables to consider, it is difficult to ascertain a commonly accepted definition of emotional and/or behavioral disorders. While the definition of emotional disturbance (ED) in Table 3.1 is accepted as a federal definition of ED, it is not always accepted as the most appropriate description of this type of disorder according to some professional associations (Heward, 2013). Because students with ED may exhibit numerous types of concerns, the discussion of characteristics associated with these individuals is often categorized into *internalizing behaviors* and *externalizing behaviors* (Heward, 2013; Rosenberg et al., 2011).

Disorders related to *internalizing* behaviors are often associated with depression, withdrawal, excessive controlling, and anxiety issues, which are more inwardly directed. Behavioral disorders that are more *externalized* are typified by disruption, aggression, and inadequately controlled behaviors (Shepherd, 2010).

Internalizing Behaviors

Disorders related to depression and anxiety have been reported as the most prevalent of the internalizing behaviors (Webber & Plotts, 2008). Major depression is considered to be a mood disorder. However, when students have issues with anxiety, their behavior may be focused on such conditions as specific phobias, social anxiety, and separation anxiety, to name just a few examples (Austin & Sciarra, 2010). Both depression and anxiety as internalizing disorders encompass a myriad of behaviors and conditions not described herein. Those mentioned are simply examples to provide you with a sampling of issues related to the *internalizing* behavior classification often associated with the disability referred to as emotional disturbance.

Externalizing Behaviors

While students who appear anxious or withdrawn are generally not a disruption or a source of classroom behavioral issues (Kirk et al., 2003), students with behavioral issues of the external variety may be very overt in the presentation of their characteristics. "Children with externalizing problems exhibit antisocial and aggressive behavior" (Heward, 2013, p. 230).

For example, conduct disorder is a common issue for students with this type of externalizing behavioral manifestation (Hallahan et al., 2009). It is "characterized by persistent antisocial behavior that violates the rights of others as well as age-appropriate social norms [and] includes aggression ..., destruction of property, ... theft and serious violation of rules" (Kauffman & Landrum, 2013, p. 234). Students with such behavioral characteristics can be a major concern not only for school personnel, peers, families, and other pertinent individuals, but also for their own personal growth. As with the aforementioned discussion of internalizing behaviors, these characteristics for externalizing behavior are again just a sampling of the numerous potential behavioral indicators that may be associated with more overt types of behavioral disorders.

An important point to also consider in the discussion of characteristics of students with emotional and behavioral disorders is the potential for comorbidity of disorders. It is not unlikely that students may have more than one co-existing disabilities, one of which is an emotional or behavioral disorder. For example, a student may be diagnosed with ED and also have some sort of learning disability (Shepherd, 2010).

EXAMPLES OF POSSIBLE APPROACHES AND SUPPORTS

School counselors should be aware that there are specific practices often associated with the provision of services to students with ED, namely the completion of a

Functional Behavioral Assessment and the development of a Behavioral Intervention Plan. These approaches will be discussed in Chapter 5, which relates to the design of an IEP. Moreover, there is a system called Positive Behavioral Interventions and Supports (PBIS), a tiered approach to providing interventions for students with behavioral concerns, which will be discussed in Chapter 4. To avoid redundancy, these topics will not be discussed in this chapter, but it is important for you to appreciate that there are specific steps and practices available for implementation in the provision of services to students with ED, which will be explained in later chapters.

In addition to the forthcoming discussions of FBAs, Behavioral Intervention Plans, and the system of PBIS, it is beneficial to provide a brief overview of academic and social/behavioral interventions often associated with students with ED. An overriding principle of many approaches for working with students with ED is noted by Werts et al. (2007, p. 187): "Two types of interventions are needed: (a) those that reduce the problematic behaviors or the likelihood of those behaviors, and (b) those that increase the likelihood of active engagement and acquisition of skills." To this end, these authors note the implementation of such strategies as positive reinforcement, negative reinforcement, extinction of inappropriate behaviors, and time-out, which are strategies generally affiliated with behavioral management systems.

Werts et al. (2007) also focus on cognitive strategy approaches, which Kirk et al. (2003, p. 284) describe as: "self-monitoring, self-instruction or self-control … [which] rely on the cooperation of the child and encourage the development of effective conscious coping skills." Along these same lines, Bock and Borders (2012) note the importance of small group and peer-assisted approaches.

As well as the pursuit of increasing academic skills, students with ED may also be participants in social skills instruction. "Best practice in social skills instruction includes screening when selecting students for intervention, identifying targeted skills and competing problem behaviors, conducting a functional assessment, and evaluating the effect of intervention" (Casey, 2012, p. 43). Since weaknesses in social skills are part of the profile for many students identified as having emotional or behavioral disorders, instruction related to the acquisition of proficiency in socialization should be a primary consideration for assisting these students (Rosenberg et al., 2011).

Clearly, the category of emotional disturbance is complex and varied both in its characteristics and application of appropriate interventions. As with the aforementioned discussion of characteristics of individuals with ED, this discussion of potential approaches is a sampling of options available to both educational personnel and school counselors as they work with students with emotional or behavioral issues. More in-depth information on counseling options will be presented in later chapters.

Specific Learning Disability

When you review the definition of specific learning disability (SLD) in Table 3.1, it will become apparent that the description is not only focused on what SLD is, but also on what it is not. The initial part of the definition notes the association between SLD and language, followed by examples of behaviors in which the disability may manifest itself, such as reading and writing. The definition then goes on to delineate specific conditions that are covered in the category of SLD, such as perceptual disorders and dyslexia. It closes with what are essentially exclusionary criteria. To be categorized as a student with SLD, certain other issues must be excluded as the primary reason for the behavior(s) in question, namely, "visual, hearing, and motor impairments; mental retardation; ED; and disadvantages in the areas of environment, culture, or economic status" (Witte et al., 2015, p. 94). This definition may be the most widely cited of the definitions for SLD because of its inclusion in the federal law, and as such is the foundation for most state definitions of SLD (Lerner & Johns, 2012), but other definitions by other associations have been generated. Please note that the identification process for a student with SLD, including the implementation of the Response to Intervention (RTI) approach, is discussed in Chapter 4.

BACKGROUND INFORMATION AND CHARACTERISTICS

The characteristics of students with SLD may be varied. It is difficult, if not impossible, to provide a profile of a *typical* student with SLD because of the broad range of characteristics across this population. Therefore, this discussion will provide some generalizations in this regard, but they may not all apply to all students with SLD.

"Academic problems are the most widely accepted characteristic of individuals with learning disabilities" (Mercer & Pullen, 2009, p. 22). Reading difficulties, in particular, are the most commonplace, with the great majority of students with SLD exhibiting issues with these skills (Mercer & Pullen, 2009). An example of a learning disability which involves a severe reading problem is dyslexia.

> Dyslexia is a specific learning disability that … is characterized by difficulties with accurate and/or fluent word recognition and by poor spelling and decoding abilities. These difficulties typically result from a deficit in the phonological component of language that is often unexpected in relation to other cognitive abilities and the provision of effective classroom instruction. Secondary consequences may include problems in reading comprehension and reduced reading experience that can impede the growth of vocabulary and background knowledge.
>
> (International Dyslexia Association, 2008, para. 1)

Many students with SLD also have problems with aspects of mathematics or oral and/or written language skills (Rosenberg at al., 2011). Examples of difficulties with mathematics include problems with computational skills, spatial relationships, and word problems, while deficits related to written language may focus on handwriting or spelling (Gargiulo, 2015).

It is clearly difficult to provide a comprehensive listing of academic characteristics of students with SLD because of the unique profile of each individual. It is also difficult to narrow the topic of characteristics of students with SLD when it relates to social and emotional issues. As with academic skill deficits, problems in the domain of social/emotional behaviors will be exhibited by some students with SLD and not by others. Some students with SLD may have problems in the areas of self-concept or self-esteem (Mercer & Pullen, 2009), social skills, or self-efficacy (Heward, 2013). In addition, the professional literature has also discussed the possibility of attention difficulties, perceptual problems, and memory issues (Mercer & Pullen, 2009; Rosenberg et al., 2011; Turnbull et al., 2013).

EXAMPLES OF POSSIBLE APPROACHES AND SUPPORTS

The heterogeneity of characteristics of students with SLD also makes it difficult to narrow the possible options for educational approaches, for discussion purposes. A few of the more common techniques/approaches, however, are provided as examples.

One example of an instructional approach that may be implemented with students with SLD is *explicit instruction*. Explicit instruction involves direct and clear teaching of concepts and/or skills, with multiple opportunities for student practice and application and instructor feedback (Heward, 2013). A related approach is known as *direct instruction*. Direct instruction is concerned with the specific steps of the instructional activities. Task analysis, the delineation of the academic goal into its components, is a major piece of this process. The specific components are taught individually and then pulled together for mastery of the complete concept and/or skill (Hallahan et al., 2012).

An approach that can be successfully implemented in the general education classroom and that may be very beneficial for students with SLD is *differentiated instruction*. This instructional approach involves differentiating instructional content and practice to promote the opportunity for all the students to master the material (Turnbull et al., 2013). Students are provided with multiple alternatives to engage with the learning process (Lerner & Johns, 2012).

A related practice is the provision of *accommodations* for students with SLD. Making appropriate accommodations or modifications for students with SLD in the general education classroom can lend itself to more student success and a more positive learning environment (Werts et al., 2007). Some types of accommodations focus on instructional materials and practice, including the provision of guides for reading, audio materials, and reduced workload for assignments (Mercer et al., 2011). Other accommodations may be concerned more with alternative aspects of the instructional process. Lerner and Johns (2012, p. 95) delineate accommodations which may be of assistance to students with SLD as: "(1) increasing attention, (2) improving the ability to listen, (3) adapting the curriculum, and (4) helping students manage time."

Content enhancement is another approach that may be very advantageous for students with SLD in a general education inclusive environment. Content enhancement strategies provide students with SLD more accessibility to the content of the curriculum (Heward, 2013), while also assisting students to organize their learning activities and retain content (Smith et al., 2014). Other educational approaches/ techniques of potential benefit for students with SLD include *study skills* and *learning strategies*, which promote such activities as the acquisition and expression of knowledge, problem-solving, completion of tasks, and independent functioning (Mercer et al., 2011).

Peer-mediated instructional approaches, such as peer tutoring, are also implemented with students with SLD. Peer tutoring is concerned with the pairing of two students to work collaboratively with an academic or behavioral issue, and its efficacy has been widely exhibited (Polloway et al., 2013). Moreover, both the student with a disability and the students who are non-disabled may benefit academically from this peer-mediated technique (Mercer & Pullen, 2009).

Conceptual Application Activity 3.1

Working with a Student with Dyslexia

Directions: Reflect on the student description and respond to the questions/comments that follow the description.

Allan is in eighth grade and has been diagnosed with dyslexia. He has recently transferred to your school system. Allan is a capable individual with a keen interest in science. He has very few issues understanding the information if it is presented orally to him, instead of only through print. He has participated successfully in general science courses at his former school, but your school has numerous options for advanced placement classes in science. Allan and his parents would like to see Allan attend one of these advanced classes instead of the general science course the students generally take in the eighth grade at your school. The concern, obviously, is how to accommodate the issue of dyslexia in such a class, where reading is a strong requirement.

The ASCA (2013, para. 4) notes the following as one of the responsibilities of a professional school counselor: "consulting and collaborating with staff and families to understand the special needs of a student and understanding the adaptations and modifications needed to assist the student."

- Based on the description of Allan, how might school counselors fulfill this responsibility? With whom should the school counselor be consulting and collaborating?
- Based on the approaches discussed in this section for students with SLD, are there any you might consider for Allan to address his dyslexia? Which ones?
- In which ways could you assist the teachers and staff members, particularly the science teacher, as they work with Allan and the issue of dyslexia?
- In which ways could you act as a consultant to Allan's family in regard to adaptations or modifications for him to succeed in the inclusive classroom in general, and the science classroom in particular?

Intellectual Disability

Intellectual disability (ID) is the name of the classification that essentially replaces the former name for individuals with mental retardation. Upon review of the definition of intellectual disability in Table 3.1, it is clear that students who have been identified as having ID have an IQ that is measured to be substantially below average, as well as adaptive behavior skills that are also considerably below average. Adaptive behavior includes those skills that are beneficial for engaging in daily living activities (Rosenberg et al., 2011).

As with other areas of disability, students with ID have varying levels of involvement and functioning, ranging from mild to profound. As a way of distinguishing among the ranges of functioning, various approaches toward classifications have been promoted. Some of these classification systems focused on the student's expectation for educability or a description of the biological basis for the condition (e.g., chromosomal deviations, such as Down Syndrome), while another model centered on the severity of the disability (mild, moderate, severe, profound) (Hardman et al., 2008). The American Association on Intellectual and Developmental Disabilities (AAIDD) supports the approach of classifying individuals with IDs according to their levels of needed support (intermittent, limited, extensive, or pervasive) to function effectively in their lives (Luckasson et al., 1992, 2002, as cited in Gargiulo, 2015).

BACKGROUND INFORMATION AND CHARACTERISTICS

As is obvious from the previous discussion of the varying approaches for classifying individuals with ID, it is difficult to provide a conclusive overview of characteristics for this population of students. Students will not necessarily exhibit all of the characteristics mentioned, or if they do exhibit some or all of them, they may do so at varying levels of severity. Some of the more commonly discussed characteristics include: (a) mild to considerable deficits in ability to learn; (b) low attainment in academic pursuits; (c) difficulties with adaptive behavior skills; (d) inattention and distractibility; and (e) difficulties with social skills (Rosenberg et al., 2011). Some students with ID also have deficits related to language (Kirk et al., 2003) and in the ability to generalize a learned skill or behavior from one situation to another (Turnbull et al., 2013). Challenging behaviors may also be an issue for some students with ID (Taylor et al., 2005), as well as delayed motor development and sensory difficulties (Beirne-Smith et al., 2006). In addition, students who have the more involved types of ID may also have related physical concerns (Hardman et al., 2008; Rosenberg et al., 2011). As with previously discussed disability areas, it is difficult to provide a *typical* profile of a student with ID, as each student is unique and has distinctive strengths and needs. As you will see in the section that follows, it is also problematic to discuss educational approaches and expect to cover a comprehensive list of options.

EXAMPLES OF POSSIBLE APPROACHES AND SUPPORTS

As with all other students with disabilities, students with ID have access to the general education curriculum. This involvement with the general education curriculum may be with or without modifications/accommodations, dependent on the issues of concern for the students. For some students with ID, the most appropriate curricular content may be a combination of instruction in traditional subject matter via the general education curriculum and learning about life skills, again depending on the student's particular needs (Gargiulo, 2015). Some students with ID are instructed through the content of a *functional* curriculum. "A functional curriculum is one that teaches everyday life skills in order to maximize the student's potential for independence" (Beirne-Smith et al., 2006, p. 303). In this type of curriculum, skills are learned and practiced through practical life applications (e.g., practicing subtraction through making change) (Gargiulo, 2015).

Polloway et al. (2013, p. 344) describe functionally oriented academics as "the real-world application of core academic content and related skills that are meaningful and relevant to an individual's life now and in the future." These authors also provide examples of such activities: reading a newspaper (reading), comparing prices (math), practicing proper hygiene (science), and registering to vote (social studies) (Polloway et al., 2013). Instruction in functional academics may accomplish "a merger of functional and academic curricular standards" (Hallahan et al., 2012, p. 132).

When students with ID are instructed in functional academics and life skills, it is recommended that they be taught as much as possible through an approach called community-based instruction, where the students are acquiring and practicing the skills in natural environments (Gargiulo, 2015). The students should also be working with authentic materials (Hallahan et al., 2012) and being instructed through systematic instructional techniques, which include such activities as task analysis, generalization strategies (Heward, 2013), direct instruction (Rosenberg et al., 2011), and instructional learning prompts (Hallahan et al., 2012). Instruction in communication and social skills is also of critical importance (Hardman et al., 2008; Taylor et al., 2005).

Another area of importance to students with ID is assistive technology. According to IDEA 2004, an assistive technology device is:

> any item, piece of equipment, or product system, whether acquired commercially off the shelf, modified, or customized, that is used to increase, maintain, or improve functional capabilities of a child with a disability … The term does not include a medical device that is surgically implanted, or the replacement of such device.
>
> (Individuals with Disabilities Education Improvement Act of 2004, Public Law 108–446, Part A, Sec. 602 [1] [A] [B])

There are numerous devices that may be beneficial to students with ID, which may range from low-tech to high-tech options (Dell et al., 2012; Marchel et al., 2015) and may be applicable to such issues as mobility, positioning, access to computers, augmentative and alternative communication, aids for instruction, and daily living aids (Bryant & Bryant, 2012).

Traumatic Brain Injury

BACKGROUND INFORMATION AND CHARACTERISTICS

From reviewing the reference to traumatic brain injury (TBI) in Table 3.1, it is obvious that students identified as having a TBI have acquired an injury or insult to the brain from an external influence and consequently may exhibit learning issues, behavioral concerns, or both (Rosenberg et al., 2011). TBI may affect individuals in various areas, and the characteristics of students with TBI may share similarities with characteristics related to other areas of disability, such as "learning disabilities … communication disorders … emotional or behavioral disorders … intellectual disability … health impairments … and physical disabilities" (Turnbull et al., 2013, p. 293). As such, depending on the nature and intensity of the injury, many characteristics that have been discussed in regard to previous disabilities may be applicable to a student with TBI. For example, when there is serious injury to the brain, different cognitive and motoric factors may be involved, including the ability to complete daily life skills, process intellectually, communicate, pay attention, and recall information (Trovato & Schultz, 2013).

EXAMPLES OF POSSIBLE APPROACHES AND SUPPORTS

Because there are numerous variables that may affect the functioning of a student with TBI, it is difficult to discuss interventions with much specificity. "Each child's

injury is unique and the consequences of their injury can be predicted only after care-
ful assessment, individualized instructional and behavioral planning, and continuous
monitoring of progress" (Bullock et al., 2005, p. 8). Although each child and his/her
injury are unique, as was noted previously, many of the interventions and supports
that have been discussed in regard to other areas of disability may be appropriate
for the student with TBI, depending on the specific needs and concerns. In addition to implementing appropriate interventions based on the student's specific academic and/or behavioral needs, providing this instruction in a structured style may
be very effective with students with TBI. Moreover, having a daily routine marked
by consistency, order, and predictability, as well as an educational environment that
is structured in an organized manner and free of distractions, may prove beneficial
in the instruction of students with TBI (Rosenberg et al., 2011). It is also important
to note that for individuals to be aware and responsive to the medical, academic,
and behavioral needs of a student with TBI, there should be cooperation and collaboration across various disciplines involved with the student's care and education
(Arroyos-Jurado & Savage, 2008).

Multiple Disabilities

BACKGROUND INFORMATION AND CHARACTERISTICS

As Turnbull et al. (2013) note, there is no single description that would provide an accur-
ate profile of all the conditions related to multiple disabilities (MD). The terminology
implies a diversity of individuals and heterogeneity of characteristics, the commonality being related to the gravity of the individual's educational needs. Individuals with
MD may have difficulties in a number of areas, including intellectual performance,
motoric growth, sensory operations, communicative functioning, and adaptive behaviors (Turnbull et al., 2013). Additions to this list of potential characteristics are deficits in
personal and social functioning, behavioral concerns (sometimes of an unusual nature,
e.g., self-injurious behaviors) and serious medical issues (Rosenberg et al., 2011).

The issue of intellectual functioning is a particularly interesting one in regard to students with MD. Educational professionals should be aware that "depending on the type
of multiple disabilities, cognitive functioning may vary from giftedness to profound
intellectual disability" (Gargiulo, 2015, p. 500). Communication and physical issues
may conceal an authentic measure of intelligence for some students with MD (Turnbull
et al., 2013).

EXAMPLES OF POSSIBLE APPROACHES AND SUPPORTS

As has been discussed previously in regard to students with TBI, cross-disciplinary models of service provision should be enacted for students with MD, as they have issues of
concern in more than one area (Hallahan et al., 2012). Within this context, educational
adjustments should take into consideration: (a) adaptation of the learning environment;
(b) adaptation of the curriculum, for example, focusing on functional skills for daily
life and age-appropriate skills; and (c) adaptations of teaching techniques, including
instructional approaches for students with communication issues and assistive technology (Kirk et al., 2003).

Assistive technology, in general, and AAC devices specifically, may be particularly beneficial for some students with MD, in that they may promote communication through technology for students who have difficulty communicating verbally or through another option like sign language (Turnbull et al., 2013). The implementation of visual modality techniques, such as the provision of visual supports (e.g., objects or picture symbols), may also be advantageous for students with MD (Snell & Brown, 2011).

In regard to examples of instructional techniques, the implementation of sequential instruction and prompts, as well as the promotion of opportunities for immediate instructor feedback, and generalization activities may all be valuable when working with students with MD (Heward, 2013). Moreover, "Student-directed learning strategies such as antecedent cue regulation, self-instruction, and self-monitoring are research-based ways to teach students to self-regulate learning; they contribute to enhanced inclusion, generalization, and student empowerment" (Turnbull et al., 2013, p. 239).

If the student's behavior is problematic, an FBA and positive behavioral supports should be considered (Hallahan et al., 2012). Self-management skills are also important skills for students with MD. "When students are taught to self-manage their own behavior, they are less dependent on others and may have mastered improved engagement, better work completion, and appropriate social behavior" (Snell & Brown, 2011, p. 145). The practice of self-determination and the skills required for making choices are two particularly important areas of focus in regard to behavioral concerns (Hardman et al., 2008; Heward, 2013).

Physical Disabilities (Orthopedic Impairments) and Other Health Impairments

The reader will note in Table 3.1 that the choice of terminology for students with physical disabilities is *orthopedic impairments (OI)*, and the terminology for health disabilities or special heath care concerns is *other health impairments (OHI)*, according to the language found in IDEA 2004 (Smith et al., 2014). Although IDEA 2004 distinguishes orthopedic impairments from other health impairments, Smith et al. (2014, p. 258) note that there are similarities between the two classifications and that "some conditions typically grouped under physical disabilities or orthopedic impairments also result in long- term health problems and vice versa." Both areas of disability will be discussed individually according to background information and characteristics, and will be discussed in combination in regard to possible approaches and supports and post-secondary concerns.

BACKGROUND INFORMATION AND CHARACTERISTICS

A wide variety of conditions falls within the category of OI. These disorders can be categorized into three major classifications: neuromotor disorders (e.g., spina bifida and cerebral palsy), degenerative conditions (e.g., muscular dystrophy), and musculoskeletal impairments (e.g., juvenile idiopathic arthritis and limb deficiency) (Gargiulo, 2015). These types of conditions may range from mild to serious and may be focused on one or many parts of the body (Spooner et al., 2011).

Other health impairments (OHI) is the categorization that applies to "students with chronic health conditions such as asthma, epilepsy, and HIV/AIDS, which may or may not be terminal, that cause weakness or fatigue or in some other way adversely affect school performance" (Rosenberg et al., 2011, p. 373). These students may have many absences from school and have issues with stamina, weakness, pain, and—because of the missed school—a lack of socialization (Rosenberg et al., 2011).

EXAMPLES OF POSSIBLE APPROACHES AND SUPPORTS

Clearly the degree to which the physical or health impartments manifest themselves will have an impact on whether or not the students will require specialized services. For example, a student whose asthma is controlled may only require minor modifications, if any, in regard to the instructional environment. However, a student with an involved physical disability may require a number of accommodations (e.g., feeding tube, catheter) related to his/her particular needs. Consequently, the array of possibilities for educational supports is vast and should be considered according to each student's particular needs.

Many students with OI or OHI are instructed according to the general education curriculum and as much as feasible in the general education setting. Easy access to areas of the classroom and other instructional environments should always be a consideration. For some students, their specialized services will involve a team of professionals, perhaps including a physical therapist and/or a speech language pathologist, as well as assistive technology devices (Heward, 2013; Rosenberg et al., 2011). Because of the absence rates due to their heath or medical treatments, students with OI or OHI may require accommodations to assist them in keeping up with their work (Werts et al., 2007). Instructional accommodations may be warranted such as extended time for assignments, flexible deadlines, and having another student act as a note taker (Smith at al., 2014).

A WORD ABOUT ATTENTION DEFICIT HYPERACTIVITY DISORDER

According to the APA in the *Diagnostic and Statistical Manual of Mental Disorders* (DSM-5), it has been reported that 5 percent of children have attention deficit hyperactivity disorder (ADHD) (cited in Division of Human Development, National Center on Birth Defects and Developmental Disabilities, Centers for Disease Control and Prevention, 2014a). ADHD has not been listed as a separate classification of disability according to IDEA 2004, as is obvious from Table 3.1. Yet it still should be addressed in this chapter because of its prevalence. Although it could be discussed in relation to Section 504, it is also appropriate to discuss ADHD in regard to the category of OHI. ADHD may enable an individual to be eligible for specialized services within the classification of OHI, which, as we are aware, is a specific category of disability within IDEA 2004.

The rationale for the potential for inclusion of ADHD within OHI appears to be related to issues of alertness as designated in the definition of OHI (US Department of Education, Office of Special Education Programs, n.d.). Consequently, if a student with ADHD is categorized as OHI, the protections and services addressed in IDEA are available to that individual. Nonetheless, it is also important to note that students with ADHD may be eligible for specialized services according to the stipulations of Section 504 of the Rehabilitation Act of 1973. Moreover, it should be noted that the disability area of ADHD has at times been identified as co-existing with other disability areas, such as learning disabilities, and as such "many students with ADHD may receive services because they have a primary disability such as a learning disability" (Mercer & Pullen, 2009, p. 79).

Background Information and Characteristics
A major source of information for characteristics and behaviors that are associated with the area of ADHD is the APA in its *Diagnostic and Statistical Manual of Mental Disorders, fifth edition* (DSM-5) (APA, 2013b). Upon review of its criteria, it is clear that an emphasis is being placed on the issues of inattention and hyperactivity-impulsivity. The manual also notes that there are three types of ADHD which may be exhibited: (a) predominantly inattentive; (b) predominantly hyperactive-impulsive; and (c) combined, which would involve meeting the criteria for both inattention and hyperactivity-impulsivity (APA, 2013, as cited in Division of Human Development, National Center on Birth Defects and Developmental Disabilities, Centers for Disease Control and Prevention, 2014b). For more in-depth information about the DSM-5 criteria for ADHD, refer to *Attention Deficit/Hyperactivity Disorder (ADHD): Symptoms and Diagnosis*, from the Division of Human Development, National Center on Birth Defects and Developmental Disabilities, Centers for Disease Control and Prevention (2014b) at www.cdc.gov/ncb-ddd/adhd/diagnosis.html.

If inattention is the primary concern, students may have difficulty with staying on-task and may be highly distractible. If the student's major issue is more hyperactivity-impulsivity, he or she may have difficulty sitting still or being quiet when the situation warrants it. Individuals with the combined type of ADHD may exhibit behaviors of both of the aforementioned types of actions (Gargiulo, 2015). Clearly, these are just a few examples of behaviors and activities in which students with ADHD may engage. Many times, the characteristics associated with ADHD are apparent in the existence of social or behavioral issues and/or academic concerns (Rosenberg et al., 2011).

Some of the social and behavioral concerns may involve the student with ADHD having problems interacting with their peers and teachers, having issues with following rules and testing limits, and exhibiting inappropriate social skills (Kewley, 2011). In academic situations, examples of behaviors of students with ADHD may include inattention to the activity, lack of organization, and problems with staying on-task (Smith et al., 2014).

Examples of Possible Approaches and Supports
There are various interventions that may be implemented with students with ADHD, whether they are related to social/behavioral and/or academic issues. An in-depth discussion is beyond the scope of this book, but a few examples will provide you with a general overview of potential interventions and supports. Hallahan et al. (2012) note the importance of classroom structure, instructor-guided activities, self-management, and FBA. Self-monitoring strategies are also important skills for addressing the issues of decreasing inattentiveness and increasing on-task performance, as well as instruction in social skills attainment (Mercer & Pullen, 2009). Many of these strategies will be addressed in later chapters.

Upon review of Table 3.1, we see that there are four categories of disabilities that fall within the classification of sensory impairments: deaf-blindness, deafness, hearing impairment, and visual impairment including blindness. In this section, to avoid being

Figure 3.1 Students learn and work together in inclusive educational environments.
Source: ©*iStockphoto.com, www.istockphoto.com/photo/elementary-school-students-34010682.*

too cumbersome, deafness and hearing impairment will be discussed together, and in conjunction with the supposition of Rosenberg et al. (2011) that the more serious hearing loss is described as deafness and less serious hearing loss is indicative of a hearing impairment.

Hearing Impairments and Deafness

BACKGROUND INFORMATION AND CHARACTERISTICS

"Hearing impairment is a generic term referring to all types, causes, and degrees of hearing loss" (Paul & Whitelaw, 2011, p. 4). Classifying hearing loss can be accomplished through consideration of the individual's sensitivity to pitch and loudness, age of onset of the difficulties, and the site of the hearing loss (Hardman et al., 2008). A hearing loss that is classified according to age of onset may be congenital (being born with a hearing issue) versus adventitious (acquiring a hearing issue after birth) or pre-lingual versus post-lingual (hearing issue is present before versus after the development of speech and language) (Hallahan et al., 2012). In regard to the site of the hearing problem, a conductive hearing loss is related to an issue in the parts of the outer and middle ear and sensorineural loss is associated with a difficulty in the inner ear or with involvement of the nerve pathway on its way to the brain (Turnbull et al., 2013). A hearing loss can also be described as mixed, which is marked by a combination of sensorineural and conductive hearing issues (Hardman et al., 2008).

In regard to educational performance, achievement, specifically in reading and writing, is of major concern for students identified with hearing impairments (HI) (Turnbull et al., 2013). As Hardman et al (2008, p. 399) note: "any difficulties in performance appear to be closely associated with speaking, reading, and writing the English language but are not related to level of intelligence."

With respect to language specifically, a seriously affected developmental area for a student with HI is oral language and this may affect both language and speech (Werts et al., 2007). Naturally, the degree to which these areas may be affected relates to the extent of the hearing loss. With some students with HI, there will be slower acquisition of vocabulary and because they may not hear their voices, they may have issues with speaking such as loudness, pitch, and rate of speech (ASHA, n.d.b). The issues with speech and language may also be accompanied by concerns with socialization and interpersonal relationships. Social relationships may also be a challenge for students with deafness as their opportunities for social interaction may be more limited (Hallahan et al., 2012). The difficulties with communication may lead to self-concept issues and/or social isolation (ASHA, n.d.b).

EXAMPLES OF POSSIBLE APPROACHES AND SUPPORTS

In regard to options for communication, students with HIs are generally instructed through oral/aural communication, manual communication, or total communication, if their needs require such approaches (Turnbull et al., 2013). A program with an oral approach focuses on the students developing their residual hearing and their speaking ability, and integrates the implementation of such tactics as amplification, speech reading, auditory learning, and assistive technology (Heward, 2013). Manual communication focuses more on sign language for communication. Sign language is a systematic and involved combination of hand movements that communicate complete words and thoughts instead of individual letters. One of the most common examples of a sign language is American Sign Language (ASL) (Hardman et al., 2008). Total communication is a combination of numerous options, including simultaneously communicating with sign and oral language, with amplification for residual hearing and speech reading (Turnbull et al., 2013).

In addition to the provision of sign language interpreters, numerous technological options may be beneficial for a student with HI, depending on his/her unique needs; for example, hearing aids, cochlear implants, and group assistive tools for listening (Heward, 2013). Whichever system of communication is implemented and whichever technological options are in place, in all educational environments, the rooms should be organized to enhance listening to others and seeing them without obstructions (Farrell, 2011).

Visual Impairments Including Blindness

BACKGROUND INFORMATION AND CHARACTERISTICS

As was the case with HI, visual impairments (VI) may also be classified in a variety of ways. One approach is to differentiate according to level of available vision. For example, one category is referred to as low vison (some sight that is functional) versus blindness (no vison that is functional but perhaps with movement or shadows). Another classification system focuses on age of onset: congenital (since the child's birth or infancy) versus adventitious (loss of one's sight after two years old). A third example of categorizing visual impairments is according to the type of loss of vision; for example, a loss may be related to peripheral vision or a color vision deficit (Smith et al., 2014).

A major problem for students with VI is their limitations for incidental learning from their environments, and consequently they may have to be directly taught skills and concepts. As such, certain considerations must be taken into account in instructional situations. VIs may have an impact on the manner in which the students acquire knowledge and skills, but do not preclude the students from learning (Turnbull et al., 2013).

In regard to social and behavioral characteristics, some students with VI may experience social isolation and difficulties with social interactions due to such issues as difficulty with eye contact with the speaker/listener, or problems with facial expressions (Heward, 2013). This points to a major concern for students whose VI is affecting their incidental learning, as they will not have access to visual models from whom to learn particular socialization skills. Consequently, they may have to be instructed in personal interaction skills and appropriate social behaviors (Gargiulo, 2015).

EXAMPLES OF POSSIBLE APPROACHES AND SUPPORTS

According to the US Department of Education, 87 percent of students with VI participate in general education environments for at least a portion of the day (cited in Rosenberg et al., 2011). Students with VI may also receive specialized instruction from a vision specialist in an educational setting as determined on the IEP or on an itinerant basis (Farrell, 2012; Heward, 2013; Rosenberg et al., 2011).

The physical educational environment is a consideration for students with VI. Materials may require adaptation and the setting may require adjustments for the student to have optimum participation opportunities (Gargiulo, 2015). Moreover, for more serious visual losses, students will require instruction in orientation and mobility, as well as access to specialized equipment (Heward, 2013).

As far as instructional concerns, there are a number of assists available to students with VI, whose effectiveness would be dependent on the degree of vision loss. Some of these options include: (a) reading through Braille; (b) large print text; (c) magnification devices; (d) possible implementation of external supports, such as a cane or guide dog; (e) tactile representations of information, such as maps; and (f) technological devices, whether they be for assistance with communication, information accessibility, or orientation and mobility (Hallahan et al., 2012). The opportunities afforded through assistive technology are varied and can provide support to the students through alternative sensory modalities, (e.g., auditory and tactile), and technology, software, and apps are assisting in the removal of barriers to various critical aspects of life for students with VI (Smith et al., 2014).

There should also be a systematic progression of listening skills, and in addition to the academic curriculum, systematic instructional opportunities to learn functional daily living skills (Heward, 2013). Another point to consider in regard to the instruction of students with VI is the implementation of a hands-on approach to instructional activities, which would encourage the involvement of the other senses, and increased opportunities for practice (Turnbull et al., 2013). The implementation of accommodations or modifications of instructional materials or assessment activities may also be warranted. For example, a student with VI may require a scribe or reader and/or extended time for a particular evaluation activity. The key is for the adaptation or modification to remove a bias toward vision (Farrell, 2011). These are just a few of the major points that should be considered when determining the most appropriate education for a student with VI.

Deaf-Blindness

BACKGROUND INFORMATION AND CHARACTERISTICS

Progressing from a separate discussion of HI and VI, we move now into a review of the disability area of deaf-blindness. Obviously, many of the basic characteristics that we have discussed in regard to the two aforementioned disability areas will have application to individuals with deaf-blindness. Yet, it is important to take into account that the combination of affected modalities will also have unique effects in regard to the functioning of the students. "Because the primary avenues for receiving information—sight and sound—are limited, those who are deaf-blind are at risk for having extensive problems in communicating and in navigating their environments" (Hallahan et al., 2012, p. 375).

An important point to consider, however, when working with students who have been identified as deaf-blind is that although the term implies a loss of hearing and vision, the majority of children with this disability have some functional degree of hearing and/or vision (Heward, 2013). Moreover, the population of individuals with deaf-blindness is varied and diverse, and the majority of individuals have additional health issues or disabilities (Malloy & Killoran, 2007). There is some aspect of commonality among the individuals in this classification as the concomitant loss of some hearing and vision may often lead to communication issues and difficulties with mobility and isolationism (Smith et al., 2014).

EXAMPLES OF POSSIBLE APPROACHES AND SUPPORTS

In addition to the approaches and supports already discussed in regard to HI and VI that may be appropriate for a student with deaf-blindness, even more particular consideration may be required for accommodating the student's mobility issues, perhaps through providing more of a tactile environment (Farrell, 2011). As well as a focus on mobility and safety issues, instructing students with deaf-blindness "requires direct teaching, predictable, structured routines, and emphasis on communication" (Hallahan et al., 2012, p. 394).

In regard to communication specifically, the system of choice will depend on the degree of hearing and vision available to the student. The communication approach should be taught in a systematic manner and the techniques should be implemented on a consistent basis (Spooner et al., 2011). If the student has inadequate hearing to learn speech, and inadequate vision to see signing, he/she may require a tactile type of sign language, for example a hand-over-hand approach. In this form of sign language, symbols are expressed through touch and resemble a type of finger spelling (Smith et al., 2014). Additional examples of tactile approaches include finger braille and braille communication cards (Parker et al., 2011). Moreover, as with other areas of disability, assistive technology and AAC options should be considered in the education for students with deaf-blindness.

Speech or Language Impairment

BACKGROUND INFORMATION AND CHARACTERISTICS

Speech is the "dynamic neuromuscular process of producing speech sounds for communication; a verbal means of transmission" (Owens, 2012, p. 440). Impairments in speech may affect three aspects of the speaking process: articulation (e.g., addition, substitution, distortion, omission of sounds), voice (e.g., issue with intensity, pitch, resonance, or phonation), and fluency (e.g., repetitions of word parts or hesitations disrupting flow) (Smith et al., 2014). There is also a group of motor-speech disorders, such as dysarthria (difficulty in controlling speech sounds production) and apraxia (difficulty with coordinating and planning speech), which result from neuromotor impairment (Hallahan et al., 2012). According to ASHA (n.d.c, para. 1, emphasis in original) "when a person is unable to produce speech sounds correctly or fluently, or has problems with his or her voice, then he or she has a *speech disorder.*"

Language is described as:

> a system used by a group of people for giving meaning to sounds, words, gestures, and other symbols to enable communication with one another. Languages can use vocal (speech sounds) or nonvocal symbols, such as American Sign Language, or use movements and physical symbols instead of sounds.
>
> (Heward, 2013, p. G-8)

Language impairments are characterized by difficulties in one or more of the following components of language: phonology (rules related to the structuring, distributing, and sequencing of patterns of speech-sounds), morphology (focus on words' internal organization), syntax (rules related to word ordering), semantics (rules related to the meaning of words or their content and combinations of words), and pragmatics (practice of language for communication) (Owens, 2012). In other words, "when a person has trouble understanding others (*receptive language*), or sharing thoughts, ideas, and feelings completely (*expressive language*), then he or she has a *language disorder*" (ASHA, n.d.c, para. 2, emphasis in original). Although speech or language impairments are listed as a unique area of disability in IDEA 2004, it is important to recognize that students with many other types of disabilities may also have communication disorders (Rosenberg et al., 2011; Smith et al., 2014).

EXAMPLES OF POSSIBLE APPROACHES AND SUPPORTS

One of the most effective ways to assist students with speech or language impairments is through the services of a speech-language pathologist (SLP) (Smith et al., 2014). Based on diagnostic information, the SLP designs an intervention plan with goals, monitors the progress toward these goals, and modifies these interventions, if warranted. The SLP may provide the assistance through various models, ranging from therapeutic sessions with the student to consultation activities. Classroom teachers and other stakeholders should collaborate and partner with the SLP and support the interventions through reinforcing them in their particular environments and keeping track of the student's progress to enable them to provide feedback to the SLP (Rosenberg et al., 2011). Collaboration and even co-teaching are vital components for consideration by personnel who work with students with speech and language disorders (Hallahan et al., 2012).

There is a variety of techniques that may be employed with students with communication issues in the instructional environment, in addition to the techniques recommended by the SLP. Although an in-depth discussion is beyond the scope of this chapter, a few examples of activities in which educators may engage will be provided as examples: (a) modeling of appropriate speech and language; (b) encouragement of students to appropriately employ language skills and social communication; (c) employment of alternative types of question-asking techniques to encourage the students' problem-solving skills; and (d) when implementing appropriate instructional strategies, exhibition of an awareness of areas of particular academic concern for students with speech or language issues, namely literacy, reading, and written expression (Hallahan et al., 2012). Smith et al. (2014) also recommend the provision of language-rich and language-sensitive environments, where students have the opportunity to interact and explore with objects in the classroom, engage in interesting activities that may encourage language, and be supported in the development of their language needs. Moreover, Smith et al. (2014) recognize the importance of the provision of early training in phonological awareness, which may be accomplished through various approaches including books, songs, and pre-writing activities (Levey & Polirstok, 2011). Further, as another example of a consideration for interventions, Reed (2012) recommends the implementation of generalization with naturalistic reinforcement in a variety of contexts.

Another example of a support for students with communication disabilities is AAC modes. "It is important for all children to have functional communication systems, whatever their levels of ability" (Reed, 2012, p. 456). AAC systems provide options for students with speech and language disorders to communicate, and include devices that are identified as low-tech or high-tech (Smith et al., 2014). As we are aware from a previous discussion, AAC systems are also characterized as aided or unaided. Unaided devices can be employed without external support mechanisms (e.g., sign language) and aided techniques may be as complex as a speech output instrument (Kuder, 2013). The increase in availability of technological assistance though AAC devices, software programs, and apps should continue to open opportunities for students with speech and language disabilities.

A Word about Students Who Are Twice-Exceptional

School counselors should also be aware that it is possible for some students to have dual diagnoses, with some type of disability and giftedness. These students are often referred to as twice-exceptional. "Twice Exceptional means a gifted and talented student with a co-occurring disability" (Council for Exceptional Children, n.d., para. 20). This population of students has the potential to be overlooked to some extent since "giftedness occurs in combination with disabilities of nearly every description" (Hallahan et al., 2012, p. 440).

Concerns, of course, with this population of students include the determination of the most appropriate approach and focus of their education. Hallahan et al. (2012) encourage the consideration of the complete range of programs available for gifted students for these individuals who are identified as twice-exceptional. Moon et al. (2008) reiterate the importance of not overlooking the nurturing of the giftedness aspect, noting that an educational approach focusing solely on remediation due to the disability will likely not be effectual unless there are also options for the student to be engaged with his/her gifted areas. This is an important consideration in the education of students who are twice-exceptional, as their post-school life and their pursuits in their areas of giftedness may be affected by their school experiences. This is a crucial consideration in that, as Lerner and Johns (2012) note, students with giftedness and learning disabilities, have the potential to become adults with considerable achievements.

As with the other areas discussed in this chapter, the school counselor can play a major role in assisting twice-exceptional students not only within the confines of the school environment, but also as they progress into their future roles as adults. In particular, a school counselor can be a liaison and facilitator of communication among all the stakeholders in the student's education, which should assist in the enactment of recommended practices (Assouline et al., 2006). They can also assist the twice-exceptional students to address social and emotional concerns to promote their potential for achievement and social/emotional growth (Reis & Colbert, 2004).

> School counselors are in a unique position to make a positive difference in the academic lives of twice-exceptional students. They can advocate for services to meet the multifaceted educational needs of these students and also can serve as supportive adults who understand the special social-emotional needs of students who are both gifted and disabled.
>
> (Assouline et al., 2006, para. 57)

Conclusion

The school counselor must be familiar with the various areas of disability that are addressed within IDEA 2004, as many of the students with whom they will be working will be identified as having a disability. To this end, this chapter presented information about various areas listed as disabilities in this law, with specific emphasis on: (a) background information and characteristics; and (b) examples of possible approaches and supports. It is hoped that this information will assist school counselors in fulfilling many of the activities mentioned in the position paper of the ASCA (2013), *The Professional School Counselor and Students with Disabilities*, which specifically notes the importance of school counselor involvement in: (a) the provision of counseling services; (b) the contribution of information for the identification of students with disabilities; (c) consultation with other stakeholders in the design of academic and transitions plans and adaptations and modifications as appropriate to the student; and (d) advocacy on behalf of the student in the school environment and in the community.

References

APA (2013a). Attention-deficit/hyperactivity disorder (ADHD). In *Diagnostic and Statistical Manual of Mental Disorders*, 5th edn. Arlington, VA: American Psychiatric Association. Retrieved from www.cdc.gov/ncbddd/adhd/diagnosis.html.

APA (2013b). Autism spectrum disorder (ASD). In *Diagnostic and Statistical Manual of Mental Disorders*, 5th edn. Arlington, VA: American Psychiatric Association. Retrieved from www.cdc.gov/ncbddd/autism/hcp-dsm.html.

Arroyos-Jurado, E. & Savage, T. A. (2008). Intervention strategies for serving students with traumatic brain injury. *Intervention in School and Clinic*, 43(4), 252–254.

ASCA (2013). *The Professional School Counselor and Students with Disabilities*. Retrieved from www.schoolcounselor.org/asca/media/asca/PositionStatements/PS_Disabilities.pdf.

ASHA (n.d.a). *Augmentative and Alternative Communication (AAC)*. Retrieved from www.asha.org/public/speech/disorders/AAC.htm.

ASHA (n.d.b) *Effects of Hearing Loss on Development*. Retrieved from www.asha.org/public/hearing/Effects-of-Hearing-Loss-on-Development.

ASHA (n.d.c). *Speech and Language Disorders and Diseases*. Retrieved from www.asha.org/public/speech/disorders.

Assouline, S. G., Nicpon, M. F., & Huber, D. H. (2006). The impact of vulnerabilities and strengths on the academic experiences of twice-exceptional students: a message to school counselors. *Professional School Counseling*, 10 (1), 14–24.

Austin, V. L. & Sciarra, D. T. (2010). *Children and Adolescents with Emotional and Behavioral Disorders*. Upper Saddle River, NJ: Pearson Education, Inc.

Beirne-Smith, M., Patton, J. R., & Kim, S. H. (2006). *Mental Retardation: An Introduction to Intellectual Disabilities*, 7th edn. Upper Saddle River, NJ: Pearson Education, Inc.

Bock, S. J. & Borders, C. (2012). Effective practices/interventions for students with emotional and behavioral disorders. In J. P. Bakken, F. E. Obiakor, & A. F. Rotatori (eds.), *Behavioral Disorders: Practice Concerns and Students with EBD* (pp. 61–82). Bingley: Emerald Group Publishing Limited.

Boutot, E. A. & Myles, B. S. (2011). *Autism Spectrum Disorders: Foundations, Characteristics, and Effective Strategies*. Upper Saddle River, NJ: Pearson Education, Inc.

Bryant, D. P. & Bryant, B. R. (2012). *Assistive Technology for People with Disabilities*, 2nd edn. Upper Saddle River, NJ: Pearson Education, Inc.

Bullock, L. M., Gable, R. A., & Mohr, J. D. (2005). Traumatic brain injury: a challenge for educators. *Preventing School Failure*, 49(4), 6–10.

Casey, K. J. (2012). Social skills training and students with emotional and behavioral disorders. In J. P. Bakken, F. E. Obiakor, & A. F. Rotatori (eds.), *Behavioral Disorders: Practice Concerns and Students with EBD* (pp. 43–60). Bingley: Emerald Group Publishing Limited.

Council for Exceptional Children (n.d.). *Special Ed Topics: Who Are Exceptional Learners?* Retrieved from www.cec.sped.org/Special-Ed-Topics/Who-Are-Exceptional-Learners.

Dell, A. G., Newton, D. A., & Petroff, J. G. (2012). *Assistive Technology in the Classroom: Enhancing the School Experiences of Students with Disabilities*, 2nd edn. Upper Saddle River, NJ: Pearson Education, Inc.

Division of Human Development, National Center on Birth Defects and Developmental Disabilities, Centers for Disease Control and Prevention (2014a). *Attention Deficit/Hyperactivity Disorder (ADHD): Data and Statistics*. Retrieved from www.cdc.gov/ncbddd/adhd/data.html.

Division of Human Development, National Center on Birth Defects and Developmental Disabilities, Centers for Disease Control and Prevention (2014b). *Attention Deficit/Hyperactivity Disorder (ADHD): Symptoms and Diagnosis*. Retrieved from www.cdc.gov/ncbddd/adhd/diagnosis.html.

Farrell, M. (2011). *The Effective Teacher's Guide to Sensory and Physical Impairments, Sensory, Orthopaedic, Motor and Health Impairments and Traumatic Brain Injury*, 2nd edn. London & New York: Routledge.

Farrell, M. (2012). *Educating Special Children: An Introduction to Provision for Pupils with Disabilities and Disorders*, 2nd edn. New York: Routledge.

Gargiulo, R. M. (2015). *Special Education in Contemporary Society: An Introduction to Exceptionality*, 5th edn. Thousand Oaks, CA: Sage.

Hall. L. J. (2013). *Autism Spectrum Disorders: From Theory to Practice*, 2nd edn. Upper Saddle River, NJ: Pearson Education, Inc.

Hallahan, D. P., Kauffman, J. M., & Pullen, P. C. (2009). *Exceptional Learners: An Introduction to Special Education*, 11th edn. Boston, MA: Pearson Education, Inc.

Hallahan, D. P., Kauffman, J. M., & Pullen, P. C. (2012). *Exceptional Learners: An Introduction to Special Education*, 12th edn. Upper Saddle River, NJ: Pearson Education, Inc.

Haney, M. R. (2013). *Understanding Children with Autism Spectrum Disorders: Educators Partnering with Families*. Thousand Oaks, CA: Sage.

Hardman, M. L., Drew, C. J., & Egan, M. W. (2008). *Human Exceptionality, School, Community, and Family*, 9th edn. Boston, MA: Houghton Mifflin Company.

Heflin, L. J. & Alaimo, D. F. (2007). *Students with Autism Spectrum Disorders: Effective Instructional Practices*. Upper Saddle River, NJ: Pearson Education, Inc.

Heward, W. M. (2013). *Exceptional Children: An Introduction to Special Education*, 10th edn. Upper Saddle River, NJ: Pearson Education, Inc.

IDEA Partnership @ NASDSE (2012). *Presenter's Guide: Autism Spectrum Disorders, Supports and Intervention*. Retrieved from www.ideapartnership.org/documents/ASD-Collection/2-2013/ASD_Interventions-PresenterGuide.pdf.

Individuals with Disabilities Education Improvement Act of 2004, Public Law 108–446 (2004). *An Act to Reauthorize the Individuals with Disabilities Education Act, and for Other Purposes. Title I: Amendments to the Individuals with Disabilities Education Act*. Retrieved from www.copyright.gov/legislation/pl108-446.pdf.

International Dyslexia Association (2008). *Just the Facts... Definition of Dyslexia*. Retrieved from www.interdys.org/ewebeditpro5/upload/Definition.pdf.

Kauffman, J. M. & Landrum, T. J. (2013). *Characteristics of Emotional and Behavioral Disorders of Children and Youth*, 10th edn. Upper Saddle River, NJ: Pearson Education, Inc.

Kewley, G. (2011). *Attention Deficit Hyperactivity Disorder: What Can Teachers Do?* 3rd edn. London & New York: Routledge.

Kirk, S. A., Gallagher, J. J., & Anastasiow, N. J. (2003). *Educating Exceptional Children*, 10th edn. Boston, MA: Houghton Mifflin Company.

Kuder, S. J. (2013). *Teaching Students with Language and Communication Disabilities*, 4th edn. Upper Saddle River, NJ: Pearson Education, Inc.

Lerner, J. W. & Johns, B. H. (2012). *Learning Disabilities and Related Mild Disabilities*, 12th edn. Belmont, CA: Cengage Learning.

Levey, S. & Polirstok. S. (2011). *Language Development: Understanding Language Diversity in the Classroom*. Thousand Oaks, CA: Sage.

Malloy, P. & Killoran, J. (2007). Children who are deaf-blind. In National Consortium on Deaf-Blindness. *Practice Perspectives: Highlighting Information on Deaf-Blindness*. Retrieved from http://files.eric.ed.gov/fulltext/ED531770.pdf.

Marchel, M. A., Fischer, T. A., & Clark, D. M. (2015). *Assistive Technology for Children and Youth with Disabilities*. Upper Saddle River, NJ: Pearson Education, Inc.

Mercer, C. D. & Pullen, P. C. (2009). *Students with Learning Disabilities*, 7th edn. Upper Saddle River, NJ: Pearson Education, Inc.

Mercer, C. D., Mercer, A. R., & Pullen, P. C. (2011). *Teaching Students with Learning Problems*, 8th edn. Upper Saddle River, NJ: Pearson Education, Inc.

Moon, T. R., Brighton, C. M., Callahan. C. M., & Jarvis, J. M. (2008). Twice-exceptional students: being gifted and learning disabled—implications of the IDEIA. In L. E. Grigorenko (ed.), *Educating Individuals with Disabilities: IDEIA 2004 and Beyond* (pp. 295–317). New York: Springer.

Owens, R. E. (2012). *Language Development: An Introduction*, 8th edn. Upper Saddle River, NJ: Pearson Education, Inc.

Parker, A. T., McGinnity, B. L., & Bruce, S. M. (2011). *Educational Programming for Students Who Are Deafblind*. Position paper of the Division on Visual Impairments. Arlington, VA: Council for Exceptional Children. Retrieved from http://community.cec.sped.org/DVI/resourcesportal/positionpapers.

Paul, P. V. & Whitelaw, G. M. (2011). *Hearing and Deafness: An Introduction for Health and Education Professionals*. Sudbury, MA: Jones and Bartlett Publishers.

Polloway, E. A., Patton, J. R., Serna, L., & Bailey, J. W. (2013). *Strategies for Teaching Learners with Special Needs*, 10th edn. Upper Saddle River, NJ: Pearson Education, Inc.

Reed, V. A. (2012). *An Introduction to Children with Language Disorders*, 4th edn. Upper Saddle River, NJ: Pearson Education, Inc.

Reis, S. M. & Colbert, R. (2004). Counseling needs of academically talented students with learning disabilities. *Professional School Counseling*, 8(2), 156–167.

Rosenberg, M. S., Westling, D. L., & McLeskey, J. (2011). *Special Education for Today's Teachers: An Introduction*, 2nd edn. Upper Saddle River, NJ: Pearson Education, Inc.

Shepherd, T. L. (2010). *Working with Students with Emotional and Behavior Disorders: Characteristics and Teaching Strategies*. Upper Saddle River, NJ: Pearson Education, Inc.

Smith, D. D., Tyler, N. C. and Smith, S. (2014). *Introduction to Contemporary Special Education: New Horizons*. Upper Saddle River, NJ: Pearson Education, Inc.

Snell, M. E. & Brown, F. (2011). *Instruction of Students with Severe Disabilities*, 7th edn. Upper Saddle River, NJ: Pearson Education, Inc.

Spooner, F., Browder, D. M., & Mims, P. J. (2011). Sensory, physical, and health care needs. In D. M. Browder & F. Spooner (eds.), *Teaching Students with Moderate and Severe Disabilities* (pp. 241–261). New York: Guilford Press.

Taylor, R. L., Richards, S. B., & Brady, M. P. (2005). *Mental Retardation, Historical Perspectives, Current Practices, and Future Directions*. Boston, MA: Pearson Education, Inc.

Trovato, M. K. & Schultz, S. C. (2013). Traumatic brain injury. In M. Batshaw, N. Roizen, & G. Lotrecchiano (eds.), *Children with Disabilities*, 7th edn. (pp. 473–485). Baltimore, MD: Paul H. Brookes Publishing Co.

Turnbull, A., Turnbull, R., Wehmeyer, M. L., & Shogren, K. A. (2013). *Exceptional Lives: Special Education in Today's Schools*, 7th edn. Upper Saddle River, NJ: Pearson Education, Inc.

US Department of Education, Office of Special Education Programs (n.d.). *IDEA '97: Final Regulations, Major Issues*. Retrieved from www.ideapractices.org/law/addl_material/majorissues.php.

Webber, J. & Plotts, C. A. (2008). *Emotional and Behavioral Disorders: Theory and Practice*, 5th edn. Boston, MA: Pearson Education, Inc.

Werts, M. G., Culatta, R. A., & Tompkins, J. R. (2007). *Fundamentals of Special Education: What Every Teacher Needs to Know*, 3rd edn. Upper Saddle River, NJ: Pearson Education, Inc.

Witte, R. H., Bogan, J. E., & Woodin, M. F. (2015). *Assessment in Special Education*. Upper Saddle River, NJ: Pearson Education, Inc.

4 Identification Process for Students with Disabilities

The following CACREP standards are addressed in this chapter:

ASSESSMENT AND TESTING
b. methods of effectively preparing for and conducting initial assessment meetings
e. use of assessments for diagnostic and intervention planning purposes
l. use of assessment results to diagnose developmental, behavioral, and mental disorders

Chapter Objectives

After you have completed this chapter, you should be able to:

- Describe the steps and process involved with the identification of a student with a disability for specialized services.
- Self-reflect on the role of the school counselor in the identification of students with disabilities.

Identification Process for Students with Disabilities, IDEA 2004

With a foundation in the field of special education and an awareness of the definitions and characteristics of students with disabilities provided by the preceding chapters, this chapter progresses to a discussion of the identification process of students with disabilities and accompanying regulations. As school counselors will often be participants in activities related to this process, they should have a strong working knowledge of the sequence of steps in the process and the elements of each step.

Students who are suspected of having a disability must be evaluated to determine their eligibility for special education services. As we have learned from the discussion of IDEA 2004 in Chapter 2, there are legal regulations that apply to the assessment procedures, including the assurance of non-discrimination, the implementation of multiple instruments and strategies (Werts et al., 2007), and the evaluation completed by a multidisciplinary team of individuals (Pierangelo & Giuliani, 2012).

This chapter will focus on issues such as the following: (a) pre-referral activities; (b) the Response to Intervention (RTI) approach as an option for consideration particularly in the identification of students with specific learning disabilities (SLD); (c) multifactored and multidisciplinary evaluation procedures; (d) the consideration of data and information in regard to the identification of a disability; and (e) the re-evaluation process and criteria for continued eligibility for students to receive special education services. There will also be a discussion of the specific role of the school counselor in this process, focusing on such activities as gathering data for the evaluation process and being an active team member in the steps of the process and resulting meetings.

Pre-Referral Activities According to IDEA 2004

The assessment process for determining whether or not a student meets the eligibility criteria for specialized services generally begins with some type of pre-referral activities or a system of pre-referral interventions. Generally, at this stage of the assessment process, the classroom teacher/educator has identified an area or areas of concern with a particular student and initiates specific interventions with him/her. The teacher may often also collaborate with other educational personnel for other alternatives or strategies to assist in alleviating the concerns. In many cases, this determination of pre-referral intervention techniques is managed by a team of individuals, which may be referred to by various titles, such as intervention assistance teams or building-level teams. Such a team may also be called a student support team (Rosenberg et al., 2011), an instructional support team, an "early intervening assistance team … teacher assistance team, or problem-solving team" (Heward, 2013, pp. 47–48). This team of individuals may be composed of various professionals at the school including teachers, administrators, and other resource personnel (Smith, 2006). Clearly, a school counselor may be involved in such a team and become an active participant in the pre-referral process for students with difficulties, both as a contributor to the process and as a supportive resource and liaison to the parents and families of the students being addressed. The relationship between the school counselor and family can provide an enabling foundation for the parents to become informed of and/or actively engaged in the discussion and implementation of pre-referral intervention activities.

The pre-referral intervention team may be of assistance to the students and teacher in a variety of ways, but a primary focus is to identify strategies that the teacher may implement with the student. This may involve instructional or curricular accommodations/modifications, behavioral interventions, or assistive technical options, among other alternatives. Pierangelo and Giuliani (2012) make particular note of in-school counseling as a potential pre-referral strategy, lending further credibility to the importance of school counselor involvement in this process.

If the team determines that the outcomes of the pre-referral interventions did not achieve a satisfactory level of success, often the next step is the initiation of a formal referral for an assessment of a suspected disability. Before progressing to the next step in the assessment process for a suspected disability, however, it is important to discuss a pre-referral process that is being increasingly implemented by school systems: the Response to Intervention (RTI) model (Heward, 2013).

RESPONSE TO INTERVENTION

Before discussing the specific role of RTI on the determination of eligibility as it relates to students with suspected disabilities, it is important to discuss a brief overview of the process and its implementation. The RTI approach is one that may be implemented across all the levels of a school to identify students who may be having academic and/or behavioral difficulties. It is a multilevel system that integrates screening, evaluation, scientifically validated intervention, student progress monitoring, and data-based decisions, accompanied by more intensive interventions as the situation warrants (National Center on Response to Intervention, 2010). As a school-wide process, RTI is applicable to all students who may be in need of interventions. It is also a system whose activities may contribute to the identification of a disability, in particular, SLD.

While various models of RTI have been developed, a commonly implemented framework consists of three levels of interventions. In Level 1, the environment is the general education classroom in which is implemented scientifically validated instructional strategies and curricular options. At this level, interventions are implemented on a class-wide basis for at-risk students. If the identified students make appropriate progress at Level 1, they may continue with the intervention process at this level or be considered no longer a participant in the RTI process. Those students who have not progressed as expected in Level 1 generally move to Level 2, and are involved with more targeted intensive interventions on a small group basis. If the students are still not making adequate progress even with the more focused small group assistance of the interventions being provided at Level 2, they may progress to Level 3. At Level 3, the students are provided with more individualized and intensive intervention. Level 3 is considered by some to either involve special education services or a referral to services through special education (Hallahan et al., 2009; Heward, 2013; McDougal et al., 2010; National Center on Response to Intervention, 2010; Wilmshurst & Brue, 2010).

POSITIVE BEHAVIORAL INTERVENTIONS AND SUPPORTS

As you may have surmised, the RTI model has an association with academic concerns, although behavioral issues have also been noted in the discussion thus far. For behavioral issues specifically, however, the name of the model most often implemented is referred to as Positive Behavioral Interventions and Supports (PBIS). Although consistent with the fundamental tenets of RTI, the primary focus of PBIS is behavior. Like RTI, PBIS centers on a level approach for providing interventions, in this case to address the behavioral issues of concern. Each of the approaches delineates key elements to be included at the class-wide/school-wide or Level 1 stage, as well as at the small group/ Level 2 stage, and Level 3 or individualized intervention phase (Sandomierski et al., 2007). Additional information will be provided in regard to both the RTI and PBIS systems, particularly focusing on the school counselor's role in these processes, in Chapter 10.

Whether the intervention is focused on academic and/or behavioral issues, the level approach of RTI and PBIS provides systematic frameworks that have the advantages of assisting at-risk students, as well as functioning as a potential springboard for additional assessment for students who may require the specific services of special education. As Rosenberg et al. note:

> Whether addressing academic or behavioral struggles of students … RTI models are designed to improve services in the general education classroom, provide students with interventions that may prevent the development of more severe problems, and provide the teacher with a more systematic approach to determine who should be referred for possible special education services.
>
> (Rosenberg et al., 2011, p. 85)

It is important to note, however, that RTI or other types of pre-referral activities may not be implemented to delay more formal evaluation of an individual who is eligible for services through special education (Yell, 2012, cited in Heward, 2013). Parents have the right to seek a complete assessment for the child to determine eligibility for special education at any point during the pre-referral procedures (Heward, 2013).

THE CASE OF RTI AND SPECIFIC LEARNING DISABILITIES

As you will see in the sections of this chapter that follow, there is a particular process for the evaluation of students to determine eligibility for special education services mandated by IDEA 2004. However, there is one specific area of disability, specific learning disabilities (SLD), for which an alternative approach has been introduced that relates directly to the topic at hand. IDEA 2004 and the accompanying regulations provide to local school districts the option of employing RTI as an alternative method for the identification of SLD (Kovaleski et al., 2013).

Based on the federal definition of SLD, most of the states require the following three criteria to identify a student with this type of disability:

1. A severe discrepancy between the student's intellectual ability and academic achievement.
2. An exclusion criterion: the student's difficulties are not the result of another known condition that can cause learning problems.
3. A need for special education services (Heward, 2013, p. 160).

There have been various concerns regarding the focus on a discrepancy model between ability and achievement and how this discrepancy may be accurately measured (McLaughlin & Ruedel, 2012). Options for the identification of SLD were increased in the 2004 reauthorization of IDEA to include what is commonly known as RTI (Zumeta et al., 2014).

> A State must adopt, consistent with 34 CFR 300.309, criteria for determining whether a child has a specific learning disability as defined in 34 CFR 300.8(c) (10). In addition, the criteria adopted by the State:
>
> • Must not require the use of a severe discrepancy between intellectual ability and achievement for determining whether a child has a specific learning disability, as defined in 34 CFR 300.8(c)(10);

- Must permit the use of a process based on the child's response to scientific, research-based intervention; and
- May permit the use of other alternative research-based procedures for determining whether a child has a specific learning disability, as defined in 34 CFR 300.8(c)(10).

(US Department of Education, Office of Special Education Programs, 2006, para. 2).

Essentially with the aforementioned changes, states and their local school systems have expanded their options for decisions of eligibility for SLD to now also include the results of a student's achievement within the RTI process with its focus on evidence-based interventions (Gargiulo, 2012). The reader should also notice that the aforementioned regulatory wording indicates that the implementation of the discrepancy formula as a means of assessing SLD is no longer a *requirement* of IDEA 2004 (McLaughlin & Ruedel, 2012).

Conceptual Application Activity 4.1

School Counselors and Pre-Referral Activities

Directions: Interview at least two school counselors to determine the extent of their school's implementation of the RTI process as a school-wide system. Further, ask the school counselors to relate their perspectives on the employment of the RTI process as a potential contributing factor to the identification of a disability. Discuss your findings with your peers.

Referral Activities and the Multifactored Evaluation According to IDEA 2004

If the pre-referral interventions do not assist the student in making adequate progress, the student may be referred for a formal evaluation of a suspected disability. Written notification must be provided to the parents and include such information as a complete explanation of the procedural safeguards available to them and a description and discussion of the proposed activities. The school must follow up this notice by seeking written consent from the parents in order to progress with the assessment process (Hardman et al., 2008).

This formal assessment is often referred to as a multifactored evaluation (MFE), in that the assessment focuses on multiple areas of the student's functioning and abilities, including the areas of focus for the suspected disability. In addition to being multifactored in its approach, the MFE for a suspected disability must be non-discriminatory and comprehensive in that various assessment instruments and techniques are to be implemented. The specific areas to be evaluated may include physical aspects, such as visual ability, hearing, and health factors, as well as such factors as intellectual ability, social emotional issues, communicative status, mobility proficiency, and academic performance (Heward, 2013). In its paper entitled, "Comprehensive assessment and evaluation of students with learning disabilities," the National Joint Committee on Learning Disabilities (2011) emphasizes the importance of making the assessment comprehensive and based on multiple sources of data.

Figure 4.1 Assessing a student's present levels of performance is critical to the formulation of an appropriate educational profile.
Source: ©iStockphoto.com, www.istockphoto.com/photo/special-needs-18817496.

Examples of assessments and approaches that may be implemented include formalized evaluation instruments such as those focused on testing intellectual ability and academic achievement, as well as more informal methods, which may include curriculum-based measures work samples, classroom observations, and interviews. The evaluation process must also be conducted by a multidisciplinary team of individuals including such professionals as the school psychologist, speech language pathologist, audiologist, and other appropriate contributors (Smith, 2006). The multidisciplinary aspect of the MFE process should assist in a broader and more informed assessment of the student's abilities and areas of difficulty. The school counselor may be an active participant at this stage of the process in a variety of ways, including data collection and reporting, providing pertinent anecdotal information about the student, and acting as a liaison between the school and the parents of the student. The American School Counselor Association (ASCA) in its paper, *The Professional School Counselor and Students with Disabilities*, emphasizes the importance of the role of the school counselor in evaluation activities by noting that the responsibilities of a school counselor may involve "contributing to the school's multidisciplinary team within the scope and practice of the comprehensive school counseling program to identify students who may need to be assessed to determine special education eligibility" (ASCA, 2013, para. 4).

Determination of a Disability According to IDEA 2004

After the MFE process is concluded and a complete picture of the student's abilities and concerns is available, the next step in the process is the determination of whether or not the student has met the criteria for one of the disability areas as designated in IDEA 2004 (see Table 3.1 in Chapter 3 for a review of the areas of disability that are covered in IDEA 2004). "The determination of whether the child is a child with a disability ... and the educational needs of the child shall be made by a team of qualified professionals and the parent of the child" (Individuals with Disabilities Education Improvement Act, Public Law 108–446, 2004, Section 614 [b] [4] [A]). The law clearly notes that a child should not be determined to be a child with a disability if the determining factor is a lack of instruction in the areas of reading and/or math, or limited proficiency in English (Individuals with Disabilities Education Improvement Act, Public Law 108–446, 2004, Section 614 [b] [5] [A] [B] [C]). In addition to providing a basis for the determination of eligibility for special education services, IDEA 2004 further mandates that the evaluation reports must present information regarding the student's educational concerns and approaches for addressing these issues (Heward, 2013). If the information supports the determination of a disability and the need for special education services, as determined by the previously mentioned team of professionals and parents, the discussion of placement options and the development of an individualized education program (IEP) will follow. Specific information regarding placements and IEPs will be discussed in Chapter 5.

To determine if students who are receiving special education services continue to be in need of such specialized instruction, a re-evaluation is completed every three years, unless the school and parent agree that there is no necessity for such an assessment. This type of evaluation may also be completed more frequently if the situation merits it, or if a re-evaluation is requested by a parent or teacher (McLaughlin & Ruedel, 2012).

A BRIEF WORD ABOUT ASSESSMENT OF BEHAVIORS

For students whose behaviors are interfering with their own educational experience or that of other individuals, schools are required to complete a Functional Behavioral Assessment (FBA) (Flick, 2011, p. 105). This assessment not only provides essential information for consideration regarding the individual student's concerns, but also provides a foundation upon which to design an intervention plan. As such, FBA will be discussed in more depth in Chapter 5, which focuses on the development of the IEP.

Conceptual Application Activity 4.2

The School Counselor and the Multifactored Evaluation Process and Determination of Eligibility for Special Education

Directions: Reflect upon the role of the school counselor in regard to the questions that follow:

1. In which ways can a school counselor be actively engaged in the MFE process for potential identification of a disability? Can you provide examples of ways in which the school counselor may be actively engaged in the evaluation of the student's skills, behaviors, etc.?

2. What types of information could the school counselor gather and provide about the student that may be relevant to the evaluation process and to the discussion of determining eligibility for special education for a particular student?
3. As a member of the team that determines the eligibility of a student for special education services, how could you specifically participate in the team meetings?
4. Provide an example of how your expertise in counseling may be advantageous to the group dynamics of a team meeting when discussing the determination of eligibility for special education for a particular student.

Identification Process for Students with Disabilities, Section 504

As previously discussed, a second piece of legislation that impacts the identification of students with disabilities for specialized services is Section 504 of the Rehabilitation Act of 1973. In Chapter 2, it was noted that Section 504 (as well as Americans with Disabilities Act—ADA) is broader in its scope of delineating areas of disability and less systematized in its regulations for identifying individuals with disabilities. Unlike IDEA 2004, Section 504 is not related to specific categorizations of a disability, but is rooted in the implications of an impairment—mental and/or physical—on what is regarded as a major life activity (Smith, 2002). Consequently, even if an individual does not qualify for specialized services through IDEA 2004, he or she may still be eligible for safeguards form Section 504 and/or ADA (Rothstein & Johnson, 2010).

There should be a specific delineated procedure for the identification of students who are entitled to protections from Section 504 and the ADA. "This includes referral, evaluation, program planning, placement, and reevaluation" (Smith, 2001, p. 340).

Referral Activities and the Evaluation Process According to Section 504

Although there are no stipulations regarding who may initiate a referral for services through Section 504 and ADA, the majority of the referrals are made by teachers and/ or parents (Smith, 2001). In response to the referral, the school completes an assessment to determine if the student is in fact eligible for services and which services may be required (Smith & Patton, 1998). Local educational systems are mandated to provide standards for the assessment and placement of individuals who are suspected to require services according to Section 504 standards, and they must evaluate the student on an individual basis (OSSE, 2012).

The assessment process must be overseen by an individual(s) who is familiar with the student and his or her situation (Miller & Newbill, 2006). Various sources of information and important factors in relation to learning should be considered and there should be assurances that assessment materials:

- have been validated for the specific purpose for which they are used, and are administered by trained personnel in conformance with the instructions provided by their producer;

- are tailored to assess specific areas of education need and are not designed merely to provide a single general intelligence quotient; and
- are selected and administered so as best to ensure that, when a test is administered to a student with impaired sensory, manual, or speaking skills, the test results accurately reflect the student's aptitude or achievement level or whatever other factor the test purports to measure, rather than reflecting the student's impaired sensory, manual, or speaking skills (except where those skills are the factors that the test purports to measure) (US Department of Education, Office for Civil Rights, 2010, para. 20).

Determination of a Disability According to Section 504

After the evaluation is completed, eligibility decisions are made. The group that is involved in the placement decision-making is composed of individuals who are familiar with the student, and are knowledgeable in the interpretation of assessment data and options for placement. (McLaughlin & Ruedel, 2012). To be eligible for the protections afforded by Section 504:

> a student must be determined to: (1) have a physical or mental impairment that substantially limits one or more major life activities; or (2) have a record of such an impairment; or (3) be regarded as having such an impairment.
> (34 CFR 104.3 (j) (1), as cited in OSSE, 2012, p. 3)

Please refer to Chapter 2 for an in-depth review and discussion of the meaning of "disability" within Section 504 and the ADA.

The members of the committee must conclude if the evaluation information is adequate as a basis for making an informed decision of whether or not the student meets the eligibility requirements for a determination of a disability. The regulatory stipulation of Section 504 at 34 CFR 104.35 (c) mandates that the assessment process includes a variety of informational sources to ensure that the potential for error is reduced, with documentation of pertinent information related to the student's process of learning (US Department of Education, Office for Civil Rights, 2013).

As for the process of evaluation, the same process may be implemented for eligibility for Section 504 protections as is employed in IDEA 2004 in relation to assessing the student's needs. If a distinct process is adopted for implementation regarding the assessment of the needs of students for Section 504 protections, the requirements for assessment stipulated in the Section 504 regulation of 34 CFR 104.35 must be followed. The regulation stipulated in 34 CFR 104.35 (c) (3) mandates that the determination of student eligibility for specialized services be made by a group of individuals including those who are knowledgeable regarding the interpretation of the assessment data and options for placement (US Department of Education, Office for Civil Rights, 2013). For additional specific information regarding the Section 504 regulation of 34 CFR 104.35, *Evaluation and Placement,* please refer to US Department of Education (1980).

If the evaluation information supports the determination of a disability according to Section 504, and the need for special education services, as determined by the previously mentioned team, the discussion of options for placement and the development of a 504

Plan will follow. Specific information in regard to placement options and 504 Plans will be discussed in Chapter 5.

To determine if students who are receiving special education services and protections within Section 504 continue to be in need of such specialized educational options, a re-evaluation on a periodic basis is required. These re-evaluations may be conducted according to the re-evaluation mandates of IDEA 2004, which stipulates that a re-evaluation be completed every three years, unless the school district and parent are in accord that one is not necessary, or even more often if warranted by the situation or requested by the child's teacher or parent (US Department of Education, Office for Civil Rights, 2010). It is important to also note that Section 504 demands that school districts complete a re-evaluation prior to making a major change in placement for the student involved with its protections (Miller & Newbill, 2006; US Department of Education, Office for Civil Rights, 2013).

A Brief Word about the Identification of Young Children for Specialized Services

Although the focus of this book is on K-12 level students, it is vital for school counselors to recognize that some of the children with whom they will be working at the elementary level may already have been involved with specialized assistance and requirements. IDEA 2004 is the basis for the provision of specialized services to children with disabilities between the ages of three and five and to infants, toddlers and their families. Early intervention for infants and toddlers is provided according to a program reflected on an Individualized Family Service Plan (IFSP) and the education of preschoolers is involved with the implementation of an IEP (Heward, 2013). For a summary of specific legislatively based information regarding infants and toddlers with special needs, please see the box below:

TITLE I—AMENDMENTS TO THE INDIVIDUALS WITH DISABILITIES EDUCATION ACT

Part C—Infants and Toddlers With Disabilities

Sec. 632. Definitions.

IDEA 2004, Part C, Section 632(5)

P. L. 108–446. 20 USC 1432, Sec. 632[5]

(5) Infant or toddler with a disability.—The term 'infant or toddler with a disability'—

(A) means an individual under 3 years of age who needs early intervention services because the individual—

(i) is experiencing developmental delays, as measured by appropriate diagnostic instruments and procedures in 1 or more of the areas of cognitive development, physical development, communication development, social or emotional development, and adaptive development; or

(ii) has a diagnosed physical or mental condition that has a high probability of resulting in developmental delay; and

---

(B) may also include, at a State's discretion—
(i) at-risk infants and toddlers; and
(ii) children with disabilities who are eligible for services under section 619 and who previously received services under this part until such children enter, or are eligible under State law to enter, kindergarten or elementary school, as appropriate, provided that any programs under this part serving such children shall include—
(I) an educational component that promotes school readiness and incorporates pre-literacy, language, and numeracy skills; and
(II) a written notification to parents of their rights and responsibilities in determining whether their child will continue to receive services under this part or participate in preschool programs under section 619.

Source: US Department of Education (n.d.).

It is also important for school counselors to appreciate that the evaluation and identification of young children with disabilities can be challenging. "Professionals often find it difficult to accurately determine if a young child has a disability unless the child shows clear physical characteristics or indicators" (Rosenberg et al., 2011, p. 89). Rosenberg et al. also note that lags in development and behavioral attributes may also be considerations. In addition, environmental influences should be taken into consideration, as there is the expectation of more inconsistency in evaluation results due to the influence of the environment on infants and preschoolers than on older students (Pierangelo & Giuliani, 2012).

The Role of the School Counselor in the Identification of Students with Disabilities

As one might expect, the school counselor can play a critical role in the identification process of students with disabilities. School counselors may be active members of the teams that review evaluation results and information and participate in the decision-making involved with the disability identification process. They may also be major contributors of relevant information for the collection of data and information as part of the assessment process, including testing information. School counselors may also be called on to be resources for pre-referral strategies for children who are suspected of having a disability (Pierangelo & Giuliani, 2012). Because school counselors have the potential of being major contributors and active participants in the evaluation and identification process of students with disabilities, it is critical that they become familiar with the aforementioned issues and activities. As Baditoi and Brott (2011, p. 133) note in their discussion of Section 504, there are "legal and ethical implications ... that counselors add this information to their body of knowledge about students with disabilities." The same can certainly be said of IDEA 2004 and its accompanying regulations and activities regarding the evaluation and identification of students with disabilities.

Conclusion

As school counselors could often be participants in activities related to the identification process of students with disabilities, they should have a strong working knowledge of the steps in the process and the components of each step. It is important that they are aware of various evaluation practices such as pre-referral activities, multifactored and multidisciplinary evaluation procedures, the summarizing of data and information for the potential determination of a disability, and the later re-evaluation process and criteria for continued eligibility for students to receive special education services, whether the students are being assessed according to the regulations associated with IDEA 2004 or those of Section 504 of the Rehabilitation Act of 1973. This type of information is critical to the design of specialized programming for students with disabilities, which may also include the involvement of school counselors. Consequently, a strong cognitive and pragmatic foundation related to this topic will enable the school counselor to be an informed contributor in the determination and implementation of these specialized services, whether it be designated on an IEP or Section 504 Plan.

References

ASCA (2013). *The Professional School Counselor and Students with Disabilities*. Retrieved from www.schoolcounselor.org/asca/media/asca/PositionStatements/PS_Disabilities.pdf.

Baditoi, B. E. & Brott, P. E. (2011). *What School Counselors Need to Know About Special Education and Students with Disabilities*. Arlington, VA: Council for Exceptional Children.

Flick, G. L. (2011). *Understanding and Managing Emotional and Behavior Disorders in the Classroom*. Boston, MA: Pearson Education, Inc.

Gargiulo, R. M. (2012). *Special Education in Contemporary Society: An Introduction to Exceptionality*. Thousand Oaks, CA: Sage.

Hallahan, D. P., Kauffman, J. M., & Pullen, P. C. (2009). *Exceptional Learners: An Introduction to Special Education*, 11th edn. Boston, MA: Pearson Education, Inc.

Hardman, M. L., Drew, C. J., & Egan, M. W. (2008). *Human Exceptionality, School, Community, and Family*, 9th edn. Boston, MA: Houghton Mifflin Company.

Heward, W. M. (2013). *Exceptional Children: An Introduction to Special Education*, 10th edn. Upper Saddle River, NJ: Pearson Education, Inc.

Individuals with Disabilities Education Improvement Act, Public Law 108–446 (2004). *An Act to Reauthorize the Individuals with Disabilities Education Act, and for Other Purposes. Title I: Amendments to the Individuals with Disabilities Education Act*. Retrieved from www.copyright.gov/legislation/pl108446.pdf.

Kovaleski, J. F., VanDerHeyden, A. M., & Shapiro, E. S. (2013). *The RTI Approach to Evaluating Learning Disabilities*. New York: Guilford Press.

McDougal, J. L., Graney, S. B., Wright, J. A., & Ardoin, S. P. (2010). *RTI in Practice: A Practical Guide to Implementing Effective Evidence-Based Interventions in Your School*. Hoboken, NJ: John Wiley & Sons, Inc.

McLaughlin, M. M. J. & Ruedel, K. (2012). *The School Leader's Guide to Special Education*, 3rd edn. Bloomington, IN: Solution Tree Press.

Miller, L. & Newbill, C. (2006). *Section 504 in the Classroom: How to Design and Implement Accommodation Plans*, 2nd edn. Austin, TX: Pro-Ed, Inc.

National Center on Response to Intervention (2010). *What is Response to Intervention (RTI)?* Washington, DC: US Department of Education, Office of Special Education Programs, National Center on Response to Intervention. Retrieved from http://files.eric.ed.gov/fulltext/ED526859.pdf.

National Joint Committee on Learning Disabilities (2011). Comprehensive assessment and evaluation of students with learning disabilities. *Learning Disability Quarterly*, 34(1), 3–16.

OSSE (2012). *Section 504 of the 1973 Rehabilitation Act: Local Education Agency Toolkit*. Washington, DC: Office of the State Superintendent of Education. Retrieved from http://osse.dc.gov/sites/default/files/dc/sites/osse/publication/attachments/OSSE_DSE_Section%20504_Toolkit%2008%2028%2012.pdf.

Pierangelo, R. & Giuliani, G. A. (2012). *Assessment in Special Education: A Practical Approach*, 4th edn. Upper Saddle River, NJ: Pearson Education, Inc.

Rosenberg, M. S., Westling, D. L., & McLeskey, J. (2011). *Special Education for Today's Teachers: An Introduction*, 2nd edn. Upper Saddle River, NJ: Pearson Education, Inc.

Rothstein, L. & Johnson, S. F. (2010). *Special Education Law*, 4th edn. Thousand Oaks, CA: Sage.

Sandomierski, T., Kincaid, D., & Algozzine, B. (2007). Response to intervention and positive behavior support: brothers from different mothers or sisters with different misters? Retrieved from www.pbis.org/common/cms/files/Newsletter/Volume4%20Issue2.pdf.

Smith, D. D. (2006). *Introduction to Special Education: Teaching in an Age of Opportunity*, 5th edn. Boston, MA: Pearson, Education, Inc.

Smith, T. E. C. (2001). Section 504, the ADA, and public schools. *Remedial and Special Education*, 22(6), 335–343.

Smith, T. E. C. (2002). Section 504: what teachers need to know. *Intervention in School and Clinic*, 37(5), 259–266.

Smith, T. E. C. & Patton, J. R. (1998). *Section 504 and Public Schools: A Practical Guide For Determining Eligibility, Developing Accommodation Plans, and Documenting Compliance.* Austin, TX: Pro-Ed, Inc.

US Department of Education (n.d.) *Building the Legacy: IDEA 2004. Statute: TITLE I/C/ 632. Sec.632 DEFINITIONS (5).* Retrieved from http://idea.ed.gov/explore/view/p/%2Croot%2Cstatute%2CI%2CC%2C632%2C.

US Department of Education (1980). *Title 34 Education, Subtitle B Regulations of the Offices of the Department of Education. Chapter 1: Office for Civil Rights, Department of Education. Part 104: Nondiscrimination on the Basis of Handicap in Programs or Activities Receiving Federal Financial Assistance.* Subpart D: preschool, elementary, and secondary education, 104.35 evaluation and placement. Retrieved from www2.ed.gov/policy/rights/reg/ocr/edlite-34cfr104.html#S35.

US Department of Education, Office for Civil Rights (2010). *Free Appropriate Public Education for Students With Disabilities: Requirements Under Section 504 of the Rehabilitation Act of 1973*, Washington, DC. Retrieved from www2.ed.gov/about/offices/list/ocr/docs/edlite-FAPE504.html.

US Department of Education, Office for Civil Rights (2013). *Protecting Students with Disabilities, Frequently Asked Questions about Section 504 and the Education of Children with Disabilities.* Retrieved from www2.ed.gov/about/offices/list/ocr/504faq.html.

US Department of Education, Office of Special Education Programs (2006). *IDEA Regulations, Identification of Specific Learning Disabilities.* Retrieved from http://idea.ed.gov/explore/view/p/%2Croot%2Cdynamic%2CTopicalBrief%2C23%2C.

Werts, M. G., Culatta, R. A., & Tompkins, J. R. (2007). *Fundamentals of Special Education: What Every Teacher Needs to Know*, 3rd edn. Upper Saddle River, NJ: Pearson Education, Inc.

Wilmshurst, L. & Brue, A. W. (2010). *The Complete Guide to Special Education, Proven Advice on Evaluation, IEPs, and Helping Kids Succeed*, 2nd edn. San Francisco, CA: Jossey-Bass, John Wiley & Sons, Inc.

Zumeta, R. O., Zirkel, P. A., & Danielson, L. (2014). Identifying specific learning disabilities. *Topics in Language Disorders*, 34(1), 8–24.

5 Individualized Education Programs (IEPs) and Educational Placement Issues

The following CACREP standards are addressed in this chapter:

SECTION 5: ENTRY-LEVEL SPECIALTY AREAS
G. SCHOOL COUNSELING
2. CONTEXTUAL DIMENSIONS
   b. school counselor roles in consultation with families, P-12 and postsecondary school personnel, and community agencies
   d. school counselor roles in school leadership and multidisciplinary teams
3. PRACTICE
   d. interventions to promote academic development
   l. techniques to foster collaboration and teamwork within schools

Chapter Objectives

After you have completed this chapter, you should be able to:

- Describe the structure and content of the IEP and a Section 504 Plan.
- Relate the composition of IEP teams and their activities.
- Relate the composition of Section 504 teams and their activities.
- Self-reflect on the role of the school counselor in the design and implementation of an IEP and Section 504 Plan.

Individualized Education Programs (IEPs), Section 504 Plans, and Educational Placement Issues

As the preceding chapters have followed a logical sequence for school counselors to gain a firm foundation in special education practice, the next area to be covered relates specifically to providing services to the student identified with a disability. This chapter will center on the structure and content of the individualized education program (IEP) as well as the IEP meeting. The elements of 504 Plans and Section 504 planning meetings will also be discussed in this chapter. The discussion will focus on the components of the IEP and/or Section 504 Plan, which are of particular relevance to the school counselor, such as the interpretation of the evaluation results, the transition aspect, inclusion and other educational placement options, and the potential delineation of school counseling as a related service. The roles and responsibilities of the IEP team and Section 504 team members will also be outlined, again with particular attention being paid to the role of school counselors, as they participate in program development and delineation of educational goals and support services.

The Development of Individualized Education Programs

As we have seen in Chapter 4, the evaluation process and identification of a disability according to IDEA 2004 involve the steps of: (a) pre-referral activities; (b) referral for assessment; (c) multifactored evaluation (MFE); (d) determination of the student's eligibility for specialized services by a qualified team of professionals and parents; and (e) a later re-evaluation to determine if students who receive special education services continue to be in need of such specialized instruction. After the student has been a participant in the IDEA 2004-related special education process leading to his/her identification as an individual with a disability, an IEP is designed and placement options are determined.

A team of individuals must meet and design a program on an individual basis "of specially designed instruction that addresses the unique needs of the child" (Gargiulo, 2012, p. 68). More specifically, the IEP team establishes the educational goals and the specialized instructional options and services, as well as the individuals responsible for providing the services and how often the services will be provided (Heward, 2013).

What Must Be Considered at the IEP Meeting for the Development of an IEP?

According to IDEA 2004, the IEP team must consider the issues that follow:

(3) DEVELOPMENT OF IEP.—

    (A) IN GENERAL.—In developing each child's IEP, the IEP Team, subject to subparagraph (C), shall consider—
        (i) the strengths of the child;
        (ii) the concerns of the parents for enhancing the education of their child;
        (iii) the results of the initial evaluation or most recent evaluation of the child; and
        (iv) the academic, developmental, and functional needs of the child.
    (B) CONSIDERATION OF SPECIAL FACTORS.—The IEP Team shall—
        (i) in the case of a child whose behavior impedes the child's learning or that of others, consider the use of positive behavioral interventions and supports, and other strategies, to address that behavior;
        (ii) in the case of a child with limited English proficiency, consider the language needs of the child as such needs relate to the child's IEP;
        (iii) in the case of a child who is blind or visually impaired, provide for instruction in Braille and the use of Braille unless the IEP Team determines, after an evaluation of the child's reading and writing skills, needs, and appropriate reading and writing media (including an evaluation of the child's

future needs for instruction in Braille or the use of Braille), that instruction in Braille or the use of Braille is not appropriate for the child;
(iv) consider the communication needs of the child, and in the case of a child who is deaf or hard of hearing, consider the child's language and communication needs, opportunities for direct communications with peers and professional personnel in the child's language and communication mode, academic level, and full range of needs, including opportunities for direct instruction in the child's language and communication mode; and
(v) consider whether the child needs assistive technology devices and services.
(Individuals with Disabilities Education Improvement Act, Public Law 108–446, 2004, Sec. 614 [d] [3] [A] [B])

It is important to note that once a student has been provided with an IEP, a review of the IEP must be completed on a periodic basis, but not less often than annually, to ascertain if the student's goals are being attained, with revisions being completed as appropriate (US Department of Education, n.d.a, Part B, Section 614 [d] [4] [A] [i] [ii]).

Who Are the Members of the IEP Team?

The design of an IEP should be accomplished through a partnership between the local education agency (LEA) and the parents (Burns, 2006). School personnel and parents should be prepared to discuss the student's strengths and weaknesses as well as pertinent goals and objectives (McLaughlin & Ruedel, 2012). Parents are equal partners in the development of the IEP and are required members of the IEP team.

The law is very specific in regard to the membership of an IEP team as you will appreciate by the membership listing that follows:

The term "individualized education program team" or "IEP Team" means a group of individuals composed of—

(i)   the parents of a child with a disability;
(ii) not less than 1 regular education teacher of such child (if the child is, or may be, participating in the regular education environment);
(iii) not less than 1 special education teacher, or where appropriate, not less than 1 special education provider of such child;
(iv) a representative of the local educational agency who—
    (I)   is qualified to provide, or supervise the provision of, specially designed instruction to meet the unique needs of children with disabilities;
    (II) is knowledgeable about the general education curriculum; and
    (III) is knowledgeable about the availability of resources of the local educational agency;
(v)   an individual who can interpret the instructional implications of evaluation results, who may be a member of the team described in clauses (ii) through (vi);
(vi) at the discretion of the parent or the agency, other individuals who have knowledge or special expertise regarding the child, including related services personnel as appropriate; and

(vii) whenever appropriate, the child with a disability.
(Individuals with Disabilities Education Improvement Act,
Public Law 108–446, 2004, Sec. 614 [d] [1][B]).

You will note that the point marked as (vi) refers to related services personnel as being potential members of the IEP team. Although related services will be discussed in more depth later in this chapter, it is important to recognize that IDEA 2004 lists *counseling services* as a related service (Individuals with Disabilities Education Improvement Act, Public Law 108–446, 2004, Sec. 602 [26] [A]), therefore affirming the potential importance of the school counselor as an active participant in the IEP process and team meeting. As Jasper (2004, p. 57) notes, if a student requires "a particular related service in order to benefit from special education, the related service professional should be involved in developing the IEP."

It is also important to note that although school counselors are valued and relevant contributors and members of the IEP team, there should not be the expectation that they will be responsible for what the American School Counselor Association (ASCA, 2013, para. 5) refers to as "inappropriate administrative or supervisory" activities, including:

•   making singular decisions regarding placement or retention;
•   serving in any supervisory capacity related to the implementation of the IDEA;
•   serving as the school district representative for the team writing the IEP;
•   coordinating, writing or supervising the implementation of the IEP.

Components and Content of the IEP

Just as IDEA 2004 has specific stipulations regarding IEP team membership, it also has specific requirements for the content of the IEP. It is critical that all pertinent personnel, including school counselors, and parents have a working knowledge of these various components to act as informed participants and contributors to the IEP process. Section 614 [d] [1] [A] of IDEA 2004 requires the components that follow, in regard to the composition of an IEP:

(I)   a statement of the child's present levels of academic achievement and functional performance, including-
(aa) how the child's disability affects the child's involvement and progress in the general education curriculum;
(bb) for preschool children, as appropriate, how the disability affects the child's participation in appropriate activities; and
(cc) for children with disabilities who take alternate assessments aligned to alternate achievement standards, a description of benchmarks or short-term objectives;
(II) a statement of measurable annual goals, including academic and functional goals, designed to—
(aa) meet the child's needs that result from the child's disability to enable the child to be involved in and make progress in the general education curriculum; and
(bb) meet each of the child's other educational needs that result from the child's disability;
(III) a description of how the child's progress toward meeting the annual goals described in sub-clause (II) will be measured and when periodic reports on the progress the

child is making toward meeting the annual goals (such as through the use of quarterly or other periodic reports, concurrent with the issuance of report cards) will be provided;

(IV) a statement of the special education and related services and supplementary aids and services, based on peer-reviewed research to the extent practicable, to be provided to the child, or on behalf of the child, and a statement of the program modifications or supports for school personnel that will be provided for the child—

(aa) to advance appropriately toward attaining the annual goals;

(bb) to be involved in and make progress in the general education curriculum in accordance with sub-clause (I) and to participate in extracurricular and other nonacademic activities; and

(cc) to be educated and participate with other children with disabilities and non-disabled children in the activities described in this subparagraph;

(V) an explanation of the extent, if any, to which the child will not participate with non-disabled children in the regular class and in the activities described in sub-clause (IV)(cc);

(VI) (aa) a statement of any individual appropriate accommodations that are necessary to measure the academic achievement and functional performance of the child on State and districtwide assessments consistent with section 612(a)(16)(A); and

(bb) if the IEP Team determines that the child shall take an alternate assessment on a particular State or districtwide assessment of student achievement, a statement of why—

(AA) the child cannot participate in the regular assessment; and

(BB) the particular alternate assessment selected is appropriate for the child;

(VII) the projected date for the beginning of the services and modifications described in sub-clause (IV), and the anticipated frequency, location, and duration of those services and modifications; and

(VIII) beginning not later than the first IEP to be in effect when the child is 16, and updated annually thereafter—

(aa) appropriate measurable postsecondary goals based upon age appropriate transition assessments related to training, education, employment, and, where appropriate, independent living skills;

(bb) the transition services (including courses of study) needed to assist the child in reaching those goals; and

(cc) beginning not later than 1 year before the child reaches the age of majority under State law, a statement that the child has been informed of the child's rights under this title, if any, that will transfer to the child on reaching the age of majority under section 615(m).

(Individuals with Disabilities Education Improvement Act, Public Law 108–446, 2004, Sec. 614 [d] [1] [A] [i])

For an example of an IEP format, see Ohio Department of Education (2012).

Conceptual Application Activity 5.1

Comparing IEPs from Various School Districts

Directions: Obtain blank copies of IEPs from two different school systems. Meet in small groups to compare formats and to locate the required elements of the IEP in each.

The previous information provides a general overview of the legally required content of an IEP. Although school counselors may not specifically write parts of the information that are included in these various IEP components, it is essential that school counselors have, at minimum, a basic knowledge of this content to ensure their active participation in the development of a student's IEP. While an in-depth discussion of each of these elements is beyond the scope of this book, it is important to highlight some of the components of particular interest to school counselors as they work with students with disabilities.

RELATED SERVICES

One of the IEP components which may have direct applicability to school counselors is the area of *related services*. As the previous legislatively based discussion noted, a statement of related services is a component to be addressed on the IEP. According to IDEA 2004, the purpose of related services is to assist the student with a disability to gain from special education (McLaughlin and Ruedel, 2012). For a specific legal explanation of the term "related services," see the box below.

Related Services

IN GENERAL—The term "related services" means transportation, and such developmental, corrective, and other supportive services (including speech-language pathology and audiology services, interpreting services, psychological services, physical and occupational therapy, recreation, including therapeutic recreation, social work services, school nurse services designed to enable a child with a disability to receive a free appropriate public education as described in the individualized education program of the child, counseling services, including rehabilitation counseling, orientation and mobility services, and medical services, except that such medical services shall be for diagnostic and evaluation purposes only) as may be required to assist a child with a disability to benefit from special education, and includes the early identification and assessment of disabling conditions in children.

(Individuals with Disabilities Education Improvement Act, Public Law 108–446, 2004, Sec. 602 [26] [A])

Again, it is critical to note that counseling services are specifically delineated in this explanation of related services in the box above. Therefore, there is the potential that school counselors will be specifically designated as providers of services on the IEP. As such, they should have direct input as to the frequency and type of counseling activities with which they will be involved with the students. For example, either group counseling activities or individual counseling approaches may be provided (Salvia et al., 2007). Further, school counselors should also actively contribute to the discussion of the educational environment in which these counseling services will be provided (e.g., inclusion classroom, individualized session in location separate from the classroom, etc.).

An in-depth discussion of individual counseling activities with students with disabilities is found in Chapter 6. Chapter 7 discusses creative counseling strategies and Chapter 8 focuses on group counseling approaches for school counselors to implement with students with disabilities. These chapters assist the reader with specific concepts and activities which may be beneficial to include as part of the related service of counseling on the IEP for those students with disabilities in need of such support.

COUNSELING GOALS AND BENCHMARKS/OBJECTIVES FOR THE IEP

As school counselors may be related services providers according to the IEP, they should have a strong working knowledge about the specific parts of the IEP that relate to the delineation of goals and benchmarks/objectives. It is important for them to be proficient in writing goals and benchmarks/objectives that can be measurably evaluated.

Terminology

There are three specific terms with which the school counselor should be knowledgeable in order to gain proficiency in completing the section on *measurable annual goals* of the IEP form: (a) annual goals; (b) benchmarks; and (c) objectives.

Annual Goals—Statements on an Individualized Education Program (IEP) that describe what a student can be expected to accomplish in one year in the identified area of need.

Benchmark—A specific statement of what a child should know and be able to do in a specified segment of the year. Benchmarks describe how far the child is expected to progress toward the annual goal and by when. Benchmarks establish expected performance levels that allow for regular checks of progress that coincide with the reporting periods for informing parents of the child's progress toward achieving the annual goals.

Objective—A smaller, more manageable learning task that a child must master as a step toward achieving an annual goal. Objectives break the skills described in the annual goal into discrete components that, when mastered, allow the child to successfully obtain the goal.

(Ohio Department of Education, 2013, glossary terms 4, 12, 62)

Either objectives or benchmarks may be employed on the IEP, or both may be delineated. Generally, however, one annual goal would not note both benchmarks and objectives. The determination of which is more appropriate for the particular annual goal is a decision that should be made by the IEP team (Ito, 2001; New York State Education Department, 2010).

Writing Measurable Annual Goals, Benchmarks, and Objectives

You will notice that the term "measurable" is a consistent modifier of the previously mentioned terminology. The practice of measurability is not a recommendation; it is a requirement (Twachtman-Cullen & Twachtman-Bassett, 2011). "To be measurable, an annual goal should, in language parents and educators can understand, describe the skill, behavior or knowledge the student will demonstrate and the extent to which it will be demonstrated" (New York State Education Department, 2010, para. 12).

In regard to the description of the behaviors and skills, in general, measurability implies that they are *observable*. Action words are commonly preferred over terms that are not as concrete in description. For example, if the focus was on an instructional goal: "The student will *consider his/her actions* before disrupting the class." Can you readily observe a student *considering* his/her actions? To make this goal more measurable, the following could be considered: "Given a large group discussion setting, *the student will raise his/her hand before speaking*, 80 percent of the time."

In addition, measurability also implies a criterion by which to measure the student's progress with the goal. The first example of the goal given in the previous paragraph does not note any information as to the extent by which the skill will be exhibited. There must be some type of specific criterion by which to determine mastery of the goal by the student. The second example of the goal clearly specifies a frequency criterion of *80 percent of the time*. Noting practical criteria assists in determining a more precise profile of the student's performance (Pratt & Dubie, 2003). Please see the box below for an example of potential counseling annual goals and how they can be addressed either through measurable benchmarks or measurable objectives.

Examples of Writing Goals and Benchmarks/Objectives for IEPs

Annual Goal: In an academic school year, during individualized seatwork assignments, the student will work independently for a period of 20 minutes.
Benchmarks:

- By the end of the first grading period, during independent seatwork time, the student will stay at his/her desk and work quietly on the assignment for a period of 5 minutes.
- By the end of the second grading period, during independent seatwork time, the student will stay at his/her desk and work quietly on the assignment for a period of 10 minutes, ETC.

Annual Goal: In an academic school year, at the end of each school day, the student will write in his/her journal about positive experiences from that day, noting at least 3–5 experiences.
Objectives:

- Given a personal journal, at the end of each school day, the student will write in the journal about one positive experience from that day.
- Given a personal journal, at the end of each school day, the student will write in the journal about two positive experiences from that day, ETC.

Source: Author.

Conceptual Application Activity 5.2

Writing Measurable Counseling Goals and Benchmarks/Objectives

Read the following description of Donna, who has just been identified as a student with an emotional disturbance through the requirements of IDEA 2004. Reflect on the questions and issues that follow the description.

Donna is in the fifth grade and has been identified as a child with an emotional disturbance (ED) according to the stipulations of IDEA 2004. Based on numerous sources of information, one of the major concerns in regard to Donna's behavior is her verbally aggressive behavior toward her classmates. While she has never been physically aggressive toward her peers, she has verbally attacked several of her classmates at various times. There is no one student who is the focus of her aggressive behavior. It simply appears that if something is bothering Donna, her coping mechanism is to verbally lash out at whichever student is nearest to her at the time.

You are a participant at the meeting where an IEP is being written for Donna. Although you, as the school counselor, have provided input in regard to various academic and behavioral issues for which the general and special education teachers will be the persons primarily responsible for their implementation, you are now requested to take the lead in the discussion as the team has also determined that Donna will require the related service of counseling as part of her specialized programming. Based on what you have learned about writing measurable goals and benchmarks/objectives, and based on the fact that the writing of these goals and benchmarks/objectives will be the result of a team discussion and decision, provide at least two examples of annual goals with two benchmarks or objectives for each goal, which you could foresee potentially resulting from this team discussion and that could possibly be included as part of the IEP for the related service of counseling.

Annual Goal 1	*Benchmark or objective 1*
	Benchmark or objective 2
Annual Goal 2	*Benchmark or objective 1*
	Benchmark or objective 2

ADAPTATIONS AND/OR MODIFICATIONS TO MEET STUDENT NEEDS

In its discussion of the role of the professional school counselor when working with students with disabilities, the ASCA (2013) emphasizes the collaborative role of the school counselor with other pertinent parties in the implementation of services, as well as the provision of assistance with the design of academic programming. Moreover, it specifically notes the school counselor's responsibility for "consulting and collaborating with staff and families to understand the special needs of a student and understanding the adaptations and modifications needed to assist the student" (ASCA, 2013, para. 4). While an in-depth discussion of adaptations and modifications is beyond the scope of this chapter, it is beneficial to provide a brief overview of some of the more commonly implemented techniques.

There are numerous examples of potential academic and instructional interventions that have been discussed to assist students with disabilities as they work to meet their goals. A few representative options include: (a) peer-assisted learning; (b) direct instruction; (c) hands-on instruction; (d) self-monitoring; and (e) instruction in study and organizational skills (McLaughlin & Ruedel, 2012; Wilmshurst & Brue, 2010). Examples of commonly implemented adaptations for instructional purposes include: (a) extended time on assignments or tests; (b) oral alternatives to written requirements; (c) reduction on length of tasks or tests; (d) environmental adaptations (e.g., for a student who is easily distracted, placement in quieter areas for completing assessments); and (e) the support of assistive technological options (Jung and Guskey, 2012).

With an appreciation of examples of the academic interventions and adaptations that may be employed as a result of the determination of the student's needs, school counselors can work toward fulfilling their critical roles of information resources and collaborative partners in IEP development and implementation. Their training and expertise also enable them to contribute vital information in relation to more counseling-related issues, such as the promotion of self-concepts, self-advocacy, and the meeting of personal/social needs (Marshak et al., 2010), as accompaniments to the fulfillment of academic or instructional activities. Chapter 10 will provide more information in relation to the supportive role that school counselors play in collaboration with teachers when working with students with disabilities, while Chapter 11 highlights the consultative aspect of school counseling in regard to families of students with disabilities and members of the community.

FUNCTIONAL BEHAVIORAL ASSESSMENT AND BEHAVIOR
INTERVENTION PLANS

Another topic relates to the writing of goals and benchmarks/objectives on the IEP but with the specific focus on students with behavioral issues: the completion of an assessment process and a plan addressing the behaviors in question. The evaluation process is called a *Functional Behavioral Assessment (FBA)* and is an organized approach for obtaining information in regard to the students and their particular behaviors, potential cause(s) of the behaviors, and predictors of the behaviors' presentations or lack thereof (Heward, 2013; Marshak et al., 2010).

The completion of a FBA is not only a pedagogically sound approach for students with emotional or behavioral issues, but there is a legal mandate for such a practice: "Schools are ... obligated by law to provide functional behavioral assessment (FBA) for students whose problem behaviors interfere with their education or the education of others" (Flick, 2011, p. 105). Examples of techniques for implementation in a functional assessment are rating scales, anecdotal information reporting, interviews, and systematically completed observations (Alper et al., 2001).

Bock and Borders (2012) identify the following steps for the implementation of the FBA process: (a) identification of the target behavior; (b) gathering of information regarding the behavior through indirect means; (c) development of a hypothesis; (d) accumulation of data from observations; (e) representing of the data through graphs; (f) design of a plan for behavioral support; and (g) evaluation of the plan. The plan is referred to as a Behavior Intervention Plan (BIP). The BIP is designed by the team and integrated into the IEP procedure (Marshak et al., 2010). "The BIP should include information obtained from the FBA, specific behavior goals, intervention strategies, and a method to assess the effectiveness of the plan" (Shepherd, 2010, p. 123).

TRANSITION

The transition process and services were previously discussed in Chapter 2, as they related to IDEA 2004. In addition, the focus of Chapter 9 is on the transition from secondary school to post-school life and career development for students with disabilities. A full chapter (Chapter 9) is concentrated on transitional services because not only is it a major emphasis of programming for students with disabilities but it is one for which the training and expertise of school counselors should be a natural fit. The discussion in Chapter 9 focuses on both the process and activities with which the school counselor may become involved in regard to transition services. For example, there will be coverage of the role of school counselors in ensuring the provision of appropriate post-secondary academic and/or training options and/or employment, as well as support regarding areas of personal growth and independent living.

Because transition and career development is covered in depth in Chapter 9, the discussion herein will focus briefly on transition as it relates specifically to IEP development. A major point in this regard is that transition is a required focus of the IEP. Furthermore, there are particular age stipulations for completing parts of the transition section. There is generally some type of statement of the student's transition requirements on his/her course of study. The US Department of Education describes the information that should be considered in that section in this manner:

Transition planning, for students beginning at age 14 (and sometimes younger)—involves helping the student plan his or her courses of study (such as advanced placement or vocational education) so that the classes the student takes will lead to his or her post-school goals.
(US Department of Education, 2007, Sec. 7, para. 21)

There is also a section of the IEP that should be focused on students 16 years of age and older—or younger if considered appropriate—for transition evaluation data for programming. Again, the US Department of Education provides guidance as to the focus of this section of the IEP.

Transition services, for students beginning at age 16 (and sometimes younger)—involves providing the student with a coordinated set of services to help the student move from school to adult life. Services focus upon the student's needs or interest in such areas as: higher education or training, employment, adult services, independent living, or taking part in the community.
(US Department of Education, 2007, Sec. 7, para. 21)

A review of an IEP generally also reveals the necessity of addressing three major categories when completing the transition portion of the IEP, namely: (a) post-secondary education and training; (b) employment; and (c) independent living. Moreover, for each of these areas, the service or activity is to be specified along with the duration of the service provision and the individual(s) responsible for the particular service/activity. Moreover, measurable goals and courses of study must be noted.

Students should be participants in discussions of transitional programming by the time they are 16 years old, if not before. The school counselor can assist in preparing students by discussing their interests and needs with them. The student can then be more equipped as an IEP team member to engage in the discussions at the meeting to ensure that the IEP transitional information does reflect his/her interests and goals (Marshak et al., 2010).

Again, more specific information will be covered in Chapter 9, but it is still important to note here the importance of the school counselor in the IEP process, and especially, in their contributions to the aspects of the IEP that center on transitional programming. By virtue of their expertise and training, school counselors will be prepared to lead and/or participate in many of the activities that will assist in the transition of the students with disabilities. Particularly at the secondary level, school counselors focus on such issues as academic and career guidance, as well as personal and social skills. School counselors generally assist students with choices of courses and activities that will prepare them for their goals after graduation, in addition to providing guidance on post-secondary educational options and vocational training opportunities (Kochhar-Bryant, 2008).

PLACEMENT AND LEAST RESTRICTIVE ENVIRONMENT

Obviously, because of the possibility of being listed as a related services provider and engaged in various activities and services related to an IEP, school counselors will necessarily be concerned with the determination of the location and environment in which the services will be presented. Clearly, there is a very pragmatic motive for school counselors to be knowledgeable of the options for a student's educational and service-related placement. However, an appreciation for these options for placement will further enable school counselors to actively engage in the activities and discussion related to the IEP process and meetings. This background will not only be beneficial in assisting them to function as active participants on the IEP team, but will also assist them in gaining a clearer profile of the students with whom they will be working, specifically, the student's needs, and where these needs will be addressed.

To assist school counselors in their appreciation of the issue of educational placement, some background information is warranted. Once the student's needs and educational and related services to assist with those needs are determined, the IEP team delineates the educational environment in which the student will receive his or her education according to the stipulation of *least restrictive environment (LRE)* (Heward, 2013).

What is "Least Restrictive Environment"?

The mandate for placement options for service provision to students with disabilities is the assurance that the environments reflect the least restrictive settings for the student. The concept and practice of LRE relates to the provision of services to the students with disabilities in environments that meet their needs *and* are the closest to the general educational setting as is appropriate (Rosenberg et al., 2011). According to IDEA 2004, LRE is described as follows:

To the maximum extent appropriate, children with disabilities, including children in public or private institutions or other care facilities, are educated with children who are not disabled, and special classes, separate schooling, or other removal of children with disabilities from the regular educational environment occurs only when the nature or severity of the disability of a child is such that education in regular classes with the use of supplementary aids and services cannot be achieved satisfactorily.

(Individuals with Disabilities Education Improvement Act,
Public Law 108–446, 2004, Sec. 612 [a] [5] [A])

Although this description is somewhat general, the determination of the LRE is specific to the individual student.

When determining the LRE for each student with a disability according to IDEA 2004 regulations, it is clear that there is a preference for providing services to students in a general education environment.

(5) Almost 30 years of research and experience has demonstrated that the education of children with disabilities can be made more effective by—
(A) having high expectations for such children and ensuring their access to the general education curriculum in the regular classroom, to the maximum extent possible.

(Individuals with Disabilities Education Improvement Act,
Public Law 108–446, 2004, Sec. 601 [c] [5] [A])

The general education setting should be the beginning point for placement considerations for students with disabilities and alternative placements should only be taken into account if it is determined that it is not feasible for the services to be provided in the general education setting while providing the students with a successful experience (Bateman et al., 2007). Furthermore, if it is determined that a student will not be instructed in the general education setting, the IEP team must provide a rationale for this decision and clear documentation that, even with a variety of accommodations and/or modifications, the student is unable to advance within the general education curriculum (McLaughlin & Ruedel, 2012).

The term commonly employed to represent the situation where a student with a disability receives his/her services in the general education environment is *inclusion* or *inclusive education* (Hardman et al., 2008).

Inclusive education, according to its most basic definition, means that students with disabilities are supported in chronologically age-appropriate general education classes in their home schools and receive the specialized instruction delineated by their individualized education programs (IEPs) within the context of the core curriculum and general class activities.

(Halvorsen & Neary, 2001, cited in FSU Center for
Prevention & Early Intervention Policy, 2002, para. 3)

It is important to recognize, however, that *least restrictive environment* and *inclusion* do not in fact always have the same meaning. In some cases, the inclusive classroom is the same as the LRE for those students who are receiving their education in general education classrooms. The tenet of *least restrictive environment*, however, mandates that students with disabilities receive their education in a setting that is as close to the general education class as is feasible, while providing an appropriate program for the student to make progress (Heward, 2013). Not every student with a disability will receive all their specialized services in the general education classroom. Obviously, the least restrictive placement will depend on his/her individual profile and needs.

With that noted, it is still important to reiterate that the general education environment is the foundation and starting point from which LRE determinations are considered. If general education is not the appropriate and least restrictive environment for a particular student, other options must be considered. There must be a continuum of alternative placement options available to meet the needs of specific students with disabilities. According to the US Department of Education, in *Building the Legacy: IDEA 2004*, there is a requirement that this continuum of alternative placements includes "instruction in regular classes, special classes, special schools, home instruction, and instruction in hospitals and institutions" (US Department of Education, n.d.b, Sec. 300.15 [b] [1]) and there are stipulations for the provision of supplemental services along with placement in the regular classroom (US Department of Education, n.d.b, Sec. 300.15 [b] [2]).

While the general education classroom is considered to be the least restrictive placement and homebound or hospital placement is generally viewed as being the most restrictive placement on a continuum of alternative placements (Heward, 2013), various other options fall between these two extremes. For example, Salvia et al. (2007) note some other options: (a) the general education classroom with instructional support provided by a special educator in the general education setting; (b) instructional services from a special educator in a resource room setting where the student leaves the general education classroom for a period of time for this specialized instruction; (c) part-time general education placement and part-time placement in a special education environment; (d) instruction in the special education setting on a full-time basis with some integration; and (e) instruction in the special education environment on a full-time basis, such as a special day school for students with disabilities.

What does all this mean to the school counselor? The key to placement decisions is to focus on the LRE that would provide the most appropriate setting for the implementation of the IEP (Hardman et al., 2008). Being knowledgeable about the legal and ethical issues involved in determining the most appropriate educational placement for a student with a disability, such as the principle of LRE, will enable the school counselor to actively engage in the IEP process, whether it be as a direct provider of information and services, consultant, liaison, advocate, or some other supportive role. Moreover, an awareness of placement issues will assist school counselors in knowing the "where" and to some extent the "how" of service provision as they directly provide support to the students with disabilities and as they collaborate with other pertinent personnel involved with the students' education. As they participate in the provision of the LRE for the students with disabilities, the school counselor may work with students on an individual basis, in group situations, in special education class environments, and/or general education classrooms (ASCA, 2013).

Figure 5.1 Student-centered instruction is a characteristic of effective educational programming.
Source: ©iStockphoto.com, www.istockphoto.com/photo/junior-kindergarten-class-32751266.

The Development of Section 504 Plans

After the student has been identified as a student with a disability, according to the afore-mentioned assessment stipulations associated with Section 504 of the Rehabilitation Act of 1973, a Section 504 Plan is designed and services are determined. Various recommendations and/or requirements have been discussed in regard tó this process.

Considerations for the Development of a Section 504 Plan

The team of individuals involved with the design of the service plan should consider all of the evaluation information available in regard to the student (Smith & Patton, 1998). In *Guidelines for Educators and Administrators for Implementing Section 504 of the Rehabilitation Act of 1973: Subpart D*, several items are listed as factors to consider in the determination of services and accommodations.

a. Evaluation results
b. Section 504 identification determination
c. The student's unmet needs
d. Services and/or accommodations based on needs
e. Least restrictive environment for services
f. Discussion of and plan for possible staff training

(US Department of Education, Office for
Civil Rights, 2010, p. 30)

The US Department of Education, Office for Civil Rights also specifies other critical requirements in regard to Section 504 Plans. It notes that: (a) "Written consent from the parent should be obtained for an initial Section 504 placement" (2010, p. 30); (b) a case manager must be assigned the responsibility for the completion and management of each student's Section 504 file; (c) a Section 504 Plan must ensure that the services will be provided in the least restrictive environment; and (d) once designed, a Section 504 Plan is to be reviewed, at minimum, on an annual basis or at a time when a member of the 504 team regards it as necessary.

Team Composition for the Design of a Section 504 Plan

The team whose responsibility it is to develop a Section 504 Plan should be composed of individuals who are knowledgeable about the student with a disability, the assessment process, and the educational and instructional options (Miller & Newbill, 2006). The US Department of Education, Office for Civil Rights (2010) notes the composition of such a team would focus on a core group of individuals that would include the parents, school principal or administrator, general education and/or referring teacher, and school counselor. In their discussion of individuals involved with the implementation of Section 504 Plans, Shaw and Madaus (2008) also discussed the roles of other school-based personnel, such as special education teachers and school psychologists. It is important to note that participating in the development of a Section 504 Plan is only one aspect of the Section 504 process with which parents should be involved. The parents should be participants in the various aspects of the Section 504 Plan process, including the assessment, determination of a disability, and the placement (US Department of Education, Office for Civil Rights, 2010).

Focus/Components of a Section 504 Plan

The format of the 504 Plan is not as formally dictated as that of the IEP. In fact, there may be a wide variety of written formats (Smith & Patton, 1998). It is important to appreciate, however, that although a Section 504 Plan "is not as expansive as an IEP, … it is still a legal document that is to be precisely followed" (Baditoi & Brott, 2011, p. 147). There are various examples of Section 504 Plans. For a sample Section 504 Plan format, please refer to US Department of Education, Office for Civil Rights (2010, Form B-8, pp. 69–70).

Conceptual Application Activity 5.3

Comparing Section 504 Plans from Various School Districts

Directions: Obtain blank copies of Section 504 Plans from two different school systems. Meet in small groups to compare formats and to discuss the elements in each. In addition, compare the formats of the previously obtained IEPs (Conceptual Application Activity 5.1) to the Section 504 Plan formats.

The focus of a Section 504 Plan is on the provision of accommodations and/or modifications for the student to experience success in the school environment (Bateman et al., 2007; Smith & Patton, 1998). In other words, "the [Section 504] plan reflects the needs of the student for both classroom (academic) and extracurricular participation and … specifies accommodations that allow the student the opportunity to participate in or benefit from the school's programs and activities" (Baditoi & Brott, 2011, p. 147).

ACCOMMODATIONS AND MODIFICATIONS

Clearly, the emphasis on the design and implementation of a Section 504 Plan is on the provision of appropriate accommodations and modifications to meet the student's particular needs. While an in-depth discussion of accommodations and modifications that may be appropriate for Section 504 Plans is beyond the scope of this chapter, it is important for the school counselor to be provided with an overview of types of accommodations and/or modifications and a few pertinent examples that may be included on a student's Section 504 Plan.

A cohesive approach to a discussion of adaptations and modifications that may be included on a Section 504 Plan is to categorize the types of approaches. Polloway et al. (2008) categorize adaptations for curriculum and instruction as follows: (a) adaptations of materials (e.g., textual materials); (b) adaptations in instructional delivery (e.g., providing multisensory learning activities); (c) adaptations in products and assignments (e.g., reduced length in assignments); (d) adaptations to homework (e.g., implementation of organizational tools such as assignment journals or books); (e) adaptations in testing (oral vs. written responses); and (f) adaptations in grading (e.g., weighted grading for assignments). Assistive technology is also a major area of potential options for adaptations to be included on a Section 504 Plan (Cohen & Spenciner, 2005; Karten, 2005; National Center for Learning Disabilities, n.d.; Polloway et al., 2008).

As is obvious, numerous examples of adaptations may be included within each of these categories. For an in-depth discussion of adaptations that may be included on a Section 504 Plan, see "Examples of Disabilities and Accommodations" of US Department of Education, Office for Civil Rights (2010).

PLACEMENT AND LEAST RESTRICTIVE ENVIRONMENT

Similar to the procedures affiliated with IEPs and services, placement decisions for students with Section 504 Plans must be rooted in the concept of the LRE (Bateman et al., 2007). In other words, the students are to receive services in the general education environment unless it is has been determined that their education in the regular setting with the implementation of supplementary assistance cannot be adequately achieved (US Department of Education, n.d.c, 34 CFR Subpart D, Part 104.34 [a]).

Consequently, the student with a Section 504 Plan may receive specialized instructional services, adaptations in the general education classroom, and/or related services depending on his/her particular situation. A major stipulation of Section 504 in this regard is that programs and services are accessible to the students with disabilities (deBettencourt, 2002). In fact, as Smith (2002, p. 262) notes, "the key to determining the

Figure 5.2 School counselors should be engaged contributors in designing the educational environment for all students.

Source: ©iStockphoto.com, www.istockphoto.com/photo/education-is-necessary-17973413.

need for a related service is if it is required for the student to be able to access the educational program," a point of particular interest to school counselors.

It should be clear that the school counselor may play a critical role not only in the IEP process and its implementation, but also in the procedures and activities involved with services related to Section 504 of the Rehabilitation Act of 1973. As with IEP-related services, the involvement of school counselors can again be focused on their provision of counseling as a related service (deBettencourt, 2002). They may also function as information resources regarding the tenets and requirements of Section 504 and its implementation, and as participants in procedural activities regarding the assessment process and eligibility determination (Baditoi & Brott, 2011).

The Role of the School Counselor in the Program Design and Educational Placement of Students with Disabilities

Throughout this chapter there have been examples provided of how a school counselor may be an engaged and active participant and contributor in the design of educational programming and placement options for students with disabilities. If school counselors are ever unable to attend and actively participate in IEP meetings, they should be certain to communicate their positions and recommendations. This section will reiterate that school counselors should not only actively participate in IEP and programming activities, but they can accomplish this involvement in a variety of ways.

Although the role of school counselors may be multidimensional when working with students with disabilities and other pertinent individuals during the IEP and Section 504 processes, perhaps a classification of role functions may be the easiest method of summarizing their varied responsibilities. The classification should not be perceived as an oversimplification of the school counselor role: on the contrary, it exemplifies the various facets of their contributions. As such, three major classifications of the role of the school counselor in regard to the IEP and Section 504 processes and their implementations are the school counselors as: (a) direct service providers and contributors; (b) information resources and consultants; and (c) liaisons and collaborative advocates.

Direct Service Provider and Contributor

As noted earlier in this chapter, school counseling may be provided as a related service on the IEP or as a service affiliated with a Section 504 Plan, in which case the school counselor will be directly involved in service provision to the student with a disability, as well as a direct contributor to the determination of the goals and benchmarks/objectives for that service. As alluded to previously, the types of services provided may include such activities as individual and/or group counseling techniques and sessions. The focus of the related service of counseling may be on a variety of possibilities including personal and social issues, academic performance, behavioral concerns, and career development, to name a few.

By virtue of their training and expertise, school counselors are enabled to assist the members of the IEP and Section 504 teams to appreciate the relationship between students' personal characteristics and social behaviors and their success or lack thereof in academic areas (Milsom et al., 2007) and, as such, may become directly involved in attending to improving the areas of need. In addition, school counselors may become directly involved in providing counseling and/or behavioral support for students with challenging behaviors (Baditoi & Brott, 2011). Moreover, a school counselor's knowledge base and practical experience in the area of career development can prove to be an invaluable asset to students with disabilities as they look to their post-school futures. The school counselor again can be directly involved as a service provider by assisting students with vocational assessments and assisting them in making career/post-secondary decisions (Milsom et al., 2007). Additional ways in which school counselors may act as direct service providers in relation to the IEP and Section 504 Plans will be covered in later chapters of the book.

Information Resource and Consultant

Clearly there may be overlap between the three general classifications of the school counselor as direct service provider, information resource and consultant, and liaison and collaborative advocate. For example, a school counselor may directly teach decision-making skills to a student with a disability (Quigney & Studer, 1999) in preparation for a personal or career goal, and may simultaneously act in a consultative manner to a community agency that may play a role in a vocational placement for the student.

Despite the potential for overlap, it is still salient to recognize the distinct importance of the role of the school counselor as an *information resource and consultant* in relation to the IEP and Section 504 processes. The ASCA specifically notes the importance of the school counselor's role as a consultant in its paper, *The Professional School Counselor and Students with Disabilities*, where it lists as a responsibility of school counselors the "consulting and collaborating with staff and families to understand the special needs of a student and understanding the adaptations and modifications needed to assist the student" (ASCA, 2013, para. 4).

These two role functions related to providing information and acting as a consultant have already been addressed in the previous discussion of the school counselor as a direct service provider and will be expanded in later chapters in the text. This consultative role is also clearly applicable to educational personnel who work with students with disabilities, parents and families of these students, and individuals from community agencies who may be involved with the implementation of the IEP goals and services or in relation to Section 504 Plans. In many ways the school counselor is actively involved in networking among these groups of individuals in ensuring that the students' goals are met and inclusion is achieved (Quigney & Studer, 1998).

During the processes and meetings related to the design of IEPs and Section 504 Plans, as well as the implementation of the IEPs and Section 504 Plans, examples of ways in which school counselors may function as information resources/consultants may include: (a) presenting and interpreting evaluation data; (b) discussing the implications of the evaluation data, including this information's impact on learning and/or behavioral issues of the students; (c) acting as a source of information regarding academic and/or behavioral accommodations/modifications for the student's programming; and (d) providing multiple sources of information on post-secondary options and transitional programming. Again, the consultative activities with which the school counselor may be involved with these groups will be addressed in depth in later chapters.

Liaison and Collaborative Advocate

As with the previous roles of direct service provider and information resource/consultant, there will be overlapping of responsibilities and activities as school counselors engage in their roles of *liaisons and collaborative advocates*. An essential commonality among all these roles is that the school counselor is an active participant and advocate for the students to ensure their most appropriate education (Owens et al., 2011). The same groups of pertinent individuals, as previously mentioned, may also be involved as school counselors fulfill the particular roles of liaison and collaborative advocate: students, educational professionals, appropriate community agency personnel, and parents and families of the students.

For example, school counselors may act as liaisons for students to post-secondary educational options, like colleges, to assist with the determination of such issues as admissions procedures and availability of disability support services (Milsom et al., 2007). They may act as collaborative advocates with educational personnel in ensuring that the students' schedules of courses match their performance levels, goals, and objectives, and personal interests and expectations. In addition, school counselors may function as advocates and liaisons with community agency personnel in providing appropriate experiential learning opportunities for the students, which coincides directly with a responsibility emphasized by the ASCA (2013, para. 4), namely, "advocating for students with special needs in the school and in the community." Marshak et al. (2010, p. 77) succinctly summarize the role of liaison for the school counselor in relation to IEP activities: "The school counselor, as a member of the team, can have an instrumental role in connecting people and information in order to ensure continuity and consistency in implementation of the IEP."

Other individuals with whom the school counselor also plays a major role as a liaison and advocate are, of course, the parents and families of the students with disabilities. Numerous examples may relate to the school counselor acting as a liaison between the parents/guardians of the students with disabilities and the school and/or the community, and will be discussed later in the text. In the meantime, a very brief discussion of the critical partnership between school counselors and parents and families of students with disabilities appears warranted in a chapter related to the development of IEPs and Section 504 Plans.

A Word on Providing Support for Parents/Families at IEP Meetings or Section 504 Plan Meetings and in IEP or Section 504 Plan Activities

School counselors not only provide support and consultation to parents and families of the students with disabilities and act as liaisons and advocates during the implementation phase of the IEP and Section 504 Plan, but also in the development phase of the IEP and Section 504 Plan, and at meetings where they are the points of focus. The ASCA (2013) emphasizes the importance of school counselors to encourage family involvement and to consult and collaborate with them. The professional background of school counselors in group dynamics and interpersonal interactions enables them to function as liaisons between the parents and families of the student and educational personnel and professionals in the community, not only in the IEP and Section 504 Plan implementation phase, but also in the development of goals, objectives, and determination of services.

As IEP and Section 504 Plan meetings may be attended by various invested parties, the parent may at times be overwhelmed by the amount of information being presented. The school counselor may act as a supportive resource for the families to prevent them from being intimidated by the numerous perspectives being presented (Quigney & Studer, 1998). School counselors can assist in keeping the discussions at these meetings focused, comfortable, and conducive to open dialogue among all members of the team. Parents must be viewed and welcomed as equal partners in the process of IEP and Section 504 Plan development and implementation, and be encouraged to provide input and request clarifications of information (Quigney, 2005).

These are just a few examples of activities in which school counselors may become involved with parents and families of students with disabilities with particular focus on activities related to IEPs or Section 504 Plans. Chapter 11 will provide additional information on the role of the school counselor in regard to parents and families of students with disabilities and the importance of school counselor–family partnerships.

Conclusion

In this discussion of the processes related to the development of IEPs and Section 504 Plans, it becomes clear that it is critical for school counselors to be knowledgeable about these procedures and related activities, as they may play various critical role functions in their regard, such as: (a) interpreter of assessment information; (b) programming contributor, providing expertise on developmentally appropriate counseling options and techniques; (c) service provider; (d) resource for goals and objectives associated with the potential provision of school counseling as a related service; (e) information resource and consultant regarding academic and/or behavioral accommodations/modifications for the student's IEP or Section 504 Plan; (f) liaison between the school and parents/guardians; and (g) advocate for students and parents/guardians, as well as other pertinent personnel. These roles related to service provision to students with disabilities, their families, and personnel who work with the students with disabilities will be discussed more specifically in later chapters.

References

Alper, S., Ryndak, D. L., & Schloss, C. N. (2001). *Alternate Assessment of Students with Disabilities in Inclusive Settings*. Needham Heights, MA: Allyn & Bacon.

ASCA (2013). *The Professional School Counselor and Students with Disabilities*. Retrieved from www.schoolcounselor.org/asca/media/asca/PositionStatements/PS_Disabilities.pdf.

Baditoi, B. E. & Brott, P. E. (2011). *What School Counselors Need to Know About Special Education and Students with Disabilities*. Arlington, VA: Council for Exceptional Children.

Bateman, D. F., Bright, K. L., O'Shea, D. J., O'Shea, L. J., & Algozzine, B. (2007). *The Special Education Program Administrator's Handbook*. Boston: MA: Pearson Education, Inc.

Bock, S. J. & Borders, C. (2012). Effective practices/interventions for students with emotional and behavioral disorders. In J. P. Bakken, F. E. Obiakor, & A. F. Rotatori (eds.), *Behavioral Disorders: Practice Concerns and Students with EBD, Advances in Special Education, 23* (pp. 61–82). Bingley: Emerald Group Publishing Limited.

Burns, E. (2006). *IEP-2005: Writing and Implementing Individualized Education Programs (IEPs)*. Springfield, IL: Charles C. Thomas, Publisher.

Cohen, L. & Spenciner, L. J. (2005). *Teaching Students with Mild and Moderate Disabilities, Research Based Practices*. Upper Saddle River, NJ: Pearson Education, Inc.

deBettencourt, L. U. (2002). Understanding the differences between IDEA and Section 504. *Teaching Exceptional Children*, 34(3), 16–23.

Flick, G. L. (2011). *Understanding and Managing Emotional and Behavior Disorders in the Classroom*. Upper Saddle River, NJ: Pearson Education, Inc.

FSU Center for Prevention & Early Intervention Policy (2002). *What is Inclusion? Including School-Age Students with Developmental Disabilities in the Regular Education Setting*. Florida State University Center for Prevention & Early Intervention Policy. Retrieved from http://cpeip.fsu.edu/resourceFiles/resourceFile_18.pdf.

Gargiulo, R. M. (2012). *Special Education in Contemporary Society: An Introduction to Exceptionality*. Thousand Oaks, CA: Sage.

Hardman, M. L., Drew, C. J., & Egan, M. W. (2008). *Human Exceptionality: School, Community, and Family*, 9th edn. Boston, MA: Houghton Mifflin Company.

Heward, W. M. (2013). *Exceptional Children: An Introduction to Special Education*, 10th edn. Upper Saddle River, NJ: Pearson Education, Inc.

Individuals with Disabilities Education Improvement Act, Public Law 108–446 (2004). *An Act to Reauthorize the Individuals with Disabilities Education Act, and for Other Purposes. Title I-Amendments to the Individuals with Disabilities Education Act*. Retrieved from www.copyright.gov/legislation/pl108446.pdf.

Ito, C. (2001). *Short-Term Objectives or Benchmarks?* Williamsburg, VA: William and Mary School of Education, Training and Technical Assistance Center. Retrieved from http://education.wm.edu/centers/ttac/resources/articles/iep/shorttermobj/index.php.

Jasper, M. C. (2004). *The Law of Special Education*, 2nd edn. Dobbs Ferry, NY: Oceana Publications, Inc.

Jung, L. A. & Guskey, T. R. (2012). *Grading Exceptional and Struggling Learners*. Thousand Oaks, CA: Corwin.

Karten, T. J. (2005). *Inclusion Strategies that Work! Research-Based Methods for the Classroom*. Thousand Oaks, CA: Corwin Press.

Kochhar-Bryant, C. A. (2008). *Collaboration and System Coordination for Students with Special Needs, from Early Childhood to the Postsecondary Years*. Upper Saddle River, NJ: Pearson Education, Inc.

McLaughlin, M. M. J. & Ruedel, K. (2012). *The School Leader's Guide to Special Education*, 3rd edn. Bloomington, IN: Solution Tree Press.

Marshak, L. E., Dandeneau, C. J., Prezant, F. P., & L'Amoreaux, N. A. (2010). *The School Counselor's Guide to Helping Students with Disabilities*. San Francisco, CA: Jossey-Bass, John Wiley & Sons, Inc.

Miller, L. & Newbill, C. (2006). *Section 504 in the Classroom: How to Design and Implement Accommodation Plans*, 2nd edn. Austin, TX: Pro-Ed, Inc.

Milsom, A., Goodnough, G., & Akos, P. (2007). School counselor contributions to the individualized education program (IEP) process. *Preventing School Failure*, 52(1), 19–24.

National Center for Learning Disabilities (n.d.). *Assistive Technology*. Retrieved from www.ncld.org/students-disabilities/assistive-technology-education.

New York State Education Department (2010). *Annual Goals, Short-Term Instructional Objectives and/or Benchmarks*. Retrieved from www.p12.nysed.gov/specialed/publications/iepguidance/annual.htm.

Ohio Department of Education (2012). *IEP Individualized Education Program, PR-07 IEP FORM*. Retrieved from http://education.ohio.gov/getattachment/Topics/Special-Education/Federal-and-State-Requirements/Procedures-and-Guidance/Individualized-Education-Program-IEP/Development-of-IEP/iep_form_09_static.pdf.aspx.

Ohio Department of Education (2013). *Glossary*. Retrieved from http://education.ohio.gov/Topics/Special-Education/Federal-and-State-Requirements/Procedures-and-Guidance/Glossary.

Owens, D., Thomas, D., & Strong, L. A. (2011). School counselors assisting students with disabilities. *Education*, 132(2), 235–240.

Polloway, E. A., Patton, J. R., & Serna, L. (2008). *Strategies for Teaching Learners with Special Needs*, 9th edn. Upper Saddle River, NJ: Pearson Education, Inc.

Pratt, C. & Dubie, M. (2003). Practical steps to writing individualized education plan (IEP) goals and writing them well. *The Reporter*, 9(2), 1–3, 24. Retrieved from https://scholarworks.iu.edu/dspace/bitstream/handle/2022/9513/17.pdf?sequence=1.

Quigney, T. A. (2005). Students with special needs. In J. R. Studer (ed.), *The Professional School Counselor: An Advocate for Students* (pp.82–106). Belmont, CA: Thomson Brooks/Cole.

Quigney, T. A. & Studer, J. R. (1998). Touching strands of the educational web: the professional school counselor's role in inclusion. *Professional School Counseling*, 2(1), 77–81.

Quigney, T. A. & Studer, J. R. (1999). Transition, students with special needs, and the professional school counselor. *Guidance and Counselling*, 15(1), 8–12.

Rosenberg, M. S., Westling, D. L., & McLeskey, J. (2011). *Special Education for Today's Teachers: An Introduction*, 2nd edn. Upper Saddle River, NJ: Pearson Education, Inc.

Salvia, J., Ysseldyke, J. E., & Bolt, S. (2007). *Assessment in Special and Inclusive Education*, 10th edn. Boston, MA: Houghton Mifflin Company.

Shaw, S. F. & Madaus, J. W. (2008). Preparing school personnel to implement Section 504. *Intervention in School and Clinic*, 43(4), 226–230.

Shepherd, T. L. (2010). *Working with Students with Emotional and Behavior Disorders: Characteristics and Teaching Strategies*. Upper Saddle River, NJ: Pearson Education, Inc.

Smith, T. E. C. (2002). Section 504: what teachers need to know. *Intervention in School and Clinic,* 37(5), 259–266.

Smith, T. E. C., & Patton, J. R. (1998). *Section 504 and Public Schools: A Practical Guide for Determining Eligibility, Developing Accommodation Plans, and Documenting Compliance.* Austin, TX: Pro-Ed.

Twachtman-Cullen, D. & Twachtman-Bassett, J. (2011). *The IEP from A to Z: How to Create Meaningful and Measurable Goals and Objectives.* San Francisco, CA: Jossey-Bass, John Wiley & Sons, Inc.

US Department of Education (n.d.a). *Building the Legacy: IDEA 2004.* Public Law 108–446, Part B, Section 614. Retrieved from http://idea.ed.gov/explore/view/p/%2Croot%2Cstatute%2CI%2CB%2C614%2Cd%2C4%2C.

US Department of Education (n.d.b). *Building the Legacy: IDEA 2004.* Part 300, Subpart B, Sec. 300.15. Retrieved from http://idea.ed.gov/explore/view/p/%2Croot%2Cregs%2C300%2CB%2C300%252E115%2C.

US Department of Education (n.d.c). *Title 34 Education, Subtitle B Regulations of the Offices of the Department of Education, Chapter 1: Office for Civil Rights, Department of Education, Part 104: Nondiscrimination on the Basis of Handicap in Programs or Activities Receiving Federal Financial Assistance.* Retrieved from www2.ed.gov/policy/rights/reg/ocr/edlite-34cfr104.html#S34.

US Department of Education (2007). *Parents/My Child's Special Needs: A Guide to the Individualized Education Program.* Retrieved from www2.ed.gov/parents/needs/speced/iepguide/index.html?exp=3.

US Department of Education, Office for Civil Rights (2010). *Guidelines for Educators and Administrators for Implementing Section 504 of the Rehabilitation Act of 1973: Subpart D.* Retrieved from http://doe.sd.gov/oess/documents/sped_section504_Guidelines.pdf.

Wilmshurst, L. & Brue, A. W. (2010). *The Complete Guide to Special Education: Proven Advice on Evaluation, IEPs, and Helping Kids Succeed,* 2nd edn. San Francisco, CA: Jossey-Bass, John Wiley & Sons, Inc.

Part II

Issues for Involvement of School Counselors Specific to Working with Students with Disabilities, Educators, and Family/ Community

6 Individual Counseling for Students with Disabilities

The following CACREP standards are addressed in this chapter:

SOCIAL AND CULTURAL DIVERSITY
f. help-seeking behaviors of diverse clients
g. the impact of spiritual beliefs on clients' and counselors' worldviews

HUMAN GROWTH AND DEVELOPMENT
i. ethical and culturally relevant strategies for promoting resilience and optimum development and wellness across the lifespan

COUNSELING AND HELPING RELATIONSHIPS
a. theories and models of counseling
b. a systems approach to conceptualizing clients
n. processes for aiding students in developing a personal model of counseling

ENTRY-LEVEL SPECIALTY AREAS: SCHOOL COUNSELING PRACTICE
f. techniques of personal/social counseling in school settings

Chapter Objectives

After you have completed this chapter, you should be able to:

•   Discuss counseling theories for specific disabilities.
•   Identify strategies for assisting students with specific counseling strategies.

During the 2011–2012 academic year, approximately 13 percent of youth between the ages of three and 21 received special education services (Children and Youth with Disabilities, 2014), and school counselors are often the only mental health professionals in the schools who are able to provide individual counseling to the students with whom they work. Although school counselors are trained in numerous counseling theories that are adapted to meet the needs of their counselees, many feel ill-prepared to adjust these theories to students with disabilities. Furthermore, it is not unusual for school counselors to be reluctant to engage in activities such as teaching about disabilities, IEP meetings, or providing counseling services (Milsom, 2006).

Despite the fact that all students have a need for acceptance and support from their peers and other significant people in their lives, students with disabilities do not always receive encouragement and affirmation. For example, Hackett et al. (2011) noted that students with learning disabilities are at greater risk of developing mental health difficulties, have fewer friends and social supports, and have more negative life experiences compared with their peer group without disabilities.

Characteristics of Students with Disabilities

Students with disabilities, especially those with mild disabilities, are often not identified in early school years due to their behavior not being noticeably different from their peer group (Lerner, 1993, as cited in Bowen & Glenn, 1998). Yet, as they transition to higher grades, learning assignments become more complex and diminished academic performance may be observed (Bowen & Glenn, 1998). School counselors have a responsibility to assess personal needs of counselees, understand learning style, and determine if additional resources or supports are needed. Counseling with students requires attention to the student's developmental level, knowledge of disabilities, goal identification, and a counseling theory that will best meet these requirements. And, it requires awareness of own personal attitudes toward students with disabilities including biases, discomfort, lowered expectations, and other adversarial attitudes that could prevent these students from growing to their fullest potential (Pelsma et al., 2004).

This chapter summarizes the counseling process with attention to students with disabilities, and the most common theoretical approaches school counselors implement with these students. Although you will most likely be taking a separate course in counseling theories within your curriculum, the following sections are intended to supplement the information you will receive in this course, and to contribute to an understanding of how these approaches may be relevant in work with students with disabilities.

Interacting through Counseling

Counseling is a collaborative relationship in which two people meet and one person (the counselor) assists the other (in a school setting, this would be the student) to resolve a problem (Thompson et al., 2004). Moreover, counseling is a process that unfolds through multiple stages to prevent normal developmental problems from becoming more serious (Thompson et al., 2004). These stages include relationship-building, assessment, intervention, termination, and evaluation, which may be revisited throughout the process.

Relationship-Building

Children and adolescents do not often seek out counseling on their own, but instead are generally referred by another adult such as a parent/guardian or teacher. This is particularly evident with students with disabilities. Although literature repeatedly indicates that the quality of the counseling relationship is essential to positive counseling outcome, there is limited evidence concerning how the counseling relationship translates to students with disabilities (Jones, 2013), which limits the counselor's knowledge base as to how to establish a therapeutic relationship with these students. Counselors report that in their attempts to establish a relationship they make more accommodations such as the use of refreshments, humor, and self-disclosure for students with disabilities more frequently than with students without disabilities (Jones, 2013). These augmented efforts are, in part, due to the limited relationship experiences and social naivety often found among students with disabilities (Jones, 2013). When school-aged youth are in a counselor's office, they may be confused as to the reason they are there, who you are, and what is going to happen. After the counselor introduces him/herself students may have questions such as:

- Why am I here?
- Did I do something wrong?
- Does my teacher hate me for sending me here?
- Will I be able to make up the work I am missing in class?
- Do my classmates know I am here?
- Will you tell anyone what I tell you?

School counselors take time to answer these questions and explain the limits of confidentiality in an age and developmentally appropriate manner. Attention to this task is particularly critical for students with disabilities as they may already feel singled out from their peers. An explanation may be something like, "anything you say to me in here I will keep to myself, unless you indicate that you are going to hurt yourself or someone else. Then I will have to tell someone to keep anyone from getting hurt." Motivational interviewing (MI) is a "front-end" strategy that is often used in conjunction with any counseling theory not only to develop rapport, but also to assess the student's motivation and ability to change.

MOTIVATIONAL INTERVIEWING

Motivating students and keeping them involved and engaged in school is sometimes difficult (Turnbull et al., 2002). Addressing motivation with students with disabilities is particularly relevant since these students often exhibit learned helplessness (Bergin & Bergin, 2004) and lack self-efficacy (Turnbull et al., 2002). Throughout the counseling process, the counselor uses the basic core conditions of empathy, acceptance, and genuineness to lay the groundwork for an atmosphere conducive to change (Moyers et al., 2005), while determining commitment to change. Through MI the counselor attempts to understand the counselee's motivation for change, his/her perception of the benefits of change, and intentions for altering behavior. For instance, the counselor could ask the question, "What will happen if you don't change?" Or, "On a scale of one to ten, with one meaning you don't want to change and ten meaning you will change, what number would you give yourself at this time?" The counselor makes efforts to create an atmosphere of personal control and autonomy through active listening while affirming previous incidents of success (Miller & Rose, 2009).

Once trust is developed the counselor assumes a coaching role that encourages change (Harakas, 2013), and facilitates concrete, measurable individual goal-setting that can be assessed (Miller, 2010). Assessing the student's confidence in his/her ability to reach an identified goal can be measured on a self-efficacy scale by asking, "On a scale of one to ten, with one meaning you have little confidence in your ability to reach your goal and ten meaning that you are certain that the goal can be reached, how would you rate your likelihood of success?" If a student states "three" then the counselor responds with, "what do you need to do to move to a four?" The answers provided serve as a means for identifying steps that can be taken to move toward goal attainment. To maintain the change, the use of calendars, diaries, and self-monitoring are utilized as homework tools between sessions. For students who have difficulty with oral communication then charts, pictures, or electronic devices may be more effective concrete strategies for relaying this information.

Assessment

School counselors typically do not conduct a formal interview to gather information, but instead rely on school records and reports from teachers and other important people in the student's life. Furthermore, school counselors do not depend upon on a single artifact or score in making an assessment, but instead utilize a multimodal approach for gaining information. The HELPING model (Keat, 1990) is a useful acronym to better understand the counselee and the areas that are influencing his/her life. Once problem areas are identified, interventions and strategies are developed to offer possibilities for the student.

H Health—does the student complain of pain or illness? Has the student been to the school nurse?

E Emotions—does the student express emotions? Is *what* is said congruent with *how* it is being stated?

L Learning—are there any learning difficulties that could contribute to the problem? What are the student's grades?

P Personal relationships—who are the significant people in this person's life?

I Imagery—how does the student perceive him/herself? Does he/she have a positive self-image?

N Need—what does the student need to help resolve the issue?

G Guidance—what guidance is needed for behavior, cognition, or affect?

Intervention

Goal-setting is at the heart of counseling, and although this may seem to be a straightforward process, determining a counseling outcome is often difficult due to the numerous problems counselees discuss during a counseling session. To facilitate this process, ask the student to list or draw out three of the problems he/she is currently experiencing. From here, the student can be asked to rate the severity of the problem on a scale of one (little problem) to five (insurmountable problem). For instance, the student may list "family" with a rating of three, "grades" as a rating of four, and "bullying" with a rating of five. Since bullying was rated as the most difficult problem, the school counselor would work with the student to design strategies to reduce the bullying behaviors. Although you may not agree with the student's choice of a target area of concern, this is the student's choice, not yours. The student will also be more committed to problem resolution when he/she is given an option of choosing a goal.

Termination

Termination occurs at several points in the counseling process; at the end of each session and when the counseling goal is attained and counseling is no longer needed. At times youth have difficulty ending a relationship, but several techniques can be used to ease this transition. For one, toward the conclusion of every session, remind the student that five or ten minutes remain before the session is to end. Also, when the counseling issues are coming to an end, a discussion regarding a termination date several weeks before it is to occur helps the student prepare for closure, while the student is reminded of the coping skills that have been acquired (Thompson et al., 2004).

Once the sessions have terminated, counselors could even consider dropping periodic notes to the student throughout the school year such as, "I noticed you paying attention in your language arts class today. Way to go!" Or, "Congratulations on getting a B on your math quiz." Counselors also may evaluate and reinforce the gains that have been made through maintenance meetings throughout the school year (Thompson et al., 2004).

Evaluation

Progress toward goal assessment occurs at the end of each session (formative) and again at the end of the counseling process (summative). Accountability is a top priority in educational reform, and school counselors are part of this initiative, with a responsibility to demonstrate how their interventions have contributed to the academic mission. Assessments answer the questions, "Did this intervention help resolve the problem?" "Is the student satisfied with counseling?" and "To what extent did the student meet his/her goal?"

A ruler can be used as a concrete, quantifiable measure to track progress. At the end of each session the student can be shown a ruler with the number one representing no progress toward goal, and ten indicating goal attainment. Ask the student to use the ruler to indicate the progress he or she is making toward the goal. If the student indicates a "five", you can then ask, "What do you need to do to move to a six?" The student and counselor are then able to collaborate on homework strategies to create movement up a numeral throughout the week to reinforce progress. Although quantifiable data is preferred for determining counseling effectiveness, subjective feedback provides an indication of how well the counseling process was perceived. Examples of qualitative assessment are in Figure 6.1.

School counselors report that the numerous relationships within the student's life are crucial for reinforcing and sustaining the goals made in counseling, yet there is a degree of tension when the student leaves the counseling room and the gains that were made could be annulled by significant others in the student's life, particularly if these individuals are not in agreement with the goals (Jones, 2013). School counselors also report that the stages of counseling for students with disabilities may take longer, which requires flexibility on the part of the counselor (Smith, 2001, cited in Jones, 2013). Moreover,

Please provide feedback on your perceptions of the counseling process.
In what ways has counseling helped you achieve your goals?
What were the most helpful parts of counseling?
What suggestions do you have for your counselor?

Figure 6.1 Subjective evaluation of counseling experience.

work with this population of students could be even more emotionally consuming (Jones, 2013).

Behavior, cognition, and emotion are the categories from which counselors generally view their counselees (Dougher & Hackbert, 2000). Cognition refers to the individual's mental processes and is considered as being related to behaviors (Ellis & Hunt, 1993, as cited in Dougher & Hacker, 2000) and affect. Emotions, defined as the individual's affective state, are also related to cognition and behaviors. Counselors make a decision as to whether to work with a counselee from a cognitive, affective, or behavioral framework. Person-centered counseling, individual psychology, behavioral theory, reality theory, solution-focused brief counseling, rational emotive behavior therapy, and narrative therapy and how these theories are applicable to students with disabilities are discussed below.

Person-Centered School Counseling

Dr. Carl Rogers is credited as the theorist who developed person-centered counseling, a phenomenological, non-directive approach in which the counselor uses the skills of congruence, unconditional positive regard, active listening, and empathy (Thompson, et al., 2004) to understand the student's subjective world (Wright, 2012). The counselor creates a safe environment for students to share their thoughts without judgment while being able to grow, thrive, and develop; a concept Rogers called *self-actualization* (Hansen et al., 1986, as cited in Williams & Lair, 1991). For students with disabilities, growth may be impeded due to obstacles associated with the disability as well as the lowered expectations and/or negative perceptions of significant people. Yet, when the counselor is able to communicate positive regard and acceptance of the individual, the student is better able to attempt problem-solving strategies to cope and advance, and view the self positively (Williams & Lair, 1991). Using a person-centered approach with students with disabilities the counselor is able to communicate that the student is more than his/her disability and has a wide range of abilities. The following strategies are suggested using a person-centered focus (Williams & Lair, 1991).

- Communicate total acceptance of the child without a focus on the disability or an accommodation unless it is the heart of the student's concern.
- Students are to be considered as living to the best of their ability.
- The focus is always to be on the "whole child."

Figure 6.2 School counselors assist students with academic, vocational, and social/emotional concerns.
Source: ©iStockphoto.com, www.istockphoto.com/photo/preteen-girl-meeting-with-school-counselor-or-therapist-52233348.

Self-concept is a cornerstone of person-centered counseling, and the school counselor is instrumental in helping students develop a greater understanding of self. Self-concept has several different definitions but can broadly be defined as the attitudes and opinions one has about self (Purkey, 1988). Self-concept is impacted by perceived success and failure, and when failure is perceived in highly valued areas, evaluations in all other areas are negatively regarded. Conversely, success in a valued area increases positive regard in other areas (Purkey, 1988). Students with disabilities tend to have a lower self-perception than their non-disabled peers (Elbaum & Vaughn, 2003), and have a need for improved self-esteem and belonging (Herring, 1990, as cited in Pelsma et al., 2004).

Because the self-concept is organized, learned, and active, the school counselor is instrumental in helping students perceive themselves more favorably. Student Activity 6.1 can be used with all students and adapted for those with disabilities.

Student Activity 6.1

This is Me!

Directions: When working with a student, ask him/her to think of personal strengths in the following areas and either write or draw out these strengths.

	Academics	Non-academics
	History	Social
	English	Emotional
	Math	Physical
	Science	

My strengths—I am proud of...

Hope and a positive sense of self can be instilled through affirmations of strengths and potentials (Laursen, 2002). Self-affirmation relates to the behavioral or cognitive events that support a sense of worth and an image of oneself as successful (Shnabel et al., 2013). Studies reveal that writing about significant personal values improves academic performance of marginalized individuals (Cohen et al., 2006, as cited in Shnabel et al., 2013), reduces stress, and enhances personal support (Shnabel et al., 2013). For example, when seventh-grade students identified self-affirmations and how their values helped them feel connected with others, one result was an improved GPA (Shnabel et al., 2013). School counselors can utilize affirmations to help students recognize personal values and their sense of connectedness with others. For students who are unable to write, concrete alternatives can be utilized such as cutting out pictures from magazines, drawing pictures, or selecting photographs that represent values. Student Activity 6.2 is an example of how affirmations can be used with students.

Student Activity 6.2

My Important Values

Directions: Discuss the definition of a value with a student (e.g., something that is important and is acted upon). Ask the student to identify three values and to draw, write, or bring in photos that represent how these values connect him/her with others.

Individual Psychology

Although Alfred Adler was originally a member of Sigmund Freud's psychoanalytic group, he disagreed with the premise that behavior was based on sexual drives. Instead, he promoted the idea that personality is based in relationships.

Adler developed the premise that a sense of inferiority emerges from birth, and to overcome this dependency, a style of life is developed. The lifestyle, usually acquired by the age of four or five, is the subjective interpretation and evaluations of early childhood experiences, and is demonstrated through a need to belong, and to move from an inferior position to one in which there is a feeling of worth and respect (Dunn, 1971).

Adler's positive views on human development stressed that individuals address the various life tasks of work (school), friendship, and love to meet psychological and physical needs. A desire to belong is a basic premise behind Adlerian theory, and individuals continually attempt to find how they fit within their social settings and make decisions regarding how they relate to others (Pelsma et al., 2001). Happiness and fulfillment are gained when students are engaging in mutual cooperation through contributions to the community and the desire to contribute to the welfare of others. This sense of belonging occurs naturally within the classroom environment, yet many students with disabilities do not feel accepted by others (Pelsma et al., 2001). The school counselor views the counselee holistically (Dunn, 1971) through knowledge of the individual's culture, family, early childhood memories, and position in the family constellation (DeRobertis, 2011).

Early recollections provide clues as to the student's central interests and lifestyle (Bettner, 2005). For example, when a ninth-grade male with learning disabilities who was having trouble in school was asked his earliest memory, the counselor was able to collaboratively determine that he feigned helplessness to avoid responsibility and to get special attention. According to Adler, this was his way of avoiding life's problems and preserving his self-esteem (Bettner, 2005). In addition, the counselor gained a greater appreciation of how he saw his role within the family unit.

Student Activity 6.3

Lifestyle Inventory

1. Parents' names and ages.
   Father_____ age_____ Mother_____ age_____
   Three personality traits

   _____   _____

   _____   _____

   _____   _____

   Occupation _____   _____
2. Names of siblings, ages, and three personality traits
   a._____   _____
   name   age

   _____   _____   _____
   Personality traits
   b._____   _____
   name   age

   _____   _____   _____
   Personality traits
   c._____   _____
   name   age

   _____   _____   _____
   Personality traits
   d._____   _____
   name   age

   _____   _____   _____
   Personality traits

3. Which sibling is most like you?_____   Least like you?_____
4. Which sibling is most intelligent?_____   Leastintelligent?_____
5. Which sibling is most athletic?_____   Least athletic?_____

Additional techniques used by Adlerian counselors are below.

Could-it-be questions	*The counselor poses a question to determine the goal of misbehavior (attention, power, revenge, inadequacy). For example, "Could it be that you want your mom to give you more attention?"*
Acting as if	*The counselee acts as his/her ideal view of self. For instance, if a goal is to make better grades, the student would act "as if" they are this successful student.*
Goal-setting	*Assist the counselee to set goals and provide homework assignments to facilitate goal attainment.*
Socratic Questions	*Questions such as "What would happen if...?" or "How would your life be different if you didn't have this problem?" help the counselee develop insight. However, with students who are unable to think abstractly, a good alternative is drawing a picture.*
Encouragement	*Encouragement is a key for changing impaired beliefs that create inappropriate behaviors. Encouragement is provided to help the student gain confidence and to break self-defeating behaviors.*

Behavioral Theory

As more students with disabilities enter general education classrooms, more and more teachers are becoming involved in the implementation of behavioral interventions. However, many do not feel adequately prepared in these strategies for addressing disruptive behaviors in the classroom (Briesch et al., 2015). This lack of training, particularly in this age of evidence-based strategies, creates a need for school counselors, in collaboration with the teachers of students with special needs and/or the school psychologist, to teach behavioral strategies to promote positive classroom responses.

Despite the popularity of this approach with students with special needs, behavior theory is difficult to define due to the numerous viewpoints as to what it constitutes (Corey, 2009). Classical and operant conditioning formed the foundation for what became known as social learning theory, and later cognitive-behavioral methods were adopted (Corey, 2009). A combination of these methodologies is used based on the needs of the student.

Behavioral therapy is based on scientific principles in that academic, vocational, and/or social/emotional goals are defined and strategies are empirically tested to determine effectiveness. As depicted through the evolution of this theory, behavioralism is not limited to those behaviors that are observable, but also includes cognitions, beliefs, and emotions that are specifically defined (Corey, 2009). Furthermore, it is an action-oriented approach in which the student counselee is actively engaged in the process by learning new, productive ways of behaving.

Behaviorists look at the antecedents and consequences that precede and/or follow certain behaviors (Dougher & Hackbert, 2000). For educators who have difficulty with certain student behaviors, behavior management strategies create opportunities to manipulate the antecedents or outcomes of an identified, unwanted behavior (Turnbull et al., 2002) in order to elicit positive responses. The ABC model is used to regulate behavioral responses:

A = Antecedents (events that occur prior to a behavior)
B = Behaviors (a reaction to an antecedent or consequence)
C = Consequences (an event that follows a behavior, which could be in the form of a
    punishment or reinforcement)

Antecedent   Behavior   Consequences

For example, suppose nine-year-old Layla, who is diagnosed with autism spectrum disorder (ASD), has trouble with any unannounced changes in the classroom schedule. On numerous occasions, Layla has thrown temper tantrums when the regular school day was interrupted for any reason, such as an assembly. To change the antecedent (A), the classroom teacher or school counselor could take time at the beginning of the school day to visually and clearly outline the class schedule for the day, and to tape a visual calendar, complete with pictures, to Layla's desk. In addition, the educator could ask Layla to review the plan for the day to make certain that she understands the changes in the daily activities.

Behavior change also is possible through positive reinforcement, which serves as a consequence (C), to help students learn and increase the occurrence of displaying desired behaviors. *Differential reinforcement of behavior* is the provision of a reward (consequence) for the purpose of increasing the identified behavior. Some examples of positive reinforcers include privileges such as free time, computer usage, desired tokens, or even positive verbal encouragers (Synapse, 2008). An understanding of the child's needs facilitates the choice of behavioral interventions considered most effective to facilitate behavioral change. For instance, some students with disabilities, such as those with traumatic brain injury, do not respond well to consequential management because they are unable to remember the rules due to their memory difficulties (Turnbull et al., 2002). Moreover, the ABC model may not be effective for other students due to the student not perceiving the reward positively, not being taught the desired behavior, or if the student is not able to transfer the behavior to other settings.

Strategies for Changing Behaviors

Several types of behavioral strategies include positive verbal praise and planned ignoring, self-managed response cost, self-managed response cost with home–school notes, dependent group contingency, interdependent group contingency, fair-pair rule, shaping, the Premack principle, and behavioral contracting. Each is discussed below:

Positive praise and planned ignoring. Positive praise is a type of reinforcement in which students are given encouraging feedback when a desired behavior is displayed. Likewise, planned ignoring is meant to remove the reinforcement the student is receiving (such as peer attention when the student is misbehaving) in the hopes of removing the unwanted response (Alberto & Troutman, 2008, cited in Briesch et al., 2015).

Self-managed response cost. This behavioral management strategy is a type of token economy in which tokens (objects or symbols that are exchanged for a service or prize) are provided for acceptable behaviors and removed when inappropriate behavior is shown (Kaufman & O'Leary, 1972, as cited in Briesch et al., 2015).

Response cost with home–school notes. This collaborative strategy partners the teacher with the student's parents/guardians in that the teacher daily assesses the student's behavior and sends a report to the parents/guardians who administer home-based rewards such as stickers. If the teacher reports unacceptable behavior, the family discusses the consequences of unacceptable behaviors.

Dependent group contingency. With this behavioral strategy, a single behavior that is applicable to all students is identified, but the group reinforcement is based on the behavior of a specific student. For instance, if a student stays in his/her seat for five minutes, the entire class receives a reward.

Interdependent group contingency. With this system, a reward is given if all group members meet an identified goal, and if any group member does not meet the goal, no one receives the identified reward

Fair-pair rule. The fair-pair rule describes that whenever an unacceptable behavior is exhibited, a desired behavior is taught to replace this undesirable behavior (Martella et al., 2012) for the purpose of showing a student the behavior that is wanted.

Shaping. Shaping is also used to increase wanted behaviors in that a student is positively reinforced for staying on a specified task for a designated period of time, and as the timeframe is increased, the student is reinforced for maintaining the on-task behavior. Using this technique, the student learns acceptable behavior and feels a sense of accomplishment for maintaining his/her performance during the designated timeframes (Martella et al., 2012). Shaping or modeling behavior shows the students the type of behavior that is desired by showing them how to perform an identified behavior and then reinforcing the behavior when it is approximated. As the child performs each step of the desired behavior, he/she is reinforced for each success step that is performed successfully (Leidenfrost, 2010).

Premack principle. This concept, known as "grandma's rule," applies to the phrase that "if you eat your vegetables, you can have dessert." The principle is that behavior is likely to occur if a reinforcer follows the desired response. For example, if a student is having difficulty providing appropriate responses, this student would be taught appropriate reactions, and after the child properly displays this behavior, he/she would be reinforced with a desired incentive to increase this behavior.

Behavioral contracts. Also known as contingency contracts, these are used to increase behaviors by answering the questions "who," "what," "when," and "how well" (Martella et al., 2012). Generally these contracts include: (a) what each person needs to do to satisfy the terms of the contract; (b) the task or duty that is stated in observable terms with a designated time period; (c) how often the task is to be

Who (name of student)

What (desired behavior)

When (at what time the behavior is to occur)

How well (extent to which the behavior is to occur)

Supervisor (person responsible for monitoring student)

What (task the supervisor is to monitor)

How often (frequency that the award is to be provided)

Student signature _____

Supervisor signature _____

Monday	Tuesday	Wednesday	Thursday	Friday

*Note: The contract can be adapted based on the student's needs and ability.

Figure 6.3 Behavioral contract.

accomplished; (d) consequences for fulfilling or not fulfilling the contract, which include a statement of what the student will earn for performing the designated behavior (something the student desires); (e) an indication of how often the consequence will be delivered; and (f) a chart in which either the student or designated adult is able to record the behaviors. An example of a behavioral contract is in Figure 6.3.

An example of a behavioral approach is Check In/Check Out (CICO), a five-step process that has been effective for controlling behavioral problems.

Step 1 The student reports to an adult mentor to review his/her performance from the previous day, remind the student of his/her behavioral goals, and provide the student with target behaviors that are concretely specified throughout the day. Points are given for appropriate behaviors within the stipulated time periods.

Step 2 Throughout the day the student provides his/her daily report to the classroom teacher at the beginning of each time interval.

Step 3 At the end of the class period, the teacher completes the daily report and provides feedback and praise to the student for exhibiting acceptable behaviors.

Step 4 At the end of the day, the student returns the daily report to his/her mentor who tallies the total points accumulated throughout the day and provides a reward if the student has reached his/her goal.

Step 5 The student brings the daily report home for the parents to sign and is returned the following day.

Hunter et al. (2014) used the steps outlined in CICO to decrease problematic behaviors of students in the fourth grade. The results of the study indicated that students' internalized behaviors improved during the project, and teachers who did not receive training on intervening with internalized behaviors did learn to provide reinforcing cues to change problem responses.

In an analysis of studies (Briesch et al., 2015, p. 17), teachers reported that they were more favorable toward interventions that were easy to implement such as the use of "praise, ignoring, or reinforcement," rather than time-out strategies or the use of a token system. School counselors who wish to implement an approach similar to CICO could serve as the mentor for the students for whom this intervention is most effective.

Reality Therapy

William Glasser is credited as the founder of reality therapy (also known as choice therapy), which is based on the premise that individuals are internally motivated by the five basic needs of survival, freedom, power, fun, and love and belonging. According to Glasser all behavior, whether it is irresponsible or appropriate, is a result of attempts to fulfill these needs (Toso, 2000). The counselor using this approach views the student holistically to understand the student's thoughts, feelings, and motivation. Comprehending what the student wants and identifying needs that are not being satisfied provides an opportunity to develop a plan that has a lifelong impact (Mishler & Cherry, 1999). The acronym WDEP is used to determine a counseling goal (Wubbolding, 2000).

w   Wants—what do you want?
d   Doing—what are you doing to get what you want?
e   Evaluation—is what you are doing working?
p   Planning—what can you do to get what you want?

Once a picture of what the student desires is established, the SAMIC acronym is used to more concretely identify the goal.

s   Simple—is the goal stated specifically and easy to understand?
a   Attainable—is this something I am able to do?
m   Measurable—am I able to quantify my progress?
i   Immediate—can I start to do this as soon as possible?
c   Cost—how much am I willing to invest in this goal?

Once a concrete goal is established, the counselor does not accept excuses when a student does not accomplish a goal or take strides toward goal attainment. Instead, the student and the counselor work together in revising strategies to increase the likelihood that the identified goal will be reached. Student Activity 6.4 is a technique for goal-setting.

Student Activity 6.4

Magic Genie Bottle

1.   Bring in art supplies and a plastic bottle or a similar object that the student can decorate. After the bottle has been decorated, tell the student to rub the

bottle and to come up with three wishes he/she would like to see happen to make life easier.

2. Ask the student to draw or communicate how his/her life would be better if the wish came true. Focus on such issues as relationships with family, friends, teachers, etc.

3. Ask the student to choose one wish and to write or draw on slips of paper strategies that would need to be taken to reach this goal. Each strategy will be placed in the bottle so that the student is able to refer to it as a reminder.

4. Additional sessions will focus on how well the student is approaching his/her goal, and if progress is not being made in that direction, the counselor and student will collaboratively establish new strategies for goal attainment, or revise the goal.

Numerous philosophical approaches are used to reduce student discipline problems and disruptive behaviors, particularly with students with emotional disabilities who are often expelled and/or suspended from school due to the disruptions they create in the classroom (Coats, 1991). Reality therapy is one such approach to improve educational involvement for all students, and student behavior with students with emotional disabilities in particular. Students between five and 14 years of age who were diagnosed with emotional disturbances (EDs) participated in the Broad Street Program that incorporated reality therapy as an approach to working with these students (Coats, 1991). The tenets of Glasser's theory were incorporated into the classroom, in which a behavioral focus was emphasized over academic growth. Students who were unable to follow the rules that were established were sent to an in-school support room to develop a plan that would create more favorable consequences. Results revealed significant decreases in disruptive behaviors, and although referrals to the in-school support room did not show a significant difference in behaviors, out-of-school suspensions did decrease.

The principles of reality therapy were utilized in the classrooms of students aged 12–14 who were diagnosed with a learning disability (Omizo & Cubberly, 1983) to determine if these students could learn to develop a positive self-concept and a more internal locus of control. Teachers were trained in conducting the classroom meetings using the tenets of reality therapy and met with the students twice weekly for 11 weeks for 30–45 minutes. At the end of this time, students who participated in these meetings showed more interest and satisfaction with school experiences, with greater improvements in self-concepts compared with those members of the control group (Omizo & Cubberly, 1983).

Solution-Focused Brief Counseling

Solution-focused brief counseling (SFBC) emphasizes students' strengths and resources as a means for creating change. Steve de Shazer and Insoo Kim Berg are recognized as the founders of this approach in which there is a shift from talking about problem-saturated incidents to focusing on answers to the problem. Solution-focused counseling is based on the assertions that success leads to more success, language creates desirable possibilities, and that change is already occurring.

The counselor and student collaboratively work together to negotiate a goal, and the counselor carefully listens for times when the problem is not occurring, known as *exceptional times*, or exceptions to the problem—for instance, asking the question, "When have there been times when everything is going as you would like?" Follow-up questions such as, "What were you doing?" "Saying?" or "Who were you with?" help the student get a picture of those times when what is desired is already occurring. This vision creates a picture of occasions when life was problem-free, and also provides an opportunity for the counselor to assign homework to assist the student in reaching the desired goal. For example, the counselor could say, "Between now and the next time I see you, I want you to do more of what you just described to me." Or, "During the week, I want you to notice the times when your goal is occurring. Pay attention to whom you are with, what you are doing, and how you are feeling. We will discuss these incidents when I see you next."

For students with intellectual disabilities, videos, drawings, and role plays are helpful means for assisting in recollecting exceptional times (Roeden et al., 2012). Video recordings are also used with students with disabilities as daily activities are recorded and the material is edited to show only the successful behaviors. Viewing the desired behaviors serves as an incentive for the student to continue along this path.

There are some occasions when the student is unable to identify exceptional times, and in these cases the counselor uses what is known as the *miracle question*, or hypothetical solutions. The counselor could ask, "Suppose that one night you were sleeping and when you woke up in the morning a miracle occurred and all your problems were solved. What would be different?" Or, "Suppose I waved a magic wand that took away all your problems. How would you know that the magic worked?" Student Activity 6.5 is a solution-focused approach that can be used with students who have the ability to think hypothetically and to envision new ways of behaving. For students with intellectual disabilities, this question may be too complex. The counselor may instead change the question such as, "Talk about yourself when you are having a really good day" (Roeden et al., 2012).

Student Activity 6.5

My Special Times

1. Draw a circle, and then shade in the percentage of time that the problem occurs.

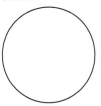

2. Next, shade in the times in which the problem doesn't occur.
3. If you are unable to think of any special times when the problem doesn't occur, think in terms of a crystal ball that can predict the future. Gaze into the crystal ball and pretend that you can see yourself at a time in the future when all

> your problems are gone. What are you doing? Who are you with? What are you thinking? Feeling? How will you know your problems have been solved? Write or draw pictures.
> 4. From now until next week, what can you do to make some of what you want happen? Write or draw a picture of your answer.

The tenets of SFBC is a practical approach for individuals with intellectual disabilities due to the emphasis on personal empowerment, the individualized interventions based on each individual's strengths and abilities, and the emphasis on desired behaviors rather than inappropriate responses (Roeden et al., 2012). Adults usually refer students with disabilities for their behavior problems, which makes it difficult for these students to establish and engage in a counseling relationship (Roeden et al., 2012). Yet, the counselor may need to adjust his/her communication by using simplistic language, being flexible with questions, and providing ample time for the student to process the information and formulate a response. For example, the counselor may consider asking questions that consist of three to five words using the student's nomenclature. Furthermore, the counselor may consider providing flexibility in the sessions by lengthening or shortening normal counseling sessions to meet the needs of the student. In addition, the use of pictures, drawings, and prompts can facilitate the counseling session (Roeden et al., 2012).

Rational-Emotive Behavioral Therapy

Rational-emotive behavioral therapy (REBT), as indicated by the name, is a therapy that incorporates cognition, emotions, and behaviors. It is based on the idea that it is not what occurs that creates emotional problems, but rather the irrational thoughts about the situation (Banks, 2011). Irrational thoughts are often expressed in terms of absolutes such as "I must," "I should," "I cannot," or "I ought." For instance, common irrational beliefs include:

- I *must* do well under all conditions.
- Other people *ought to* treat me fairly and just.
- I *should* get all As to be a success.

REBT has been used effectively with school-aged youth to address numerous issues such as low frustration (Ellis, 2003, as cited in Banks, 2011), test-anxiety, locus of control (Omizo, 1986, as cited in Banks, 2011), learning disabilities, and academic achievement (Ellis & Wilde, 2002, as cited in Banks, 2011).

REBT is based on an educational foundation in that youth are taught to identify illogical thoughts about an event to which they have problematic reactions, and to reframe the event using an objective outlook. A structured format represented by the letters A-B-C-D-E is used to teach counselees about irrational thoughts that have created difficulty. Table 6.1 defines the steps.

To assist with this shift in thinking the counselor could ask the question, "Suppose a camera were recording the event, what would a person who is not involved in the

Table 6.1. REBT and Identifying Irrational Thoughts

A = Activating event	The event that occurred is described. The counselee talks about the situation that created uncomfortable thoughts, emotions, and behaviors.
B = Belief	The person's irrational belief about the activating event is communicated.
C = Consequence	The consequences of a belief can be unhealthy and harmful and lead to destructive behaviors and emotions.
D = Dispute	When the student is taught to dispute the belief, a more realistic view of the situation emerges.
E = New effective responses	This final stage describes a new outlook of the event.

situation see?" Socratic questions are also helpful in disputing beliefs. For instance, questions such as, "What is the proof for this belief?" "Is there another way to view this situation?" "Think about the worst thing that could happen. Would it really be that awful?"

REBT was taught to elementary students through short-term guidance lessons. Fourth-grade students were given two 30-minute weekly lessons for ten days. Students were taught how to distinguish between thoughts and feelings, and differences between rational and irrational beliefs. These lessons were reviewed and practiced through active participation in groups or individual sessions. The outcome was the ability of students to demonstrate knowledge and use of REBT (Wilde, 1996) throughout their lives.

A challenge for counselors is to teach social skills to students with behavior or emotional disorders, particularly as many of these students deny responsibility for their own behaviors (Patton, 1995). Middle school students identified with behavioral and emotional disorders were given instruction in REBT in small groups for 14 weeks. Sessions included information on how the brain creates emotions, the definition of an emotion, rational and irrational thoughts, self-analysis of thoughts, practice with positive self-talk, and self-monitoring skills. At the end of the instruction, students utilized their new skills and teachers reported an improvement in student behaviors.

Students diagnosed with learning disabilities between the ages of nine and 18 were provided instruction on rational emotive education, with the purpose of improving attitudes toward self and their learning difficulties. Irrationality decreased as a result of this educational format, which also contributed to changes from an external locus of control (Patton, 1985, as cited in Hajzler & Bernard, 1991) to an internal locus of control.

Some counselors believe that this theory is inappropriate for students who have difficulty with problem-solving due to their cognitive difficulties. However, studies have shown that students' intellectual levels are not barriers to successful outcomes (Hajzler & Bernard, 1991).

Student Activity 6.6 can be implemented with students to teach the concepts of REBT.

Student Activity 6.6

How Would You Respond?

Directions: In groups, ask students to take out a piece of paper and a pen. Explain that you are going to give them a series of situations and they are to write down how they would feel in the situation. Discuss feelings and corresponding behaviors.

1. Suppose your mother bought you a new pair of shoes and asked you to keep the shoes clean. As you are walking down the street, you are talking to your friend and you don't see a mud puddle and you step in it. How would you feel? What would you do? Now, suppose you saw a younger child start across the street into the path of a turning car. You race forward to push the child out of the way and you step in a mud puddle. The driver of the car is a friend of your mother, and she said she would take you home and explain the situation to your mom. How would you feel? What would you do? _____

2. You worked hard to make a diorama for your social studies class and you put it on a bench outside the classroom. You see another student sit on it. How would you feel? What would you do? Suppose you learn that the student is blind. How would you feel? What would you do?

Narrative Counseling

Narrative counseling is based on the premise that people make meaning of their lives and how they interact in the world through the *dominant narratives* they tell. Narrative therapists believe that: (a) problems are a result of each individual's perspective of his/her connections with others and their life experiences (Lambie & Milsom, 2010); (b) people express points of view through language; and (c) individuals behave according to beliefs about self. For instance, a person who has been told he/she is angry will respond to interactions according to this label. Or a student with a disability may view themselves as being different and not as deserving of the respect given to other people. Some stories are unhelpful as they are debilitating, whereas other stories are helpful in that they elicit expressions of strength (Neukrug, 2011). Yet, many students with a disability may have difficulty viewing themselves as having abilities (Lambie & Milsom, 2010). Because unhelpful, dominant stories create hurt, distress, and dysfunction, changing perceptions is the best path to assist distressed individuals. Through a collaborative relationship, the counselor asks the student respectful questions about the context and meaning behind his/her personal stories (Seligman & Reichenberg, 2014). For instance, students who are deaf or have hearing impairments have difficult issues that need to be understood (Furlonger, 1999), and asking "curious questions" assists these individuals in recognizing instances when situations are not applicable to the problem-saturated story.

The counselor assists in *deconstructing* stories, or taking them apart, examining them, and discussing them. This process occurs through *mapping* the influence of the problem by asking counselees about how the problem affects various aspects of life such as friendships, family, school, and so on. Counselors also use *externalizing language* to separate the problem from the person, which supports the idea that the problem is a result of social labels rather than personal insufficiencies (Lambie & Milsom, 2010). The counselor and student collaboratively name the problem (e.g., Fred) to externalize the issue. Questions to facilitate externalization and extrapolate dominant themes include: "How often does Fred comes to visit?" or "When does Fred create the most difficulty?" "Are there times when you are able to control Fred?"

As the counselor carefully listens to the stories that brought the student to counseling, an investigative stance is assumed to identify contradictions to the saturated story by looking for *unique outcomes*, or times when the problem doesn't exist. Competencies, successful coping skills, and personal strengths are identified and communicated. Once these characteristics are conveyed, the process of *reauthoring* occurs, which consists of changing life perceptions, and finding exceptions to the story (Seligman & Reichenberg, 2014). Student Activity 6.7 can be used with students who have the ability to conceptualize issues abstractly and are able to verbalize their personal narratives.

Student Activity 6.7

A New Me

Write or draw your answers to the following questions in as much detail as possible.

1. Name the problem.
2. How is this a problem? (school, friends, home, etc.)
3. When are you able to control the problem?
4. When is the problem easier to handle?
5. What strengths or skills do you have that give you control over the problem?
6. From now until the next time I see you I want you to notice the times you are able to conquer the problem.

Students with learning difficulties, cognitive disabilities, or behavioral problems often fail to take an active role in their own decision-making. The school counselor is able to facilitate problem-solving and skill development through narratives to renegotiate life's difficulties.

At times, students with disabilities have difficulty viewing a situation from a larger, integrated perspective, and an integration of theoretical models and techniques may facilitate this goal. For instance, students with ASD are often focused on a single aspect of a situation and are so rigid that there is an inability to separate single aspects into an integrated whole (Abildgaard, 2014). As many of these students are visual learners, a social map with pictures can be used to help students view situations from a broader perspective. This technique is used to identify something that the student is thinking about, whether that is something that is distressing or a positive event. The following steps are used to create a more holistic picture of events (Abildgaard, 2014).

1. Identify a situational time and place.
2. Who is involved?

3. Identify the problem or positive event.
4. Identify thoughts, emotions, and feelings involved.
5. Discuss plan A for resolving the issue, and in case this plan doesn't work, create a plan B.
6. Reflect on the situation with time for role-playing plan A and B.

Other visual supports such as pictures, schedules, or calendars with sequentially arranged pictures provide cues to remind students of a specific task to perform. Or, asking the student to draw a stick-figure to illustrate problem resolution also serves as a concrete, visual aid (Studer & Brown, 2010).

Conceptual Application Activity 6.1

Interview a school counselor and ask this person the following questions:

1. What is the counseling theory that best fits your philosophy in regard to people and the change process?
2. How does this counseling theory relate to your work with students with disabilities?
3. How have you adapted your counseling theories and techniques to work with students with specific disabilities?

Discuss the responses you received with those of your peers. What are some differences or similarities?

Conclusion

Students with disabilities do not always receive the services they deserve, and school counselors do not always receive the training to work with students with physical and cognitive disabilities. The American School Counselor Association (ASCA) position statement requires that school counselors "recognize their strengths and limitations in working with students with disabilities. Professional school counselors also are aware of current research and seek to implement best practices in working with students presenting any disability category" (ASCA, 2013, para. 3). School counselors report a lack of training surrounding students with disabilities, which creates reluctance in working with this group of students. Nevertheless, counseling theories such as person-centered counseling, individual psychology, behavioral therapy, reality therapy, SFBC, REBT, and narrative approaches have been successfully adapted for work with this group of individuals, particularly when integrated with (MI) as a "front-loaded" intervention. Although the process of counseling is similar regardless of the type of theoretical approach that is used, the basic steps of assessment, intervention, termination, and evaluation guide the process.

References

Abildgaard, C. (2014). Processing the "whole" with clients on the autism spectrum. *Counseling Today*, 56, 60–63.

ASCA (2013). *The Professional School Counselor and Students with Disabilities.* Retrieved from http://schoolcounselor.org/asca/media/asca/PositionStatements/PS_Disabilities.pdf.

Banks, T. (2011). Helping students manage emotions: REBT as a mental health educational curriculum. *Educational Psychology in Practice*, 27, 383–394.

Bettner, B. L. (2005). Using early recollections to help and understand a failing student. *Journal of Individual Psychology*, 61, 100–105.

Bergin, J. W. & Bergin, J. J. (2004). The forgotten student. *ASCA School Counselor.* Retrieved from www.ascaschoolcounselor.org/article_content.asp?article=712.

Bowen, M. L. & Glenn, E. E. (1998). Counseling interventions for students who have mild disabilities. *Professional School Counseling*, 2, 16–25.

Briesch, A. M., Briesch, J. M., & Chafouleas, S. M. (2015). Investigating the usability of classroom management strategies among elementary schoolteachers. *Journal of Positive Behavior Interventions*, 17, 5–14.

Children and Youth with Disabilities (2014). *National Center for Education Statistics.* Retrieved from http://nces.ed.gov/programs/coe/indicator_cgg.asp.

Coats, K. L. (1991). *The Impact of Reality Therapy in a School for Emotionally Disturbed Youth: A Preliminary Report.* Department of Education, ERIC Document Reproduction Service No. ED355691.

Corey, G. (2009). *Theory and Practice of Counseling and Psychotherapy*, 9th edn. Belmont, CA: Brooks/Cole.

DeRobertis, E. M. (2011). Deriving a third force approach to child development from the works of Alfred Adler. *Journal of Humanistic Psychology*, 51, 492–515.

Dougher, M. J. & Hackbert, L. (2000). Establishing operations, cognition, and emotion. *The Behavior Analyst*, 23, 11–24.

Dunn, A. M. (1971). *An Introduction to Adlerian Psychology for the School Counselor.* Paper presented at the Annual Convention of the Canadian Guidance and Counselling Association, Toronto, Ontario.

Elbaum, B. & Vaughn, S. (2003). For which students with learning disabilities are self-concept interventions effective? *Journal of Learning Disabilities*, 36, 101–108.

Furlonger, B. E. (1999). Narrative therapy and children with hearing impairments. *American Annals of the Deaf*, 144, 325–332.

Hackett, L., Theodosiou, L., Bond, C., Blackburn, C., & Lever, R. (2011). Understanding the mental health needs of pupils with severe learning disabilities in an inner city local authority. *British Journal of Learning Disabilities*, 39, 327–333.

Hajzler, D. J. & Bernard, M. E. (1991). A review of rational-emotive education outcome studies. *School Psychology Quarterly*, 6, 27–49.

Hansen B. D., Wills, H. P., Kamps, D. M., & Greenwood, C. R. (2014). The effects of function-based self-management interventions on student behavior. *Journal of Emotional and Behavioral Disorders*, 22, 149–159.

Harakas, P. (2013). Resistance, motivational interviewing, and executive coaching. *Consulting Psychology Journal: Practice and Research*, 65, 108–127.

Hunter, K. K., Chenier, J. S., & Gresham, F. M. (2014). Evaluation of check in/check out for students with internalizing behavior problems. *Journal of Emotional and Behavioral Disorders*, 22, 135–148.

Jones, R. A. (2013). Therapeutic relationships with individuals with learning disabilities: a qualitative study of the counseling psychologists' experience. *British Journal of Learning Disabilities*, 42, 193–203.

Keat, D. B. (1990). Change in child multimodal counseling. *Elementary School Guidance & Counseling*, 24, 248–262.

Lambie, G. W. & Milsom, A. (2010). A narrative approach to supporting students diagnosed with learning disabilities. *Journal of Counseling and Development*, 88, 196–203.

Laursen, E. K. (2002). Seven habits of reclaiming relationships. *Reclaiming Children & Youth*, 11, 10–14.

Leidenfrost, C. (2010). *Behavior Strategies for Autism*. Retrieved from www.livestrong.com/articl e/185569-behavior-strategies-for-autism.

Martella, R. C., Nelson, J. R., Marchand-Martella, N. E., & O'Reilly, M. (2012). *Comprehensive Behavior Management: Individualized, Classroom, and Schoolwide Approaches*, 2nd edn. Thousand Oaks, CA: Sage.

Miller, N. H. (2010). Motivational interviewing as a prelude to coaching in healthcare settings. *Journal of Cardiovascular Nursing*, 25, 247–251.

Miller, W. R. & Rose, G. S. (2009). Toward a theory of motivational interviewing. *American Psychologist*, 64, 527–537.

Milsom, A. (2006). Creating positive school experiences for students with disabilities. *Professional School Counseling*, 10, 66–72.

Mishler, J. A. & Cherry, S. (1999). *Correlating Glasser's Choice Theory to the Behavioral Requirements of IDEA 97*. Retrieved from ERIC database, ED429741.

Moyers, T. B., Miller, W. R., & Hendrickson, S. M. L. (2005). How does motivational interviewing work? Therapist interpersonal skill predicts client involvement within motivational interviewing sessions. *Journal of Counseling and Clinical Psychology*, 73, 590–598.

Neukrug, E. S. (2011). *Counseling Theory and Practice*. Belmont, CA: Brooks/Cole.

Omizo, M. M. & Cubberly, W. E. (1983). The effects of reality therapy classroom meetings on self-concept and locus of control among learning disabled children. *The Exceptional Child*, 30, 201–209.

Patton, P. L. (1995). Rational behavior skills: a teaching sequence for students with emotional disabilities. *School Counselor*, 43, 133–141.

Pelsma, D., Hawes, D., Costello, J., & Richard, M. (2004). Creating helper children as natural supports. *Journal of Professional Counseling: Practice, Theory, & Research*, 32, 16–27.

Purkey, W. W. (1988). *An Overview of Self-Concept Theory for Counselors: Highlights*. Retrieved from ERIC database, ED304630.

Roeden, J. M., Maaskant, M. A., Bannink, F. P., & Curfs, L. M. G. (2012). Solution-focused brief therapy with people with mild intellectual disabilities: a case series. *Journal of Policy and Practice in Intellectual Disabilities*, 8, 247–255.

Seligman, L. & Reichenberg, L. W. (2014). *Theories of Counseling and Psychotherapy: System, Strategies, and Skills*, 4th edn. Columbus, OH: Pearson.

Shnabel, N., Purdie-Vaughns, V., Cook, J. E., Garcia, J., & Cohen, G. L. (2013). Demystifying values-affirmation interventions: writing about social belonging is a key to buffering against identify threat. *Personality and Social Psychology Bulletin*, 39, 663–676.

Studer, J. R. & Brown, N. (2010). Addressing autism spectrum disorders. *ASCA School Counselor*, 48, 10–25.

Synapse (2008). *Help with Autism, Asperger's Syndrome & Related Sisorders*. Retrieved from www. autism-help.org/index.htm.

Thompson, C. L., Rudolph, L. B., & Henderson, D. A. (2004). *Counseling Children*, 6th edn. Belmont, CA: Brooks/Cole.

Toso, R. B. (2000). Control theory. *Principal Leadership: High School Edition*, 1, 40–43.

Turnbull, R., Turnbull, A., Shank, B., Smith, S. J., & Leal, D. (2002). *Exceptional Lives: Special Education in Today's Schools*, 3rd edn. Upper Saddle River, NJ: Merrill.

Wilde, J. (1996). The efficacy of short-term rational-emotive education with fourth-grade students. *Elementary School Guidance & Counseling*, 31, 131–139.

Williams, W. C. & Lair, G. S. (1991). Using a person-centered approach with children who have a disability. *Elementary School Guidance & Counseling*, 25, 194–203.

Wright, R. J. (2012). *Introduction to School Counseling*. Los Angeles, CA: Sage.

Wubbolding, E. R. (2000). *Reality Therapy for the 21st Century*. Muncie, IN: Accelerated Press.

7 Creative Counseling Strategies for Students with Disabilities

The following CACREP standards are addressed in this chapter:

ENTRY-LEVEL SPECIALTY AREAS: SCHOOL COUNSELING PRACTICE
f. techniques of personal/social counseling in school settings
i. approaches to increase promotion and graduation rates

Chapter Objectives

After you have completed this chapter, you should be able to:

- Identify creative strategies to more effectively assist students with disabilities.
- Practice strategies to gain self-awareness of various creative approaches.

Expressive arts are implemented in counseling to improve social interaction, promote communication among students who have limited verbal skills, enhance socio-emotional growth, develop self-awareness and insight, and improve language and cognition (King et al., 2013; Lenz et al., 2010). For example, counselors in the United Kingdom revealed that creative arts were the primary strategies they used with students with disabilities (Pattison, 2010), and when used in conjunction with a counseling theory that matched the needs and abilities of the counselee, a therapeutic relationship was developed. Various media such as literature, art, dance and movement, music, and play are discussed in this chapter as viable expressive arts in a counseling relationship with students with disabilities.

Literature in Counseling

The use of literature in counseling, often referred to as bibliocounseling, utilizes a variety of genres such as reading, writing, listening to stories or poetry, or recalling stories or poetry. Of all the creative arts, writing or storytelling does not require much special equipment or environment (King et al., 2013). Through this approach, the counselor is able to tell stories using simple sentences or provide reading materials that match the student's developmental level to facilitate the student's speech and understanding. Furthermore, when the counselor uses literature in which repetitive directions are highlighted, it is possible that students may obtain a more comprehensive understanding of the material (Pattison, 2010), with the additional benefit of developing attention skills.

Scriptotherapy is a type of bibliocounseling that promotes therapeutic writing through such means as journals (Gladding, 2011) or focused writing. When a child listens to or reads a story, he/she may identify with a particular character or the experiences of individuals within the story, or share the beliefs, behaviors, thoughts, or emotional involvement presented in the literature (Geldard et al., 2013).

Story creation is another literary counseling method in which the student envisions how personal experiences, ideas, hopes, wishes, and dreams are similar to those of the characters relayed in a story (Geldard et al., 2013). As the child creates and tells a story, the counselor has the option to either write or to record the story. If the student has difficulty developing a story, the counselor is able to model how to tell a story using prompts. For instance, "We are going to work together to tell a story that has a beginning, middle, and end. I will start the story and when I stop, I would like you to fill in the blank. 'Once upon a time, in a land far, far away, there was a little prince who wanted to play.' Can you tell me what he wanted to play?" Additional questions could be "Who was with the prince?" "What were they playing?" "How was the prince feeling?" Through this storytelling method, youth are metaphorically giving the counselor a description of his/her perspective, feelings, and thoughts.

The counselor may also tell a story that parallels a situation in the student's life with the intention that the counselee is able to relate to a character and the protagonist's motives or behaviors. At the conclusion of the story, the counselor and counselee explore what was learned from the story. The use of literature in counseling can also be combined with other creative expressions, as described in Student Activity 7.1.

Student Activity 7.1

In group or individual counseling, ask students to bring in a poem or song lyrics that they like. Read or play the piece and discuss the meaning of the literature and how they believe it relates to them.

Social stories are a literary approach for addressing the needs of students with disabilities. Counselors and other significant others have been successful in implementing this approach.

SOCIAL STORIES

Social stories teach appropriate behaviors such as following rules, acquiring organization skills, undertaking social skills, adapting to new routines, and decreasing problem behaviors (Hutchins & Prelock, 2012). Social stories are presented in a concrete, visual manner that is related to the student's learning style. And, they provide opportunities for students to practice targeted skills (Hsu et al., 2012). Yet, Hutchins and Prelock (2012) caution that desired behavioral changes using social stories are more likely to occur when the child has a minimum verbal age of three.

Social stories have been successful with students diagnosed with autistic spectrum disorder (ASD), attention deficit hyperactivity disorder (ADHD), and developmental

Table 7.1. Examples of Social Story Sentences (More, 2011)

Sentences that direct	Sentences that describe
Directive sentences: *Provide guidance by providing advice for behavior* **Example:** *I will raise my hand before I speak in class.*	**Descriptive sentences:** *Sentences that provide facts about the required action.* **Example:** *Listen when the morning announcements are given.*
Control sentences: *The student provides suggestions for responding to a particular situation.* **Example:** *Before I talk in class I will STOP and take a deep breath, and then raise my hand.*	**Perception sentences:** *Statements that explain feelings, thoughts, etc.* **Example:** *Sometimes people get annoyed when I blurt out answers.* **Cooperative sentences:** *Describe how to work together* **Example:** *When someone talks to me, I will listen.* **Affirmative sentences:** *Describe a shared value* **Example:** *Listening is important.*

delays in a pre-designed or individualized format (PBIS World, 2014). In a study by Quirmbach et al. (2009, as cited in Hutchins & Prelock, 2012), social stories were effective in teaching children diagnosed with ASD to initiate interpersonal communication, retain and demonstrate the skill, and apply the acquired abilities to other situations (More, 2011). Iskander and Rosales (2013) investigated the impact of social stories with two elementary-aged students diagnosed with ADHD. Individualized stories, which included pictures that depicted the desirable behaviors, were read to the students. Following the intervention the students were asked follow-up questions to determine their understanding of the story, and subsequent assessments revealed increases in the desired behaviors following the intervention.

Social stories contain sentences that *describe* as well as *direct*. The sentences that describe include descriptive, perspectives, illustrate cooperative behaviors, and are affirmations. Sentences that direct provide directives and control (More, 2011). According to More (2011), there is a 2:1 ratio for sentences that describe versus those that direct. Table 7.1 provides examples of descriptive and directive statements.

The following steps are used to create a personal story:

- Outline the steps that reinforce the behavior that is desired (e.g., greeting a classmate) in the present tense from the perspective of the student.
- Develop one or two sentences that describe each step (e.g., "smile at the friend" or "make eye contact").
- Create a directive statement that guides the required response (descriptive, perception, cooperation, affirmative).
- Create directive statements that provide advice or self-control.
- Use language that is developmentally appropriate.
- Choose durable paper that students can easily manipulate for story repetition.
- Place a picture next to each step. The picture could be one cut from a magazine, an actual photograph of the student performing the task, or a drawing.

Figure 7.1 Elementary-aged students listening and learning through stories.
Source: ©*iStockphoto.com, www.istockphoto.com/photo/story-time-35758756.*

- The story is shown to the student every day until the steps are understood.
- The student practices the steps in the story.
- Multiple copies of the story are made if used in a classroom of students.

Involving the students in the creation of the story with consideration to different culture and language invites ownership, but before the school counselor is able to collaboratively create a "fitting" story, the school counselor has to have knowledge of cultural concepts. Hsu et al. (2012) investigated the use of social stories using multiculturally based stories with culturally and linguistically diverse students diagnosed with learning disabilities. The results indicated that the social stories positively influenced the display of desired behaviors, and an appropriate understanding of the student's culture was an essential component to engage the students in the stories and to make them meaningful. The box below provides a list of websites that can be accessed for more information on social stories.

Websites for Social Stories

www.thegraycenter.org/social-stories
This website provides several links for writing a social story and creating story movies.
http://csefel.vanderbilt.edu/resources/strategies
This site provides practical strategies for creating social stories as well as tools for building relationships.

---

www.friendshipcircle.org/blog/2013/02/11/12-computer-programs-websites-and
-apps-for-making-social-stories
This website contains applications (apps) that can be downloaded for creating
social stories and pictures for use with the stories.

Conceptual Application Activity 7.1

Using the steps for creating a personal story mentioned above, create a social
story for a student with an identified disability. Share and repeat this story with the
student and make any changes that are necessary. Are there any apparent behavioral
changes? How did you assess these changes?

Art in Counseling

Counselees may be more comfortable expressing themselves through art such as drawings,
paintings, or collages. Drawings create an opportunity for the child to communicate feelings, thoughts, ideas, and perceptions that serve as a foundation for the student and counselor to engage in a form of discussion through images without using words (Ray et al.,
2004). Through drawings, students are able to get in touch with feelings that have been
buried and unacknowledged (Webb, 1991), and this often has a calming effect, particularly
when a student feels pressured to talk about uncomfortable emotions or experiences. Art in
counseling has been used with students who are learning disabled or for those with speech
impairments (Pattison, 2010) to facilitate developmental social skills, self-awareness, anxiety reduction, and self-esteem enhancement. Art media is therapeutic, especially among
students who have limited relationships with others, those diagnosed with mental health
disorders, ADHD, and conduct disorders (Epp, 2008, as cited in Lenz et al., 2010).

Case Study 7.1

*Isaac is a ten-year-old male who has been diagnosed with conduct disorder. His
father is incarcerated and his mother has abandoned him on several occasions, which
has resulted in multiple moves and caregivers. He is verbally and physically aggressive and he doesn't take his medication on a regular basis. He has made threats to kill
himself and has tried to choke himself several times. Isaac does not complete work,
and his teacher has tried ignoring him to avoid engaging him in altercations. He is
receiving special education services for reading. Working with Isaac in counseling
was difficult since he tended to see his school counselor to avoid going to class. Art
therapy provided an opportunity to discover his deeper-rooted feelings and emotions,
and eventually he was placed in an alternative, smaller, more structured class.*

Elementary school counselor

There are no limits as to how art can be used in counseling, which ranges from the use of
play-dough to soap, construction paper, paint, crayons, or pictures from magazines. However,
an understanding of developmental performance is required to appropriately select materials
according to the child's skill level. Various types of art media are shown in Table 7.2.

Table 7.2 Suggested Art Materials

Crayons	Paint	Markers	Clay
Construction paper of different colors	Glue	Stickers	Magazines
Scissors	Finger paints	Modeling clay	Scotch tape
Pipe cleaners	Templates of various shapes	Pencils	Play-dough

Figure 7.2 Art facilitates communication.
Source: ©iStockphoto.com, www.istockphoto.com/photo/drawing-36915134.

Various adaptations of art in counseling include asking students to bring in their own artwork, or the counselor could bring in several pieces of art such as those from photograph books, magazines, or pictures from art museums. Student Activity 7.2 is an example of an art strategy in counseling.

Student Activity 7.2

My Personal Logo

Logos are symbols or emblems used to represent businesses, stores, products, etc. Students can be asked to create a logo that represents who they are. To aid in this process, have students scribble on paper until a symbol emerges that best represents who they are (Gladding, 2005). Once the student is satisfied with his/her final product, he/she can take the lead in explaining the significance of his/her representation.

Figure 7.3 Movement provides an opportunity for youth to release tension, express oneself, and contributes to socialization.
Source: ©iStockphoto.com, www.istockphoto.com/photo/elementary-gym-class-27433773.

Dance and Movement

Dance and movement can create a greater understanding of feelings, thoughts, and behaviors. Furthermore, dance and movement improves psychological and physical well-being as movement has the potential to uncover psychological blocks and memories that have been repressed (Gladding, 1992). Dance and movement can take numerous forms such as traditional dancing moves, yoga, or drama. Yet, regardless of the physical activity, the purpose of using this methodology is to release physical tension, direct self-expression positively, and assist in socialization. For example, when school counselors in the United Kingdom used movement with secondary-aged students with limited verbal ability in inclusive classroom settings, communication was enhanced (Pattison, 2010).

The flexibility of movement and drama makes expressive approaches ideal for working with children and adolescents diagnosed with ASD. Drama to teach social skills to children diagnosed with Asperger's Syndrome was first used in the 1940s by Viktorine Zak, a pioneer in the treatment of children with this disability. In addition, the use of role play and drama has been successful in teaching individuals with ASD to learn mutual communication, social cues, and socialization skills (Attwood, 2008, as cited in Tricomi & Gallo-Lopez, 2012). Drama provides an opportunity to discover and voice feelings, and fosters genuine, spontaneous interaction, and creative thought (Tricomi & Gallo-Lopez, 2012).

School-aged youth have a natural energy that makes movement an ideal means for self-expression. The school counselor can ask students to express emotions such as frustration, sadness, happiness, enthusiasm, and so on. From here, the counselor and student may engage in a discussion of how physical actions are linked to emotions, thinking, and awareness. Moreover, awareness of related behaviors such as deep breathing or muscle relaxation teaches skills to cope with a tense, stressful situation. Student Activity 7.3 is an example of the use of movement as a therapeutic tool.

Student Activity 7.3

Because I Move

In a group setting, basic emotions such as happy, mad, sad, embarrassed are written, or pictures of people displaying these emotions are displayed on index cards. Students randomly draw cards and express the effect on the card through facial expressions and movement. The group members are to guess the emotion that is enacted.

Music in Counseling

Neuroscience research reveals that neural foundations are established through the interrelated connections of memories, thoughts, and experiences that change the brain structure (Leanza, 2012). For instance, because music is an activity that communicates with different parts of the brain, exposure to music at a young age establishes efficient networks that enable the different parts of the brain to work together (Pollard, 2010). In addition, music is a flexible means for increasing attention and learning, and promoting positive behaviors, particularly for youth with autism or speech difficulties. Music interventions can include quietly listening to music, singing with others, or playing an instrument (Baker, 2010). Students with ASD are able to incorporate non-music objectives with music goals. For instance, shared attention or eye gaze on an instrument or sound are means for shifting attention (Walworth, 2012). Interestingly, children diagnosed with ASD are able to discriminate affect expressed in music (Heaton et al., 1999, as cited in Walworth, 2012), and have demonstrated outstanding auditory discrimination skills in comparison with their general education peers (O'Riordan & Passetti 2006, as cited in Walworth, 2012).

Since autistic youth often lack social interaction skills, have difficulty socially acknowledging others, and struggle with compliance, research was conducted to determine whether these skills could be improved through the use of music (Pollard, 2010). Students diagnosed with autism, who ranged in age between the ages of three and ten, were randomly placed in either an experimental or a control group. Experimental group participants were able to interact with one another while they played musical instruments and marched around the room for 15 minutes every day for weeks. The control group participants listened to music only, without the active involvement of playing and interacting. The results of this study indicated that interaction through musical activities improved social interactions, social acknowledgment, and compliance skills (Pollard, 2010).

In another study, adolescent students diagnosed with learning disabilities participated in a study in which they were taught to listen to music through the use of the iPod

Touch, which also served as a reinforcer for following the directions to access the music (Kagohara et al., 2011). Participants observed a video model in which a pair of hands was displayed to locate and start a song. The video modeling provided an easily implemented intervention with minimal assistance from others, and seemed to promote connectedness with peers who had common music interests. Furthermore, the participants often sang or hummed the songs, and danced while the music was playing. The use of the iPod Touch provided evidence that those with developmental disabilities were able to become more independent, and learning was reinforced when music followed correct application of the directions.

Play in Counseling

Play is a natural activity that facilitates self-expression in a safe, non-judgmental environment. Through play, the child is able to engage in imaginative activities, take on different roles, or perform activities that he/she was previously unable or afraid to do (Gladding, 1992). Moreover, games provide an opportunity for school-aged youth to develop a sense of self, explore personalities, improve social skills, and increase emotional growth (Rosselet & Stauffer, 2013). Play was originally used with pre-pubescent children with limited cognitive ability, but more recently adaptations of play such as in the form of games are used with non-disabled adolescents (Gladding, 1992) as well as students with disabilities.

Play is a developmental process that progresses from the sensorimotor stage to a more abstract representation in which the child is able to take another's perspective, learn reciprocity, and act creatively. Children with ASD have difficulty in these areas as evidenced through their repetitive, isolated, unimaginative play (Rubin, 2012). As a result, many have questioned whether or not children with this diagnosis are able to learn to play. To test whether or not behavioral interventions with children with ASD are effective, these students were taught the basic elements of play, were reinforced when the behaviors were displayed, and through the reinforcement of steps, these students were able to link the steps together into a structure (Stahmer et al., 2003, as cited in Gallo-Lopez & Rubin, 2012). In addition, children with ASD learned to play through the use of canine-assisted play therapy in which they were able to learn how to develop a healthy relationship with a living animal, acquire empathic understanding, improve in self-regulation, and engage in problem resolution (Van Fleet & Coltea, 2012).

Puppets are used in play as a safe means for the student to: (a) identify with a puppet; (b) project uncomfortable feelings; and (c) gain a sense of control over traumatized situations (Webb, 1991; Vernon, 1999). While the student symbolically talks about the puppet's feelings and thoughts that often serve as a metaphor for the counselee's experiences, the counselor observes and assesses the student for any anxiety that could create any re-traumatization.

Finally, games are a type of play that require numerous behaviors such as taking turns, cooperation, and rule-following (Webb, 1991). Games are a good choice in counseling, as they can be used with students who are resistant, uncommunicative, anxious, or inhibited. As in most games, winning and losing are an integral part of the game, and the counselor is given an opportunity to observe reactions to game components such as cheating, responses to winning or losing, and cooperation with other game players.

However, there are some games such as Uno or the Ungame that do not have a designated winner but do provide a safe environment for building rapport and talking without feeling pressure to engage in eye contact, or to answer questions.

Conceptual Application Activity 7.2

Interview a school counselor to learn about some of the expressive arts that are used in counseling with students with disabilities. What are some of the challenges in using expressive arts with this population? What are some of the techniques that have had the most impact? Share your responses with those of your peers.

Conclusion

Counseling theories guide the counseling process based on the needs of each individual student, but these traditional "talk therapy" approaches do not always meet the needs of students who have difficulty with verbal means of expression, or others who have difficulty expressing themselves. In these instances, a counseling theory that is used in conjunction with expressive arts facilitates the helping process. Literature, art, dance and movement, music, and play have been effectively used as interventions for students with disabilities.

References

Baker, L. M. (2010). Music therapy: diversity, challenge and impact. *International Journal of Disability, Development and Education*, 57, 335–340.

Gallo-Lopez, L. & Rubin, L. E. (2012). *Play-Based Interventions for Children and Adolescents with Autism Spectrum Disorders*. New York: Routledge.

Geldard, K., Geldard, D., & Yin Foo, R. (2013). *Couselling Children: A Practical Introduction*, 4th edn. Thousand Oaks, CA: Sage.

Gladding, S. T. (1992). *Counseling as an Art: The Creative Arts in Counseling*. Alexandria, VA: American Counseling Association.

Gladding, S. T. (2005). *Counseling as an Art: The Creative Arts in Counseling*, 3rd edn. Alexandria, VA: American Counseling Association.

Gladding, S. T. (2011). *Counseling as an Art: The Creative Arts in Counseling*, 4th edn. Alexandria, VA: American Counseling Association.

Hsu, N., Hammond, H., & Ingalls, L. (2012). The effectiveness of culturally-based social stories to increase appropriate behaviors of children with developmental delays. *International Journal of Special Education*, 27, 104–116.

Hutchins, T. L. & Prelock, P. A. (2012). Parents' perceptions of their children's social behavior: the social validity of social stories and comic strip conversations. *Journal of Positive Behavior Interventions*, 15, 156–168.

Iskander, J. M. & Rosales, R. (2013). An evaluation of the components of a social stories™ intervention package. *Research in Autism Spectrum Disorders*, 7, 1–8.

King, R., Neilsen, P., & White, E. (2013). Creative writing in recovery from mental illness. *International Journal of Mental Health Nursing*, 22, 444–452.

Kagohara, D. M., Sigafoos, J., Achmadi, D., van der Meer, L., Reilly, M. F., & Lancioni, G. E. (2011). Teaching students with developmental disabilities to operate an iPodTouch® to listen to music. *Research in Developmental Disabilities*, 32, 2987–2992.

Leanza, N. (2012). Simple therapeutic interventions for rewiring the maladaptive brain. *Counseling Today*, October.

Lenz, A S., Holman, R. L., & Dominquez, D. L. (2010). Encouraging connections: integrating expressive art drama into therapeutic social skills training with adolescents. *Journal of Creativity in Mental Health*, 5, 142–157.

More, C. M. (2011). Social stories™ and young children: strategies for teachers. *Intervention in School and Clinic*, 47, 167–174.

Pattison, S. (2010). Reaching out: a proactive process to include young people with learning disabilities in counseling in secondary schools in the UK. *British Journal of Guidance & Counselling*, 38, 301–311.

PBIS World (2014). *Social Stories*. Retrieved from www.pbisworld.com/tier-2/social-stories.

Pollard, D. J. (2010). *The Use of Music to Improve Social Skills Development in Children Diagnosed with Autism*. Doctoral dissertation, available from ProQuest Dissertations and Theses database, UMI NO. 3536911.

Ray, D. C., Perkins, S. R., & Oden, K. (2004). Rosebush fantasy technique with elementary school students. *Professional School Counseling*, 7, 277–282.

Rosselet, J. G. & Stauffer, S. D. (2013). Using group role-playing games with gifted children and adolescents: a psychosocial intervention model. *International Journal of Play Therapy*, 22, 173–192.

Rubin, L. C. (2012). Playing on the autism spectrum. In L. Gallo-Lopez & L. C. Rubin (eds.), *Play-Based Interventions for Children and Adolescents with Autism Spectrum Disorders* (pp. 19–38). New York: Routledge.

Tricomi, L. P. & Gallo-Lopez, L. (2012). The ACT project: enhancing social competence through drama therapy and performance. In L. Gallo-Lopez & L. C. Rubin (eds.), *Play-Based Interventions for Children and Adolescents with Autism Spectrum Disorders* (pp. 271–291). New York: Routledge.

Van Fleet, R. & Coltea, C. (2012). Helping children with ASD through canine-assisted play therapy. In L. Gallo-Lopez & L. C. Rubin (eds.), *Play-Based Interventions for Children and Adolescents with Autism Spectrum Disorders* (pp. 39–72). New York: Routledge.

Vernon, A. (1999). *Counseling Children and Adolescents*, 2nd edn. Denver: Love Publishing.

Walworth, D. (2012). Music therapy interventions for social, communication, and emotional development for children and adolescents with autism spectrum disorders. In L. Gallo-Lopez & L. C. Rubin (eds.), *Play-Based Interventions for Children and Adolescents with Autism Spectrum Disorders* (pp. 317–332). New York: Routledge.

Webb, N. B. (1991). Assessment of the child in crisis. In N. B. Webb (ed.), *Play Therapy with Children in Crisis* (pp. 3–42). New York: Guilford Press.

8 Group Counseling Options for Students with Disabilities

The following CACREP standards are addressed in this chapter:

GROUP COUNSELING AND GROUP WORK
b. dynamics associated with group process and development
e. approaches to group formation, including recruiting, screening, and selecting members
f. types of groups and other considerations that affect conducting groups in varied settings
g. ethical and culturally relevant strategies for designing and facilitating groups

Chapter Objectives

After you have completed this chapter, you should be able to:

- Identify group factors for students with disabilities.
- Recognize various groups for students with disabilities.
- Develop a group for a specific category under IDEA.

Groups are an effective, time-efficient method for addressing academic achievement, vocational issues, and/or social/emotional concerns (Serres & Nelson, 2011). School counselors are often the only school professionals who have special training and expertise in leading groups, and serve as leaders in numerous types of groups. As stated in the American School Counselor Association (ASCA) position statement, "The professional school counselor's training in group facilitation is unique to the school setting ... School counselors prioritize group offerings based on analysis of school data. Group counseling should be offered to all students in a PK-12 setting" (ASCA, 2014, para. 3). For instance, school counselors involve elementary-aged students with disabilities in groups to address such issues as self-esteem, behavior problems, and social skills (Serres & Nelson, 2011). Other group formats promote the achievement of students with disabilities such as: (a) groups with a focus on transition planning for middle and high school aged youth; (b) groups for school-aged youth who have siblings with learning disabilities designed to share some of their concerns; (c) psychoeducational groups that assist in educating others in the school regarding the implications of disabilities; (d) teachers in groups to address such topics as classroom management strategies, consultation, or problem-solving; and (e) parent groups surrounding such issues as parenting, child development, or methods for assisting their child with disabilities with homework. Case Study 8.1 is an example of the positive impact of groups.

Case study 8.1

Students who spend the majority of their day within the special education classroom have a very different social experience in school compared with those who are in a general education program. Unless the students with disabilities are involved in extracurricular activities after or away from school, they might only spend time with the regular education students during special related classes such as art or music, and/or lunch. Additionally, because multiple grade levels share the same space, and the classroom size is small, the opportunity to connect with peers in the special education classroom is also limited. Ironically, social skill goals are written into the IEPs of many students.

One year, the school's speech pathologist and I decided to create our own opportunity for group inclusion. We formed a "lunch bunch" that was composed of both regular education and students in special education classrooms. Anna and Sally were the only two fourth-grade girls in the special education classroom that year, and both were in need of social growth. Anna was diagnosed as a selective mute and only spoke to her family members in her home. Sally had significant physical disabilities and some cognitive delays stemming from seizures she experienced as a baby. Neither of these girls formed meaningful friendships with their general education peers, and they typically avoided social opportunities like field trips and field days that were planned for all of the fourth-graders.

Over the next two years, the five members of the lunch bunch met with the speech teacher and me every Thursday. We played games, drew pictures, read books, and had meaningful conversations. Friendship skills, feelings, manners, and bullying were a few of the topics we covered, and by the end of their fifth-grade year, Anna was participating in group activities even when speaking was required. She was also reading out loud in her classroom. Sally gained the confidence to go on an overnight field trip with the fifth grade, which turned out to be an incredible social experience for her.

The three girls from the general education classroom who participated in the group were positively affected by this experience. When the group first started, they were often frustrated with Anna's silence, and they would answer questions for Sally when she struggled to come up with appropriate responses. As time progressed, their patience and understanding grew, they took Anna and Sally under their wings during lunch and special areas, and they formed significant bonds with both of them. This small group is a testament to the role school counselors play in enhancing the school experience for all students.

Elementary school counselor

Students with disabilities often have emotional and interpersonal difficulties that influence how others see them, and how they perceive themselves (Stephens et al., 2010). Group counseling is a direct service intervention that can address multiple issues, provide members with an opportunity to learn from each other, offer a sense of universality by understanding that others experience similar issues and feelings (Stephens et al., 2010), and students can acquire methods for coping with their disability through training, practice, and rehearsal. Yet, not all individuals with disabilities may be easily integrated into group intervention activities. For instance, students who have difficulty differentiating social cues may not be good candidates for group work. Or, students diagnosed with attention deficit hyperactivity disorder (ADHD) or autism spectrum disorder (ASD) may have unique interpersonal difficulties. Those diagnosed with ADHD could have difficulties raising their hand before speaking, taking turns, or even recognizing social cues. Students with ASD may have trouble with attending skills, understanding non-verbal communication, initiating conversations, and taking different perspectives (Shepard et al., 2013). However, when students are taught skills related to social and emotional development, significant improvement has been shown in social skills and behaviors (Durlak, 2011, as cited in Shepard et al., 2013). Groups provide an abundant opportunity for teaching and learning these skills. For example, because of the association between mental health difficulties with higher functioning ASD students, teaching social skills to these individuals in a group format while attending to their emotional reactions can facilitate greater interpersonal connectedness (Shepard et al., 2013). Yet, in forming groups, screening potential members for an identified group is particularly relevant as some students with disabilities such as those with high-functioning autism do not always appear to have interpersonal difficulties.

Group process includes all the factors that occur in a group from its inception to its termination (Corey et al., 2010). Numerous types of groups are found in schools—from task groups to psychoeducational groups to counseling groups—which provide a different function and target specific activities. Psychotherapeutic groups are another type of group, but because these groups focus on individuals with acute or chronic mental or emotional disorders, these groups are not normally found in a school setting. A discussion of the various types of groups and how students with disabilities benefit from these groups is given below.

Task Groups

Task groups focus on specific, project-oriented objectives (Corey, 2012) that concentrate on an immediate issue in which there is a clear goal. Members are selected due to their specific skills with the intention of producing a final service, product, or decision. This final outcome is evaluated to determine its effectiveness (Conyne, 2014). Examples of task groups that support students with disabilities in the school, or are composed of all students, including those with disabilities, are:

- IEP meetings;
- student council meetings;
- PTA;

- class officers' meetings;
- RTI meetings;
- service group projects.

The size of the task group is dependent on the issue that is to be resolved. In larger groups, members often express dissatisfaction due to such dynamics as: (a) monopolizing behavior by some members; and a (b) reluctance of members to voice opinions. Nonetheless, too small a group can constrain the production of new ideas and does not allow for the diversity of opinions.

Psychoeducational Groups

The focus of these groups is teaching problem-solving skills, discussing common concerns, and/or providing support (Corey, 2012). At times, however, the information that is shared in the group may trigger personal concerns of individual members, and in these cases individual counseling may be required. For instance, at one point, one of the authors of this book was visiting sophomore-level health classes to provide information about warning signs of suicide. During this psychoeducational session, one of the students became visibly upset and announced that she had made a suicide attempt a few weeks earlier. As a result of this disclosure, the student received extensive individual counseling.

Case Study 8.2

Students with ADD often have issues with disorganization. In group, I work with these students to teach skills to help them become more systematic with their school work. For example, locker clean-out is one method in which I help students who struggle with losing assignments. We take a box to the locker, remove all the contents and sort the papers by subject. I keep school supplies in my office so that I can easily assist the student with creating folders and notebooks for keeping their work organized using color-coordinated notebooks so they can get to class with the materials that are color-matched to that class. We also discuss mnemonic devices that will help them remember to turn in assignments.

Middle school counselor

The school counselor serves as a teacher, facilitator, or trainer to address developmental and/or prevention issues (Conyne, 2014) either through small groups or classrooms of students. In a school setting, some of the more popular psychoeducational groups that are developed for all students, including those with disabilities, include:

- managing stress;
- learning study skills;
- learning about transitions to college or career;
- developing assertiveness skills;
- teaching about bullying behaviors.

Psychoeducational groups can range in size from large assemblies, to classrooms of 30–40 students, or smaller groups that range in size depending on the developmental needs of the participants.

Counseling Groups

Participants of counseling groups address interpersonal processes to resolve academic, career, or social/emotional concerns. These growth-oriented groups are considered as remedial as well as preventive, and designed for individuals experiencing a situational crisis and/or difficulties in living (Conyne, 2014). Group members recognize their existing, helpful coping skills, and learn additional skills to manage future dilemmas (Corey, 2012). Counseling groups are generally small and range in size from 3–5 for elementary-aged youth, 6–10 for middle school aged youth, and 10–12 for high school students. Examples of counseling groups for all students, including those with disabilities, include:

* anger management;
* social skills;
* relationship issues;
* parental divorce;
* self-esteem issues;
* loneliness.

Conceptual Application Activity 8.1

Interview a school counselor and discuss the types of groups in which this individual is involved. How does this school counselor determine the types of groups to implement and lead in the schools? Discuss your responses with those of your peers.

Considerations for Groups in Schools

Planning groups for students with disabilities follow the same guidelines as groups that are planned for non-disabled peers. Data analysis from the school report card, needs assessments, or identified student competencies provide a foundation for determining the purpose and type of group. For instance, suppose that disaggregated data revealed that students with disabilities were victims of bullying. The counselor is then able to select standards from the *ASCA Mindsets and Behaviors for Student Success* to address bullying in the group format considered most appropriate. For example, does the counselor want to address bullying and social behaviors as a part of the school curriculum to educate all students as to what behaviors constitute bullying? If so, a psychoeducational group format would be created. Or, is the formation of a counseling group to teach targets of bullying appropriate responses to bullies more suitable? Or perhaps the more critical issue is addressing school policies and procedures that impact aggressive behaviors. In this case, a task group would be applicable.

Considerations in forming a group include whether to develop a *homogeneous* group (e.g., participants all have the same disability, or are all in the same grade), or a *heterogeneous* group (e.g., students with varying disabilities, or students of all abilities). An additional consideration is whether the group should be an *open group* to students who can enter and leave the group at any point, or a *closed group* in which no new member is able to enter the group. When the group members include non-disabled students, members with disabilities are able to learn new methods of thinking and behaving, and students without disabilities are able to gain a greater understanding of disabilities and how they affect their peers. The group format would necessitate familiarity with the various disabilities and the limitations that a particular disability places on an individual group member or the other group members. Additional concerns to consider when forming a group include: the child's developmental stage, psychosocial needs, cognitive functioning, insight, and maturity.

Schools often have limited space, and at times it is difficult to identify an available private room, especially one that can accommodate assistive devices such as a wheelchair or a service dog that may be needed by any group member (Snyder, 2000, as cited in McEachern & Kenny, 2007). Moreover, therapy balls are sometimes used to enhance sensory stimulation, gross motor skills, and movement. If therapy balls are chosen for group work, space will be needed, as will monetary resources to purchase these balls. Additional attention is to be given to group promotion and member selection, informed consent, scheduling issues, and evaluation.

Group Promotion and Member Selection

Once the group goals and purpose are established, support and approval from the school administrator is critical for group success. Teachers are often reluctant to dismiss students from class, but when an administrator understands the purpose and the group, how the group promotes student growth, and how the group objectives integrate with the Common Core State Standards, teachers may be more willing to share their classroom time.

Teachers, student self-referrals, parents/guardians, the public address system, flyers placed around the building, or websites are all viable methods for promoting the group and recruiting group members. Naming the group that doesn't label students can be complicated, as not only do you want to provide a clear essence of the purpose of the group, but at the same time the group name should not be one that is regarded as a negative descriptor. Many well-meaning school counselors who have a specific purpose for a group run the risk of labeling prospective students that could create embarrassment for these students (Ritchie & Huss, 2000). For instance, instead of calling a group for students with anger issues the "Anger Management Group," this group could be retitled as the "Resources for Life Group." Asking the students to come up with a name for the group could offset this problem and may serve as an initial activity to facilitate relationships with the other group members.

Group promotion includes consideration to privacy and perhaps disclosure of information. In asking teachers to provide names of potential group members, there is a risk of teachers identifying students based on the purpose of the group. An alternative method could be to provide teachers with a checklist of behaviors that are to be addressed in the group, and to identify students based on the names that are provided on this list (Ritchie & Huss, 2000).

Figure 8.1 Group counseling is a direct service intervention that can address multiple issues in a time-effective manner.
Source: Computers. ©iStockphoto.com, www.istockphoto.com/photo/computers-15653105.

Screening of Members

The ASCA's *Ethical Standards for School Counselors* states, "professional school counselors screen prospective group members and maintain an awareness of participants' needs, appropriate fit and personal goals in relation to the group's intention and focus" (ASCA, 2010, A6 Group Work a). Screening prospective members determines suitability for the group based on students' needs, and those who have the ability to provide support and encouragement to other members. Additional factors include: (a) the nature of the student's disability; (b) whether the disability poses any limitations on the student's ability to participate; (c) the student's aptitude to adjust to the disability; (d) the student's developmental level; (e) the prospective student's intellectual and verbal skills; and (f) the student's interpersonal skills (McEachern & Kenny, 2007).

Screening can be in the form of a pre-group meeting or through individual interviews. Regardless of the approach that is chosen, best practices suggest that this is an opportunity for the leader to explain the purpose of the group, objectives, leader qualifications, number of times the group will be meeting, length of each group meeting, expectations, and how the group will be evaluated. Pre-group meetings provide an opportunity for the counselor to observe interactions, communication, behaviors that could be counterproductive to group effectiveness, already existing relationships, or possible conflicts between members (Ritchie & Huss, 2000). For instance, students who display disturbing or violent behaviors would not be good candidates for group work, and through

---

Consent for Participation in Group

At times, middle school students have many difficulties that influence their school work, goals, or personal/interpersonal issues. I will be conducting a group at Superior Middle School for students to learn coping skills. The objectives of this group are to:

1. Demonstrate the differences between passive, aggressive, and assertiveness skills.
2. Exhibit appropriate responses to bullying.
3. Identify appropriate methods of solving problems.
4. Recognize appropriate responses to anger.

School Counselor Qualifications

I have a Bachelor's degree in psychology and a Master's degree in school counseling from Constructive University, and I have received training and supervision as a group leader in the school.

The group will meet for 45 minutes for six weeks every Wednesday during lunch in the school counselor's conference office. Confidentiality is an essential part of the counselor's relationship with students and I will remind the students that they will need to respect the rights of all group members.

If you would like more information regarding the group, feel free to contact me at _____ (phone number) or _____ (email)

Student name: _____

I understand the purpose of the group and I give permission for my child to attend the group sessions.

_____ Date _____

Figure 8.2 Example of informed consent.

the screening process the school counselor would have a better idea as to how individuals are able to relate with others. If an individual is not considered to be a productive group member, individual counseling is an alternative consideration until the student is exhibiting behaviors that are acceptable in a group setting (Stephens et al., 2010).

Although group screening sessions are more time-effective than individual interviews, meeting face-to-face provides an opportunity to answer questions that a student may be reluctant to ask in a group setting. In either screening process, informed consent from the student's parent/guardian and student assent must be obtained before an individual can participate in the group.

Informed Consent

The prospective student should be given enough information regarding the group logistics, purpose, goals, and expectations to give informed consent regarding his/her participation in the group. Because school-aged youth are minors, legal and ethical issues arise particularly in regard to confidentiality. Minor students have a right to privacy and confidentiality; however, in the case of students under the age of 18, legally the rights belong to their parents (Wheeler & Bertram, 2012). The ASCA's *Ethical Standards for School Counselors* states, "professional school counselors recognize that best practice is to notify the parents/

Individual goals that are established prior to group that mirror the purpose of the group provide an opportunity for group members to work toward a target that they would like to accomplish as a result of participating in the group. The following questions assist in forming a goal.

S = specific   What is the concern that you would like to address?

M = measurable   Can this concern be evaluated?

A = attainable   Is this goal something that you can accomplish?

R = results   How will I know that I have attained this goal?

T = timing   When do I hope this goal will be accomplished?

Figure 8.3 Goal-setting.

guardians of children participating in small groups" (ASCA, 2010, A6 Group Work b). An example of an informed consent is found in Figure 8.2.

Goal-Setting

Once members are chosen and parental/guardian consent is given, group and individual goals that can be accomplished during the group are discussed. Selecting individual goals is often a process that is difficult for students, particularly for those with limited cognitive ability. To facilitate this process, the following questions could be asked, "Suppose I followed you around with my camera for the next few days, and everything was going just as you want it to be. What would I see you doing? What would you be feeling? What would you be thinking? Who would you be with?" Based on the answer, a goal could be identified for making this vision occur. Individual goals are narrow and focused on present issues and concerns as indicated by the SMART acronym shown in Figure 8.3.

Scheduling Issues

With teachers being held accountable for students' progress in accomplishing academic standards, they are often reluctant to release students from class. Therefore, finding an appropriate time for group meetings can be challenging. Obtaining the endorsement and permission from the school administrator is a first step to gaining teacher support. A well-developed group plan (with clear rationale and goals) and standards facilitates an understanding of how the school counseling program is an integral component of the school mission.

Rather than scheduling the group to meet at the same time and day every week, it may be necessary to engage in creative alternatives such a implementing a rotating schedule in which the group meets on different days and times, during lunch, or before or after school. Yet, each of these alternatives creates other problems. For instance, younger students and some students with disabilities could have difficulties when a regular routine is interrupted. Lunchtime may be a viable option, but students are often reluctant to miss socializing with their friends. In addition, lunchtimes tend to be short—around 25–30 minutes—and although this shortened time may be acceptable to address the developmental needs of younger students, it may not be long enough for high school students. Group time could be scheduled for students who are in special classes, but may restrict potential students in general education classrooms. Students could be pulled out of their elective classes, but since these are classes that students tend to enjoy the most, this may not be a good option. Regardless of the time that is chosen to conduct the group, data collection to reveal the effectiveness of the group is critical so that administrators and teachers are able to understand how the group facilitates academic success and/or reduces incidents of behavioral disruptions.

Communicating to teachers when the group will occur and indicating that any work that the student misses while participating in group will be completed will signify that students are not to use the group to get out of classwork. Many students feel self-conscious or singled-out when they are summoned out of the classroom environment, and leaving class could create embarrassment for students with disabilities, who often already feel different from their peers. Including non-disabled students who will also leave the class to attend group could make all group members feel more comfortable.

Groups proceed through common, predictable stages that are often revisited as the group progresses. After the pre-group member screening, the initial stage is characterized by an orientation to group work and building group trust. The second stage is described as a transition in which the members struggle with anxiety and defensive behaviors. The third stage, referred to as the working stage, is marked by cohesion and productivity, and the final group stage is characterized by sadness and anxiety over separation (Corey, 2012).

Stage 1

During the initial group stages group members express hesitancy and resistance, with trust as a dominant characteristic during the initial group stage. Finding commonalities, getting acquainted, and developing norms to govern behaviors are tasks during this phase. The group leader is very active and is continually emphasizing the importance of confidentiality, and reassuring group members that feelings of anxiety are common. Moreover, the leader provides an opportunity for the group members to develop rules that will give structure to the sessions. Member-created rules should be minimal, establish the groundwork for expectations, and generate a commitment to follow the procedures. Typical group rules include:

1. Things talked about in the group, stay in the group.
2. Do not interrupt when someone else is talking.
3. Encourage and support group members.
4. Be on time for group.

Student Activity 8.1 is an example of an icebreaker designed to get group members to become acquainted with each other.

Student Activity 8.1

Once...

Age: Grades 3 and up.
Objective: To learn about self and others.

Evaluation: Each member will share one thing he/she learned about another member.

Directions: On small cards write down incomplete sentences that start with the word "Once." Cards will be face down and group members will take turns drawing a card and completing the statement. For students who are unable to read, the group facilitator can read it for them. Examples are below.

Once I ate a(n)...

Once I was upset because...

Once my mom...

Once I was sad because...

Once on vacation I...

Once my teacher...

Once I saw a(n)...

Stage 2

Anxiety and resistance are still evident at this stage, and although the group members are getting to know one another better, conversations tend to focus on superficial issues as participants are still determining whether or not the group is a trustful place to express oneself. Individuals fear sounding stupid, being rejected, or not fitting in with the other members. Other typical behaviors include defensiveness, hostility, and indirect styles of interaction. The leader's role is to reiterate the importance of confidentiality, remind members about the group rules, and respectfully challenge members through Socratic questions such as:

- How do your feelings relate to this topic?
- What is an example of your experiences that are similar to what _____ said?
- Is there another way to look at this issue?
- What do you think is the reason I asked this question?

Student Activity 8.2. is an example of an activity that is appropriate for this stage; however, it is possible that some students with fine motor skill or eye-hand coordination difficulties may have difficulty with this activity. To alleviate this concern, the counselor could adapt this exercise by pairing students to work together.

Student Activity 8.2

Snowflakes and Communication

Objectives: To improve communication and listening skills.

Materials: One 8.5 × 11" paper per person.

Age: Ten and older.

Evaluation: Identify one way you could listen better.

Directions: Each group member is given a piece of paper. Explain that you want them to follow the directions you will be giving and that they are to listen without asking questions. Each person will work individually. Give the following directions quickly without clarifying what you mean:

1. Fold the paper in half and tear off a top corner.
2. Fold it in half again and tear off the top corner.
3. Fold it in half again and tear off the left corner.
4. Rotate the paper to the right three times and tear off the bottom corner.
5. Fold it in half again and tear off the middle piece.

Instruct the group members to unfold their papers and compare their snowflakes with the other members. They will find that their snowflakes will be different. Discussion: Discuss the importance of communicating and listening. Use questions such as:

1. Why is it that even though everyone received the same instructions, the snowflakes looked different? What would have changed if you had been able to ask questions?
2. How can you improve your communication skills when it is obvious that others are doing things differently than you intended?

Stage 3

As the group members become more comfortable with one another, cooperation and collaboration are hallmarks of this stage, and contribute to trustful relationships and supportive interactions. Self-disclosure is more frequent and more personal, and group members support one another as they work on personal goals. The leader's role is less active due to the energetic involvement of group members and their ability to share, discuss, and confront each other in a caring atmosphere. Student Activity 8.3 is an example of an exercise that could be used during this stage of the group, yet the counselor may need to adapt this activity for students who are in wheelchairs or have mobility challenges. Pairing students to assist one another may be one method to implement this activity.

Student Activity 8.3

Land Mine

Objective: To identify the importance of listening to instructions.
Age: Grades 5 and up.
Evaluation: To identify one listening strategy to implement in class.
Directions: A specified area in the room is set aside for the activity. Objects are scattered around this area to serve as obstacles that are identified as "dangerous or life-threatening." One of the partners is blindfolded and asked to stand on one side of the land mine. The other partner stands on the other side and guides his/her partner through verbal communication to cross the land mine in a specified period of time. The person who is instructing is to remain calm so that his/her partner's life is not in danger. After everyone has had a chance to be the instructor and person crossing the land mine, a discussion follows. Questions to facilitate this discussion include:

1. What directions were most important?
2. What made the instructions difficult to follow?
3. What directions were most helpful?
4. How can you use what you learned from this exercise in the classroom?

Stage 4

As the group comes to an end, members discuss what they have learned and how they will apply this knowledge to their lives outside of group. Isolation during the final sessions is common for group members as a strategy to protect themselves from the feelings of loss. These feelings may be expressed through avoidance such as not bringing up repeated thoughts or affect, or through sadness and remorse that they weren't able to use the group opportunity to process personal issues. Student Activity 8.4 is an example of a termination activity.

Activity 8.4

Circle Around

Objective: To identify new concepts learned from the group experience.
Age: Grade 3 and up.
Materials: Paper with the template of a circle divided into three sections.
Directions: One section of the circle is labeled "One thing I learned from group is…" The second section is labeled, "One of my biggest surprises was…" The third section is labeled "I will always remember…" Each student completes his/her own circle using words and/or pictures. A large plastic ball that is safe to throw can be brought to the group and each person can share one item from his/her own picture.

Stage 5

Post-group sessions at a designated time in the future provide the group leader with an opportunity to assess the long-term outcomes of the group, and for group members to report their success in accomplishing their goals. This post-group session also holds students accountable and responsible for goal accomplishment, a time to identify obstacles that have prevented goal attainment, and to rework personal goals.

Evaluation

Evaluation is an ethical practice that requires a realistic measure of the group's effectiveness, and how the students have changed due to group participation. This evaluation is formulated to match the group objectives related to the identified standards. Tracking data and documenting results to display to stakeholders provides concrete support that your school counseling program is making a difference to the academic, vocational, and social/emotional growth of students. It will also confirm that you are an integral member of the educational community.

Please circle the answer that you feel best represents your experience in this group.			
1 = do not agree 2 = somewhat agree 3 = strongly agree			
1. I am better able to solve my problems	1	2	3
2. I am able to communicate with my peers	1	2	3
3. This group helped me get better grades	1	2	3
4. I am able to control myself better	1	2	3
5. When my teacher scolds me I can hold my temper	1	2	3

Figure 8.4 Group counseling evaluation.

Directions: Your opinion is important for helping me understand how you felt regarding your group experience. Please provide me with your feelings related to each of the questions below.
1. What part of group did you enjoy the most? Explain_____
2. What suggestions do you have for improvement?_____
3. Would you recommend this group to your friend? Why or why not? _____

Figure 8.5 Qualitative assessment.

Quantitative data can be obtained to determine each individual's change in knowledge, behavior, or attitudes, or each member's assessment of the group experience. The evaluation is designed with the developmental level of the group members in mind. Ideally, quantitative data shown in easily understood graphs is a helpful strategy to reveal group effectiveness. Figure 8.4 provides an example of a quantitative group evaluation.

Qualitative data is another useful strategy for obtaining more in-depth information regarding members' perceptions of the group, suggestions for improvement, and perceived highlights of the experience. Figure 8.5 is an example of a qualitative assessment.

Groups for school-aged youth with disabilities will vary depending on the identified need, disability, and developmental level of the students. The information in the following section describes groups that were developed for students with various disabilities.

Group Counseling for Youth with ADHD

As discussed in previous chapters, students with ADHD have difficulty completing tasks, paying attention, not fidgeting, and concentrating (Webb & Myrick, 2003). For these students, group counseling is an intervention that is recommended over individual counseling (Braswell & Bloomquist, 1991, as cited in Webb & Myrick, 2003). For instance, Rational emotive behavioral therapy (REBT) emphasizes behavior and thought modification, and when used in a small counseling group, participants are able to recognize how ADHD influences learning, classroom behavior, thoughts, and feelings. Webb and Myrick (2003) developed a small counseling group for elementary students who were diagnosed with ADHD. The groups met for six sessions that centered around a theme of an imaginary journey in which the students identified road signs and their meaning, and recognized essential skills needed for successful travel. The group journey consisted of teaching participants about ADHD, strategies that facilitate organization and planning, recognition of signs that support or detract from school achievement, signals that target troublesome situations, and sources of support in the school setting. Teachers reinforced the skills learned in the group during classroom lessons through additional support and feedback, and at the end of the intervention teachers' assessments revealed an improvement in students' classroom behavior.

Groups for Students with Autism

Behavioral and cognitive counseling are recommended approaches for working with school-aged youth on the autism spectrum (White et al., 2010). Multimodel Anxiety and Social Skills Intervention (MASSI) is an effective approach that centers on behavior, thoughts, and feelings and has been successful with students with ASD (White et al., 2010). Psychoeducation and instruction about ASD with specific attention to cognition and feelings that contribute to anxiety and avoidance, and recognition of others' emotions and behaviors are a focus of MASSI in counseling (White et al., 2010). In group sessions, each member is given an opportunity to practice social skills, rehearse anxiety management, and apply communication skills with peers. These skills also motivate students to practice skills outside of the group setting.

When students learn to advocate for themselves, they have acquired a lifetime skill that can be used in numerous situations. A self-advocacy training program for students with autism enables students to learn their educational rights and facilitates skills for academic success. Self-advocacy programs entail several crucial steps (Smith, 2010). Researching the needs of the students in the school and identifying various programs that have worked is an essential first step. Second, collaboration with the special education department assists in locating materials, identifying personnel, and understanding district procedures. Finally, identifying students with autism and non-disabled peers who are able to demonstrate self-advocacy skills and who will benefit from this training is crucial. Peer-to-peer groups provide opportunities for self-empowerment and recognizing strengths (Smith, 2010).

Students with Emotional and Behavioral Problems

Students with severe emotional and behavioral problems need additional support in the school environment (Pearce, 2009). In a study that utilized the Response to Intervention (RTI) model, multiple interventions were conducted with nine students in grades 3–5 who were identified with emotional disorders (Pearce, 2009). These interventions consisted of an applied behavioral analysis in which teachers reinforced desirable behaviors, provided quiet areas for the students to regain behavioral or emotional control, rearranged physical aspects of the room to provide a more calming environment, and differentiated instructional approaches to meet the learning styles of each student.

In addition to these classroom-based modifications, counselors created a trusting group environment to allow students to discuss the social and academic consequences surrounding their inappropriate behavior. Students were taught social and problem-solving skills that were practiced in the group and reinforced in the classroom by their teachers. The group sessions also provided an opportunity for the school counselor to monitor students' progress and evaluate whether individual counseling sessions were necessary to reinforce the cognitive behavioral strategies that served as the foundation for the group. Overall improvements in student behaviors at the end of the interventions were revealed, and due to increased communication, parents indicated that they felt as if they were equal partners in improving their child's success (Pearce, 2009).

Students diagnosed with emotional and behavioral disabilities were the target of another group intervention through the use of the *Self-Discovery Programme* (SDP). The SDP is based on building self-efficacy, role modeling, and reframing physiological and affective states (Powell et al., 2008). Primary-aged students with emotional and behavioral disabilities were placed in either the SDP program or a control group. The SDP group met weekly for 12 sessions of approximately 45 minutes in which participants took part in activities designed to promote self-understanding through strategies such as sensory awareness, touch therapy, yoga, breathing, communication, and relaxation. At the end of the intervention, the SDP group revealed improved self-talk, enhanced listening skills, improved attention span, use of positive touch, calming breathing strategies, and less fidgeting in class in comparison to the control group.

Students with Learning Disabilities

Amerikaner and Summerlin (1982) conducted a group intervention with primary grade students diagnosed with a learning disability. Students were randomly assigned to either a control, relaxation, or social skills group. The control group members resumed normal classroom activities while those in the relaxation group attended bi weekly, 30-minute sessions for six weeks, in which they were taught to identify tension and the contrasting feelings of relaxation, as well as changes in feelings and behavior. The social skills group also met bi-weekly for 30 minutes for six weeks, with members being taught self-awareness, coping with feelings, and appropriately relating to peers. At the conclusion of these groups, those in the relaxation group revealed fewer acting-out behaviors in comparison with the other groups, and those in the social skills group showed higher social self-esteem scores in comparison with their peers in the other groups. This study emphasizes that brief group interventions with students with learning disabilities have the potential to bring about positive changes.

Transition Groups for High School Students with Disabilities

Students with disabilities do not often receive information on transition from high school to careers or higher education, and they often have numerous challenges with transition. These issues can be addressed in a group format. For instance, psychoeducational groups aimed at developing specific skills for career exploration or post-secondary training are opportunities to provide this group of individuals with skills that are needed for career or post-secondary matriculation (McEachern & Kenny, 2007). Navigating through the admissions process, financial aid, and choosing a major are issues the school counselor is able to address (McEachern & Kenny, 2007) in group. Moreover, issues such as identifying barriers to post-secondary training, demonstrating self-advocacy skills, understanding various institutional factors including size and choice of majors, learning about admissions requirements such as the ACT and SAT, and comprehending available college support services are topics that can be addressed in a group format. Students who have chosen to transition directly to work also have needs that can be addressed in psychoeducational groups.

Too often, individuals who go directly into the workforce believe that they cannot be successful without training after high school. Yet, providing information to these group members such as the prediction that by 2018, 40 percent of the available jobs will not require a college education (Las Vegas Review, 2014) provides hope that a successful career does not necessarily require post-secondary education. In this psychoeducational group, members can practice self-advocacy skills, learn the importance of work, finding a job, knowledge of salary, applying to jobs, and interviewing skills (McEachern & Kenny, 2007).

Since academic achievement is a major goal for educators and school counselors, *Empowerment Groups for Academic Success* (EGAS) was a format that was provided to nine ninth-graders who were chosen to participate in the group due to their failing grades and teacher recommendations (Johnson & Johnson, 2005). These students were matched with a control group of students according to gender, ethnicity, and failing grades in math, science, language arts, or history. Members' GPAs were gathered and analyzed before the group commenced, at the conclusion of the group, and again the following school year.

In the group sessions, the students were given information on the purpose of the group, confidentiality considerations, advice to students with academic challenges, cultural issues, family dynamics, time spent on video games, drug use, and relationships. The school counselor leaders emphasized academic achievement but specifically designed this group to be unstructured with an emphasis placed on the group process. The *Critical Incidents Questionnaire* was administered at the last group session to understand the critical factors most significant to the group experience. The results revealed that students perceived that sharing thoughts and feelings and recognizing that others shared similar experiences were the most salient, positive aspects of the group. Although there were no significant GPA differences between the intervention and control groups, the researchers suggested that the small group size was a factor that contributed to this finding. Johnson and Johnson (2005) further emphasized the importance of allowing students to initiate group discussion as an influencing factor that promotes student growth.

Conceptual Application Activity 8.2

Talk with the teacher of special education and design a group format for a particular issue that could be addressed in a group format. Use the concepts discussed in this chapter to structure your group.

Conclusion

School counselors have the unique training and skills to lead groups, and students with disabilities benefit from participating in groups designed to meet their needs. Task, psychoeducational, and counseling groups are the formats most commonly found in schools, and evidence supports the benefits for students with disabilities who participate in these groups. In developing groups to address an identified need, group promotion and screening, goal-setting, informed consent, scheduling, and attention to special accommodations are relevant to group conception and planning. The school counselor has an awareness of the group stages, dynamics, activities that promote the group goals, and knowledge of disabilities and student needs. Various types of groups for students with disabilities have been created and have shown success in the school environment.

References

Amerikaner, M. & Summerlin, M. L. (1982). Group counseling with learning disabled children: effects of social skills and relaxation training on self-concept and classroom behavior. *Journal of Learning Disabilities*, 15, 340–343.

ASCA (2010). *Ethical Standards for School Counselors*. Retrieved from www.schoolcounselor.org/asca/media/asca/Other%20Media/EthicalStandards2010.pdf.

ASCA (2014). *The Professional School Counselor and Group Counseling*. Retrieved from http://www.schoolcounselor.org/asca/media/asca/PositionStatements/PS_Group-Counseling.pdf.

Conyne, R. K. (2014). *Group Work Leadership: An Introduction for Helpers*. Los Angeles, CA: Sage.

Corey, G. (2012). *Theory & Practice of Group Counseling*, 8th edn. Belmont, CA: Brooks/Cole.

Corey, M. S., Corey, G., & Corey, C. (2010). *Groups: Process and Practice*, 8th edn. Belmont, CA: Brooks/Cole.

Johnson, S. K. & Johnson, C. D. (2005). Group counseling: beyond the traditional. *Professional School Counseling*, 8, 399–400.

Las Vegas Review (2014). *By 2018, 60% of Job Openings Will Require a College Education*. Retrieved from http://222.reviewournal.com.

McEachern, A. G. & Kenny, M. C. (2007). Transition groups for high school students with disabilities. *The Journal for Specialists in Group Work*, 32, 165–177.

Pearce, L. R. (2009). Helping children with emotional difficulties: a Response to Intervention investigation. *Rural Educator*, 30, 34–46.

Powell, L., Gilchrist, M., & Stapley, J. (2008). A journey of self-discovery: an intervention involving massage, yoga and relaxation for children with emotional and behavioural difficulties attending primary schools. *Emotional & Behavioural Difficulties*, 13, 193–199.

Ritchie, M. H., & Huss, S. N. (2000). Recruitment and screening of minors for group counseling. *Journal for Specialists in Group Work*, 25, 145–156.

Serres, S. A. & Nelson, J. A. (2011). Professional school counselor. In C. Simpson & J. Bakken (eds.), *Collaboration: A Multidisciplinary Approach to Educating Students with Disabilities*. Waco, TX: Prufrock Press, Inc.

Shepard, J. M., Shahidullah, J. D., & Carlson, J. S. (2013). *Counseling Students in Levels 2 and 3: A PBIS/RTI Guide*. Thousand Oaks, CA: Corwin.

Smith, B. (2010). Help others help themselves. *ASCA School Counselor*, September/October, 19–21.

Stephens, D., Jain, S., & Kim, K. (2010). *Group Counseling: Techniques for Teaching Social Skills to Students with Special Needs*. Retrieved from http://www.questia.com/library/journal.

Webb, L. D. & Myrick, R. D. (2003). A group counseling intervention for children with attention deficit hyperactivity disorder. *Professional School Counseling*, 7, 108–115.

Wheeler, A. M. & Bertram, B. (2012). *The Counselor and the Law: A Guide to Legal and Ethical Practice*, 6th edn. Alexandria, VA: American Counseling Association.

White, S. W., Abano, A. M., Johnson, C. R., Kasari, C., Ollendick, T., Klin, A., Oswalk, D., & Scahill, L. (2010). Development of cognitive-behavioral intervention program to treat anxiety and social deficits in teens with high-functioning autism. *Clinical Child and Family Psychology Review*, 13, 77–79.

9 The School Counselor's Role in Transition and Career Development

The following CACREP standards are addressed in this chapter:

CAREER DEVELOPMENT
  b. approaches for conceptualizing the interrelationships among and between work, mental well-being, relationships, and other life roles and factors
  d. approaches for assessing the conditions of the work environment on clients' life experiences
  e. strategies for assessing abilities, interests, values, personality and other factors that contribute to career development
  f. strategies for career development program planning, organization implementation, administration, and evaluation
  g. strategies for advocating for diverse clients' career and educational development and employment opportunities in a global economy
  h. strategies for facilitating client skill development for career, educational, and life-work planning and management
  j. ethical and culturally relevant strategies for addressing career development

ASSESSMENT AND TESTING
  i. use of assessments relevant to academic/educational, career, personal, and social development
  j. use of environmental assessments and systematic behavioral observations

ENTRY-LEVEL SPECIALTY AREAS: SCHOOL COUNSELING CONTEXTUAL DIMENSIONS
  c. school counselor roles in relation to college and career readiness

PRACTICE
  j. interventions to promote college and career readiness

Chapter Objectives

After you have completed this chapter, you should be able to:

- Identify the school counselor's role in transition planning.
- Demonstrate skills to facilitate transition planning.

Transition and Career Development

Children go through cognitive, physical, emotional, and behavioral changes through-out life that determine their new roles and responsibilities. These transformations mark one type of lifelong transition; transitioning from school to school or to various grades throughout school is another type of transition. Each transition brings new expectations and learning goals. Research reveals that school transitions are associated with lowered grades, diminished motivation, and elevated psychological stress (Akos, 2003). While these are serious moments in the lives of all students, it is important to emphasize that the types of services children with disabilities receive throughout these transitions are in many ways dependent on various legislative mandates according to the Individuals with Disabilities Education Improvement Act (IDEIA) of 2004. Please refer back to the dis-cussion of IDEA 2004 in Chapter 2 for an overview of the importance of transition and transitional programming from a legal perspective. Read Case Study 9.1 for an example of problems that may result due to a transition to a new school.

Case Study 9.1

Jason is a ten-year-old who entered the middle school from another county. Upon enrollment, his father indicated that he had a 504 Plan in that county, although his records did not indicate he was receiving this service. However, Jason exhibited many disruptive behaviors such as aggressiveness, difficulty making friends, and paranoia. When upset he would become destructive, such as ripping paper, throwing things, and tearing things from the wall, and we became concerned for his safety as he would run from the building when agitated. Upon further investigation, we learned he had been in an alternative placement for his schooling due to these violent outbursts. Since testing had not been done, he was not eligible for services in our county. Records indicated that he would move and transfer to another county before interventions can be implemented to address his emotional and behavioral outbursts. Unfortunately, his records are slow to follow his moves, and he doesn't stay in a school system long enough for an identification for special services.

Middle school counselor

Early Childhood Special Education and Transition

Although the emphasis of this book is on students with disabilities, pre-K-12, it is important to note again that provisions for services for infants and toddlers with special needs are addressed in IDEA 2004. School counselors should have a knowledge base in regard to this topic as elementary level school counselors may be involved with students with disabilities who have already been receiving specialized services before entering the K-12 environment. For a review of legislative information from Part C of IDEA 2004, relating to infants and toddlers with disabilities, please refer back to the box in Chapter 4 that addresses the subject.

Before progressing to a discussion of the transition process from preschool to the K-12 environment, a brief word in regard to the early intervention process for students with special needs is warranted. The Child Find mandate requires all school districts to locate, identify, and evaluate all children from birth to age 21. A child from birth to age two diagnosed with a developmental delay or disability may receive services based on the Individual Family Service Plan (IFSP) in which he/she may transition to services such as preschool or childcare setting. The IFSP is a written plan that is developed by professionals who represent several specialty areas with a focus on the child and the services his/her family may need to augment growth and development. IDEA 2004 also mandates that states provide specialized services to children aged three through five years of age with disabilities through the design and implementation of a specialized program (Heward, 2013).

Transition from an Early Childhood Education Perspective

In its *Recommended Practices in Early Intervention/ Early Childhood Special Education 2014*, the Division for Early Childhood of the Council for Exceptional Children explains the transition for young children with disabilities in the manner which follows:

> Transition refers to the events, activities, and processes associated with key changes between environments or programs during the early childhood years and the practices that support the adjustment of the child and family to the new setting. These changes occur at the transition from hospital to home, the transition into early intervention (Part C) programs, the transition out of early intervention to community early childhood programs, the transition into Part B/619, and the transition to kindergarten or school-age programs.
>
> (Division for Early Childhood, 2014, p. 15)

As has been discussed previously, and as a note for clarification in the previous quote, Part C of IDEA 2004 addresses infants and toddlers with special needs and Part B of IDEA 2004 focuses on individuals aged 3–21 (Wilmshurst & Brue, 2010). Transition for children with disabilities may obviously be viewed from different stages in the child's life. Although this description of transition as it relates to early intervention is broader than that of the progression of a child from preschool services to kindergarten, it does validate the importance of the transitional process for young children with special needs as they move into a K-12 environment, which as previously noted, does fall within the pre-K-12 focus of this text.

The Transition Process from Preschool-Age to School-Age Services

Once again, the school counselor may be involved as a member of the individualized education program (IEP) team that focuses on a variety of activities for the young child with a disability transitioning from preschool-age to school-age services, such as reviewing the child's needs, delineating individualized goals, participating in making recommendations for services, and determining the appropriate educational environments

Figure 9.1 With today's global market economy the need for additional education after high school is becoming increasingly important. School counselors are able to introduce youth with disabilities with an array of options.
Source: ©iStockphoto.com, www.istockphoto.com/photo/university-students-42802714.

(Vicker, 2009). Moreover, since "young children with special needs typically receive services from a multitude of professionals" (Gargiulo & Kilgo, 2005, p. 193), the school counselor may take a leadership role in the coordination of educational and community resources. The role of coordinator is particularly critical as there may be a number of stakeholders whose perspectives should be taken into consideration, including the child's family, members of the community, and individuals involved with service provision, to ascertain the needs of the child and family during this type of transition programming (La Paro et al., 2000).

A goal of the transition process is to make it as seamless as possible while ensuring continuity of service provision. In addition to making the process proactive (Fenlon, 2011), it is important to note that extensive preparation, consistent collaboration, and continuing communication among all the pertinent parties are considered (Gargiulo & Kilgo, 2005). The Division for Early Childhood (2014) also strongly supports the transition practices of information exchange and strategy implementation with the family and child pre-transition, during the transition process, and post-transition to encourage successful outcomes.

Transition Process Leading to Post-Secondary Life

Another type of transition focuses more on older students as they prepare to transition from high school to post-school adult life. This type of transition involves addressing post-secondary options including college, other post-secondary training, and employ-ment, as well as areas of personal growth such as housing, access to appropriate com-munity services, and independent living. It also includes the planning of the completion of appropriate coursework and experiences to support the students in reaching their particular post-secondary goals. While the discussion of transition in Chapter 5 focuses primarily on addressing transition on the IEP specifically, this discussion will build upon this foundation and focus even more on concepts and practices of primary interest and importance to school counselors, as they work with adolescents with disabilities.

Transition from the Perspective of Post-School Outcomes

As we have seen, the practice of transition may be addressed for students with disabilities prior to their entry to the K-12 environment. To have a clear appreciation of the meaning of transition for the older student, it is beneficial to look to the law for its description. According to the Individuals with Disabilities Education Improvement Act, *transition services* are explained as:

(34) TRANSITION SERVICES—The term "transition services" means a coordinated set of activities for a child with a disability that—(A) is designed to be within a results-oriented process, that is focused on improving the academic and functional achievement of the child with a disability to facilitate the child's movement from school to post-school activities, including post-secondary education, vocational education, integrated employment (including supported employment), continuing and adult education, adult services, independent living, or community participation;

(B) is based on the individual child's needs, taking into account the child's strengths, preferences, and interests; and

(C) includes instruction, related services, community experiences, the development of employment and other post-school adult living objectives, and, when appropriate, acquisition of daily living skills and functional vocational evaluation.

(Individuals with Disabilities Education Improvement Act,
Public Law 108–446, 2004, Sec.602 [34] [A] [B] [C])

By virtue of their training and experience, school counselors could clearly play a vital role related to many of these issues.

The Importance of Transition to Post-School Life for Students with Disabilities

With today's global market economy, the need for additional education after high school is becoming increasingly important; a high school diploma is not enough. In 2011, 63.8 percent of students receiving services according to IDEA 2004 graduated from high school (Annual Disability Statistics Compendium, 2013). Furthermore, in 2010, among students diagnosed with a specific learning disability (SLD), approximately 68 percent graduated with a diploma, 12 percent received a certificate, and 19 percent dropped out of school (National Center for Learning Disabilities, 2013). As for employment options,

Heward (2013) notes that in 2010 the Bureau of Labor Statistics reported that considerably fewer individuals with disabilities in the working age range were employed in comparison with individuals without disabilities.

Recognition of and access to services and supports that promote high school graduation and enrollment in post-secondary education, additional training, or careers are critical. Yet, school counselors are inconsistent in their knowledge of these resources and in their ability to make these provisions available. As revealed by Milsom and Akos (2003), school counselors do not feel well-prepared to work with students with disabilities, and feel even less prepared to assist in transition planning.

As stated by a school counselor who works in a private school:

> Students who need special education services are placed on a Student Support Plan (SSP), which is similar to the IEP. The SSP outlines medical needs, diagnosis, and the academic modifications and accommodations we are able to offer. One of the great things that came out of working with the Learning Center Specialist was the realization that our students need to not only be successful at our school, but we need to be preparing them for life after high school. Therefore, we developed a "Template for Transition Planning" that we use with all our students who have an SSP.

The template is in Figure 9.2.

The importance of transition services was originally mandated in the IDEA 1990 provisions (Carter et al., 2014), and was reauthorized in 2004 with the Individuals with Disabilities Education Improvement Act (IDEIA). This revised law included a "results-based process … focused on improving the academic and functional achievement of the child with a disability to facilitate the child's movement from school to post-school activities" (Wrightslaw, 2013).

As we have previously discussed in Chapter 5 on IEPs, the focus of transition planning for students beginning at the age of 14—or perhaps younger—is on the determination of the coursework and courses of study that will assist the students in the attainment of their post-secondary goals (US Department of Education, 2007). Beginning at age 16 or younger, the transition focus is on the determination of an organized group of services to assist the student in progressing from high school to post-secondary life, taking into consideration such aspects as post-secondary education or training, opportunities for employment, skills for independent living, and adult and/or community services (US Department of Education, 2007). It is imperative that by the age of 16, the student's IEP identifies the supports and interagency connections that are available to him/her. Moreover, in a discussion of the importance of the transition process for adult outcomes, it is essential to note that school counselors should be aware that the student is to be given instruction on adult rights one year before the student reaches the "age of majority," which is usually 18, although this age varies from state to state (Marshak et al., 2010).

Conceptual Application Activity 9.1

Interview a school counselor regarding how he/she plays a role in the transition process. Compare your responses with those of your classmates.

Template for transition planning	Goal to be addressed in future academic years	Progress being made	Student is proficient
Rigor of the curriculum			
Takes ownership/responsibility for academic success			
Active listening and note-taking skills			
Independent reading at college level			
Uses assistive technologies as needed			
Develops/uses study skills for test preparation			
Develops/uses study skills for completing long-term assignments			
Arranges with teacher to test at the learning center before test date			
In core subjects, takes test that are not modified			
In core subjects, takes tests without extended time			
In core subjects, does assignments without modified requirements			
In core subjects, does assignments without extended time			
Self-determination and independence			
Student participates in developing SSP			
Student, not parent, contacts learning center			
Articulates/proposes a strategy to resolve issues (vs. first asking the learning center how to resolve)			
Initiates requests for getting help from teachers or arranges for tutoring when needed			
Successfully sets short-term goals			
Successfully sets long-term goals			
Develops and uses good time management skills			
Develops and uses good organizational skills			

Figure 9.2 Template for transition planning.

Figure 9.2 (cont.)

Template for transition planning	Goal to be addressed in future academic years	Progress being made	Student is proficient

Self-advocacy

Can articulate disability to teachers
Understands documentation required to prove their disability
Can articulate realistic career or college goals
Can describe a realistic plan for reaching their goals
Can realistically describe their strengths and weaknesses
Develops good peer relationships

Transitioning to college

Realistically understands the rigors of college

Motivated to succeed in college or career

Develops a plan to visit colleges, investigates available services, and understands how to request (in a timely manner) all paperwork needed to request services

Can self-advocate independently of parents

Source: Reprinted with permission from Knoxville Catholic High School Guidance Department.

The Role of Assessment in Transition Planning for Post-School Life

Age-appropriate, functional transition assessments are key components to understanding the educational practices most essential for students with disabilities (Carter et al., 2014). An emphasis on the role of assessments is included in the transition plan to measure post-secondary, age-appropriate goals related to training, education, employment, and/or independent living skills, if appropriate (Carter et al., 2014). Furthermore, these assessments utilize a variety of measures such as interviews, contextual assessments, vocational evaluations, self-advocacy skills, and supports (Marshak et al., 2010). Multiple perspectives, identification of personal strengths, and personalized programming are essential measurement elements.

ASSESSMENT BASED ON MULTIPLE PERSPECTIVES

The observations and views of various individuals who work with students with disabilities are particularly crucial as these stakeholders often differ in their perspectives of student needs and strengths (Carter et al., 2014). The student with special needs comes in contact with various individuals who see the child in different settings, and are contributors to realistic goal formation. Goals are written in measurable, results-oriented terms, and include such activities as education, independent living, or community participation (Marshak et al., 2010). Students want to be part of their educational preparation, and transition planning is most effective when the student is involved in identifying personal goals. However, the student is often the person who understands the transition plan meeting the least of those involved (Marshak et al., 2010), their input is often overlooked (Trainor, 2005), and in some cases students report being chastised during these meetings (Trainor, 2005). The school counselor has the ability to prepare the student for the transition meeting by discussing goals, strengths, and facilitating self-advocacy skills; concepts integral to the American School Counselor Association (ASCA) National Model (Marshak et al., 2010).

School counselors are also able to promote student involvement in the transitional planning process by helping students identify when they want to graduate from high school, and the type of work they would like to do upon high school graduation. Moreover, brainstorming such practical items as how they will get from one place to another, what learning experiences they would like to have following high school graduation, and with whom they will live and where, are foundational questions for creating leisure, work, educational, or community involvement (Luckner & Sebald, 2013). Based on the results of the multi-perspective assessment, post-secondary goals are created and plans are made to identify needed transition services to address these needs.

The Importance of the Identification of Individual Strengths and Needs in the Transition Process

Too often IEP meetings focus on the student's disability or areas of limitation with an identification of accommodations that are required to aid in the student's successes. Revisions in IDEA 2004 include identification of student *strengths* in addition to the student's interests and preferred choices as components of the student's post-secondary plans (Carter et al., 2014). In fact, a student's multiple strengths can be identified when observed by diverse individuals in differing contexts. Students with communication issues who are involved in the transition process may have difficulty articulating their own needs and goals, yet supportive individuals who have opportunities to observe the child in unique contexts are able to share their perspectives regarding the student's needs, personality, limitations of disability, and personal strengths (Carter et al., 2014).

Cultural beliefs, mores, and behaviors are essential ingredients integral to transition planning. In some cases, the student's cultural background and belief system could be in conflict with the individualization that is supported by transition planning meetings (Trainor, 2005). Therefore, inviting community leaders who are members of the student's cultural group may be important sources of support for the student. For instance, in a study by Trainor (2005), African Americans revealed the importance of emotional support in making transition plans, yet unfortunately, teachers were not perceived as supportive participants in the transition process (Trainor, 2005). Hopefully, school counselors are viewed as valuable support resources.

Personalized Programming in the Transition Process

Too often, post-secondary plans are based on already existing structures or programs such as workshops or employers who hire students with disabilities. In many instances, these previously developed resources do not address unique, individual needs. Instead, plans should be tailor-designed around the needs and strengths of the individual student, with attention to personal beliefs that could impair transition planning. As an example, Trainor (2005) revealed that African American and Hispanic students were often excluded from exit examinations and were enrolled in vocational programs more often than their Caucasian peers, even when there was an expressed interest in pursuing secondary education.

Several factors shape post-secondary decisions such as the types of services, accommodations, and self-determination (Fleming & Fairweather, 2012), yet students with disabilities often depend more on personal supports such as parents and friends than on accommodations to promote success. Further, the type of disability influences post-secondary school attendance in that students with a visual impairment or those with emotional disabilities are less likely to attend these institutes than those with other health impairments (Fleming & Fairweather, 2012).

The Role of the School Counselor in Transition Planning for Older Students with Disabilities

"For an adolescent, transition planning is often one of the most important parts of the IEP" (Rosenberg et al., 2011, p. 98), and the school counselor may play a critical role in assisting the student with meeting the goals of this plan. For example, a school counselor's knowledge of the factors that make it more likely to attend post-secondary education facilitates decision-making and educational attendance. Information regarding career and educational planning are concepts that all students need, and since students with disabilities are often included in regular education classrooms, lessons on transition planning and decision-making are essential concepts to include in classroom guidance lessons. For instance, all students benefit from assignments aimed at investigating various careers and skills that are required to be successful in chosen areas (Trainor, 2005). School counselors could also provide information to help students recognize that being released for vocational opportunities could interfere with their college preparatory classes. Or students may be informed that standardized testing exemptions may preclude attendance in post-secondary education, or learn that college preparatory classes are distinctly different from honors classes, advanced placement classes, or dual-enrollment options.

The school counselor is able to provide information to all students that fulfill the student competencies that are selected within the school counseling curriculum through classroom guidance lessons, individual counseling, or group counseling. The next several sections of this chapter will focus on self-determination, decision-making and problem-solving skills, goal-setting, self-advocacy, self-esteem, and self-regulation interventions that enhance student growth.

Concepts and Interventions for Success

SELF-DETERMINISM

Self-determination (SD), incorporated into the IDEA and the Rehabilitation Act, is associated with effective transitions from school to adult living (Luckner & Sebald, 2013). Although SD is usually associated with secondary transition (Wehmeyer et al., 2013), the foundation for SD is established in early childhood through the help and support of other adults. In early childhood, children are given guidance, and opportunities to practice and refine skills (Palmer et al., 2013), including an awareness of needs, decision-making, setting goals, problem-solving, and how to act on these skills through self-regulating behaviors and thoughts, and self-advocacy (Luckner & Sebald, 2013; Trainor, 2005). As children grow and develop, they can be taught to understand that choices involve consequences. Children with disabilities may need more directed intentional support to develop these decision-making skills that often include: (a) identifying the problem; (b) brainstorming options; (c) identifying obstacles that could impede problem-solving; and (d) selecting results of each solution (Palmer et al., 2013).

Adults are also able to provide instruction designed to accommodate various disabilities. For example, students who are deaf or hard of hearing will require explicit instruction to acquire language, knowledge, and skills for SD. Helpful resources such as children's books promote self-awareness, decision-making, and learning opportunities for skill acquisition. Figure 9.3 lists books that can be used with children to teach these concepts.

DECISION-MAKING AND PROBLEM-SOLVING

The ability to make choices is associated with autonomy, and yet this skill is often difficult for children with disabilities, particularly those with cognitive difficulties. Age differences and skills impact the ability to acquire and use problem-solving skills. For instance, younger children tend to be more concrete in their thinking and have

When I'm Feeling Angry by Trace Moroney

This is a beautifully illustrated book for children three to five years of age. Different emotional concepts are discussed.

Giraffes Can't Dance by Giles Andreae and Guy Parker-Rees

This book for children aged three to six comes with a DVD, and tells the story of long-legged Gerald the giraffe who wants to dance but his legs are too thin and he has difficulty twirling. His jungle friends make fun of Gerald, but he does have one friend who believes in him.

I Like Myself by Karen Beaumont

This book, written for children aged four and older, is written to appreciate all their traits unconditionally.

Figure 9.3 Books that promote self-awareness and decision-making.

difficulty with abstract thought. In addition, the ability to use social skills influences problem-solving ability, and when students lack these skills the school counselor is able to assist in the attainment of these competences. Furthermore, school counselors are able to instruct students that:

- problems are a normal part of life;
- life's difficulties can be resolved through a systematic method of problem-solving;
- feelings are cues to a problem;
- when you realize there is a problem you need to *stop* and *think*.

Preschool children with disabilities can be taught this process through assistance with verbal or picture representations depending upon their specific disability.

SETTING GOALS

Although most youth want meaningful plans when they leave secondary education, individuals with disabilities trail behind their peers in reaching this goal (Carter et al., 2014). School counselors are able to assist students with disabilities recognize the connection between planning, identification of personal strengths, and goal attainment (Trainor, 2005). Student Activity 9.1 can be adapted for students in elementary school to facilitate career goal-setting.

Student Activity 9.1

Who Wears This Hat?

Directions: Bring in various hats that are worn by workers such as a firefighter's helmet, football helmet, chef's hat, construction worker's helmet, baseball cap. The counselor will put on one of the hats and ask the students to identify the hat. Students are asked to describe what the person does who wears the hat. Notice if the labels of "he" or "she" are used when describing the worker's role. Ask students to name jobs men usually have, and jobs women usually have. Write the names of these jobs under the categories "men" and "women." Ask students if they agree with the columns under which the jobs were listed, and explain how either a man or woman can complete the required responsibilities. Next, have the students identify what they want to be when they grow up, and explain that they should not let someone tell them they cannot do something just because they are male or female.

SELF-ADVOCACY

Test et al. (2005) define self-advocacy as including knowledge of self, knowledge of rights, communication, and leadership. The importance of understanding self in order to communicate personal needs serves as a foundation for self-advocacy, and is a vital skill that all students can learn through lessons in classroom guidance (Test et al., 2005).

One of the biggest differences between high school and post-secondary institutions is that the matriculating student now has the onus of advocating for him/herself rather than relying on the partnership that was developed under IDEA. When individuals with disabilities are sheltered and overprotected by adults in their lives, their autonomy is reduced (Test et al., 2005) and their self-knowledge may be limited. Without assertiveness, these students are unable to articulate their strengths and needs or the accommodations that are needed during and beyond this transition (Test et al., 2005).

SELF-ESTEEM

Self-esteem and self-concept impact well-being. Self-esteem is defined as the global evaluations of self, whereas self-concept refers to specific evaluations of the self in specific areas (Santrock, 2012). Each of these constructs is impacted by the individual's perception of his/her disability (Marshak et al., 2010). In this regard, youth may have developed successful methods for coping and maintaining a positive sense of self despite others' devaluation of this disability, or may have feelings of shame and inferiority that negatively impact their view of self. Additionally, environmental factors may also impede one's ability to navigate opportunities (Marshak et al., 2010). For instance, have you ever been in a wheelchair? If so, you may have recognized the difficulties in navigating around places. For instance, even though the signs outside of doors specify that the exit or entrance are handicapped accessible, doors that are operated manually with a door handle that opens outward make it difficult to enter and exit while sitting in a wheelchair. Student Activity 9.2 is designed as an activity for students to recognize strengths and to set goals.

Student Activity 9.2

Marvelous, Wonderful Me

Grade level: Elementary
Objective: To identify special characteristics that make each person unique.
"You are important—you are special. No one else is like you—you are unique." On the handout, students will write, draw pictures, or paste pictures that depict the following:

- Things that make them different from everyone else.
- Things they are able to do well.
- Things they like about themselves.
- Goals for the future.

Things that make me different from others	Things I am able to do well	Things I like about myself	My future goals

SELF-REGULATION

Self-regulation, a component of self-determination, includes controlling one's emotions and behavior through the use of cognitive and social/emotional development (Palmer et al., 2013). Some students with disabilities have negative reactions to sensory input and consequently have difficulty with self-control. Students can be taught to calm down and manage impulses by learning to filter out distractions (Palmer et al., 2013). In addition, adults are also able to provide support by altering the environment that may be responsible for triggering unwanted sensory input such as the noise from a neighboring classroom.

Planning is a self-regulating behavior. In a study by Florez (2011), when preschool children were taught to plan their daily activities, there was an increased ability to monitor themselves. For instance, a child was asked what plan he could think of to help him remember to keep his hands to himself, and his idea was to sit on his hands to remind himself to stop distracting others.

Cultural factors are also considerations when promoting self-regulation skills. Although self-determinism is seen as a Eurocentric value, it can also be viewed in collectivist cultures where children are taught to be responsible, competent members of a group such as the family or community (Palmer et al., 2013). A culturally responsive collaboration between the school and family contributes to optimal self-development through consistent adult cues, environmental accommodations, and other supports. Student Activity 9.3 is used to remind students that they have the ability to self-regulate their behaviors.

Student Activity 9.3

I Am in Charge of Me

Directions: Divide an 8½ × 11" piece of paper into three sections. At the top of each column put a picture of a stop sign, a yield sign, and a green light. Under the stop sign, the student will write or draw behaviors that are not acceptable. Under the yield sign the student writes or draws pictures that represent behaviors that may create problems. Under the green light the student will identify replacement behaviors for the behaviors identified under the first two pictures. The paper can be laminated and each day the counselor or teacher can remind the student of the behaviors he/she can perform by saying: "Instead of the stop sign behavior X, I will instead do the green light behavior Y." Or, "Instead of the yield behavior A, I will instead do the green light behavior B."

Stop sign	*Yield sign*	*Green light*

Primary Areas of Focus on the IEP for the School Counselor in Transitional Programing for Older Students with Disabilities

The preceding discussion naturally leads to a delineation of the major areas of focus in transitional programming for adolescents with disabilities. The aforementioned topics become particularly relevant when viewed within the context of the three major areas addressed in the transition section of the IEP: (a) post-secondary education and training; (b) employment; and (c) independent living (Ohio Department of Education, 2012).

Before delineating information according to these three areas of focus, it should be noted that the Vocational Rehabilitation Services (VRS) is an organization of vital importance to all the areas of focus in transition planning. School counselors are able to serve as helpful liaisons for students who may qualify for these services, particularly since there is a possibility that the VRS counselor will continue to work with the student following high school graduation (Marshak et al., 2010). Another resource for students with disabilities in regard to all the areas of focus in transition planning is the Americans with Disabilities Act (ADA). Please refer to Chapter 2 for a discussion of ADA and the Americans with Disabilities Act Amendments (ADAA).

POST-SECONDARY EDUCATION AND TRAINING

There are numerous post-secondary opportunities available to students with disabilities, including but not limited to four-year colleges, two-year colleges, and technical and vocational schools/programs (Kochhar-Bryant, 2008). While there has been a noticeable increase in the number of students who indicate that they have some type of disability on the post-secondary education level, their rates for graduation are still considerably lower than those of non-disabled students (Heward, 2013). Clearly, specific and effective transition planning should be implemented to not only afford the students with disabilities the opportunity to attend college and post-secondary training options, but to complete their programs successfully.

A focus of school counselors at the secondary level is to assist students in preparing for post-secondary educational options. School counselors already assist students with choosing the appropriate courses for their post-secondary goals, as well as being an information resource and support in regard to providing information about specific post-secondary alternatives, entrance requirements, and the completion of applications to colleges or post-secondary training options (Kochhar-Bryant, 2008). As Marshak et al. (2010, p. 206) note: "Since school counselors are very familiar with helping students make the transition to post-secondary education, it makes sense to build on this foundational expertise while addressing areas that are exceptionally different for students with disabilities."

DISCLOSURE OF DISABILITY

One of these "exceptionally different" areas for students with disabilities to which Marshak et al. (2010) refer is the issue of students disclosing their disability status. Once students graduate from high school and matriculate to a post-secondary institution, the IEP does not transfer with them. "Despite its forward-looking purpose, IDEA has no jurisdiction after a student exits the K-12 school system" (National Center for Learning Disabilities, 2006, p. 1).

However, Title 11 of the ADA and Section 504 of the Rehabilitation Act are the laws that impact students in post-secondary schools (Marshak et al., 2010). Once admitted into a post-secondary institute, students will need to disclose their disability to receive accommodations. Post-secondary educational institutions are responsible for minimal accommodations, and services beyond what is considered appropriate may be the responsibility of the student (Marshak et al., 2010).

It is vital that the students are acutely aware of this issue as it is up to them to inform the institutional staff of their disabilities if they require accommodations. These institutions are not required to identify students who may have disabilities (US Department of Education, Office for Civil Rights, 2011). College disability services offices will assist students in revealing the information about their disabilities to specific instructional personnel, "but students are in control and must initiate the process" (National Center for Learning Disabilities, 2006, p. 3). The school counselor can be a point person in the provision of this key information to the students and their families.

The school counselor may also prove to be an invaluable resource in regard to the organization of the required documentation of the student's disability that may be provided to his/her post-secondary institution of choice. In fact, the focus of a report from the National Joint Committee on Learning Disabilities (2007, p. 12) was on "the disconnect between the nature and extent of disability documentation generated during a student's public school career and the documentation required at the post-secondary education level to access services." School counselors may be in a particularly favorable position to assist the students in avoiding this disconnect of information by assisting with this process.

It is essential that school counselors are aware that there is a requirement for students who receive services according to Part B of IDEA 2004 to be provided with a summary of such pertinent information. The law specifically requires that the student be provided with a summary of his/her "academic achievement and functional performance, which shall include recommendations on how to assist the child in meeting the child's post-secondary goals" (US Department of Education, n.d., P.L. 108–446, Part B, Section 614 [c] [5] [B] [ii]).

Conceptual Application Activity 9.2

Interview a student with disabilities who is attending a post-secondary institution. Ask the student the following questions:

1.   What was most helpful in your transition from secondary school to post-secondary training?
2.   What do you wish you had known prior to entering this institution?

3. What are some of the factors that made this transition problematic? What could have been done to help you navigate these barriers?

Share your answers with your peers.

Considering Accommodations and Services in Choosing the
Post-Secondary Options

The school counselor may make valuable contributions for the student with disabilities in regard to his/her choice of college/school/program. Available services and accommodations vary from school to school, and could be significant factors in helping students choose an institution or program. The school counselor may act as an information resource in assisting the students investigate appropriate post-secondary options, with particular emphasis on the support services and accommodations available to them (Baditoi & Brott, 2011; Marshak et al., 2010).

A number of accommodations and/or services may be appropriate for particular students to succeed on the post-secondary level, however, an in-depth discussion of these options is beyond the scope of this book. It is important to note, nonetheless, that "according to Section 504 of the Vocational Rehabilitation Act of 1973, post-secondary schools must modify program requirements that are discriminatory and allow for the use of auxiliary aids" (Milsom & Hartley, 2005, p. 438). Some of these auxiliary aids may include texts on tape or assigned individuals to take notes, or to sign for the students with deafness (Milsom & Hartley, 2005). Other accommodations may include extended time for exams and/or assignments and alternative assignments. In addition to assisting the student in the consideration of appropriate accommodations and services available at particular post-secondary environments, school counselors may function as liaisons with personnel from the post-secondary institutions being considered and assist the student to make connections with these individuals to obtain extra clarification and information about available services (Milsom & Hartley, 2005). Chapter 5 provides additional information on accommodations and modifications, and more information is available from http://doe.sd.gov/oess/documents/sped_section504_Guidelines.pdf.

As well as being a liaison, facilitator, and coordinator, school counselors are also valuable sources of information, particularly in assisting the student to see how career goals should guide the investigation into post-secondary alternatives (IRIS Center, n.d.a). Table 9.1 describes commonly held myths surrounding students with disabilities who are applying for and entering post-secondary institutions (Hamblet, 2014).

Individuals with intellectual and developmental disabilities (ID) are characterized by significant cognitive impairments (IQ of 70 or lower) and compromised behaviors that are exhibited before the age of 18. Students with ID are more likely to drop out of high school, yet school counselors need to have an awareness of various post-secondary programs that are available for these students (Cook et al., 2014). In 2008, the Higher Education Opportunity Act was passed that provided post-secondary educational options available for students with ID. As a result, college-based programs such as the Pathway program at the University of California, Los Angeles (UCLA) are available, in which students with ID attend mainstream college classes and campus activities, and in some cases provide opportunities to reside on campus. The Inclusive Concurrent

Table 9.1 Myths and Facts of College for Students with Disabilities

Myth	Reality
Competitive schools do not need to provide services for students with disabilities.	All colleges have to provide basic disability services. Some institutions have a special fee for services.
Colleges make admission adjustments for students with disabilities.	Colleges are not required to adjust admission standards. Students with disabilities must meet the same admission requirements.
College personnel are aware of students who have disabilities and make special arrangements for these students.	The only way students are able to receive accommodations or services is to apply for them. Documentation as to their disability is required. Students with learning disabilities will need to submit the most recent test (conducted within a specified timeframe) indicating a learning disability.
Students must apply for accommodations.	The student is able to decide whether or not to apply for services. Once applying for services, accommodations include extended time for exams, permission to record lectures, and note-takers. Technology such as "smart pens," or software that reads texts audibly, and calculators and spellcheckers may be allowed.
Trained learning disabilities specialists such as tutors are available.	These are not services that are required by law, but there are some specialists available on some campuses on a limited basis. Specialists may be available on a payment basis.

Enrollment (ICE) Partnership Program at the University of Massachusetts in Boston is another initiative that provides opportunities for students aged 18–22 with ID who are receiving special education services. Coaches from the high school facilitate the transition to the university and students audit or take college courses for credit. Furthermore, they participate in job shadowing and internships while being mentored by undergraduate students (Cook et al., 2014). School counselors are also able to assist students with ID through such interventions as group and individual counseling, cognitive-behavioral interventions, anxiety and stress reduction techniques, and positive self-talk.

INDIVIDUALS WITH DISABILITIES AND EMPLOYMENT

The ADA prohibits an employer from discriminating against an employee with disabilities, and mandates that employers provide reasonable accommodations to an employee unless there is an undue hardship in doing so. Despite the desire for students with disabilities to work after high school, unemployment remains high for these individuals. In a study by Simonsen and Neubert (2013), only 43 percent of transitioning youth with intellectual or other developmental disabilities were employed and earning at least a minimum wage. Employment opportunities are also influenced by additional variables such as individual characteristics, family and community, and transition planning services.

Other job opportunities may be limited for some students with disabilities such as those students with autism, due to their communication difficulties and recurring and constrained patterns of behavior. In a study that investigated employment for students with autism, more than half of these individuals who left high school participated in employment, although the majority were paid less than the minimum hour wage (Chiang et al., 2013). Family characteristics such as higher income, student characteristics such as higher levels of social skills, and the formation of a collaborative partnership between the school personnel and potential employers are factors that contribute to employment among students with autism (Chiang et al., 2013).

Work-Based Learning Activities and Agency Partnerships
The possibility of work-based learning experiences while the students are still in school may prove to be beneficial for some students. "Participation in work-based learning is associated with successful outcomes for youth with disabilities" (Kochhar-Bryant, 2008, p. 414). The school counselor can play an instrumental role in establishing partnerships with employers for such work-based learning opportunities, which may even lead to potential job placements (IRIS Center, n.d.b).

The IRIS Center (n.d.b, para. 2) provides a listing of examples of work-based learning activities:

• Work-site tours.
• Job-shadowing assignments.
• Service learning with a career component.
• Unpaid internship or mentorship (high school and post-high school).
• Paid internship or work study (high school and post-high school).

The school counselor may also take the lead on assisting in the formation of partnerships with key agencies with which the student could become involved during high school and into his/her adult life. In addition to the aforementioned VRS, school counselors can facilitate a connection with such employment-related community organizations as job placement agencies, regional offices for the Department of Labor, and apprenticeship programs. These linkages should be made before the student leaves high school and addressed in the transition process to ensure that these connections are in place for the student's assistance and support (IRIS Center, n.d.b).

Types of Employment
Clearly, students with disabilities should have the same access to employment opportunities as their non-disabled counterparts. As you are aware from previous discussions, the ADA provides essential protections for individuals with disabilities who are qualified for the employment in question.

> The ADA considers an individual with a disability (an employee or job applicant) to be qualified if he or she meets the skill, experience, education, and other job-related requirements of the position in question and can execute the essential functions of the job with or without the use of reasonable accommodations.
> (Marshak et al., 2010, p. 205)

Although school counselors clearly have the expertise in supporting students to reach their employment goals, it is important for them to also become familiar with some specialized employment options available to students with disabilities whose needs require such adaptations. Particularly for students with more involved disabilities, there are three general types of employment opportunities that are often discussed, again depending on the individual's strengths and needs.

The first is *competitive* employment, which is described as employment with "competitive wages and responsibilities" (Kochhar-Bryant, 2008, p. 416). In this type of employment, there is generally no long-term assistance required for the individual with a disability to learn or maintain the job requirements (Kochhar-Bryant, 2008).

The second category of employment is referred to as *supported* employment, which involves the individual working at a job with pay but with the provision of long-term assistance and support (Pierangelo & Giuliani, 2004). An example of how this ongoing support may be provided is through the services of a job coach, who may be involved with on-the-job training and providing assistance related to other areas such as interactions with other employees and transportation concerns (Hallahan et al., 2009).

The third general category of employment options is *sheltered* employment for students whose needs are not adequately met through the other employment options. With this model, individuals work in a separate center and are generally not integrated with workers without disabilities. Pierangelo and Giuliani (2004) note that there is evidence from models of supported employment that individuals with more involved disabilities can be employed in the community if they receive appropriate assistance and support. These authors also point out that many programs with sheltered employment are being modified to include integrated alternatives.

Conceptual Application Activity 9.3

Interview an employer who has hired a student with disabilities to work in his/her place of employment. What are some of the benefits that have arisen from this decision? What are some of the issues that were created with this hire? Discuss your answers with your peers.

Clearly, school counselors should have a working knowledge of employment issues regarding students with disabilities and assist them in making the transition from school to the world of work, if this is the appropriate option for them. School counselors also work with parents and educators of students with disabilities to facilitate their transition from high school by: (a) informing others that graduating from high school is associated with greater employment opportunities; (b) discussing graduation requirements and diploma options; and (c) providing career awareness opportunities to students as early as elementary school.

INDEPENDENT LIVING SKILLS

The third category addressed on the transition portion of the IEP focuses on independent living skills. Self-determination, self-awareness, and self-advocacy are essential skills for independent living for students with disabilities, and the school counselor plays a critical role in assisting in their attainment. These skills and attributes will be invaluable to the students as they work toward independent living, and the school counselor can assist students to strengthen them by working with the students on such activities/behaviors as decision-making, negotiating, and problem-solving (IRIS Center, n.d.c).

In addition to self-determination, social skills are vital to a student's success in independent living. "School counselors should help students understand the impact of social skills in all environments and the rationale for learning appropriate behaviors" (IRIS Center, n.d.c, para. 5). With the attainment of self-determination and appropriate social skills, the student will have increased likelihood to be successful in independent living, including residential options (IRIS Center, n.d.c).

Individuals with disabilities have access to the same residential alternatives as their counterparts without disabilities. However, for those individuals who require something more, various options are available. As Heward (2013) notes, a continuum of residential alternatives may be found in the community, including living in apartments with varying degrees of supervision, foster homes, or group homes.

Independent living also includes recreational and leisure activities (Heward, 2013), as well as having access to and working with agencies for adult services. The focus of some adult service organizations is pointedly on assisting individuals with disabilities to function more independently. These agencies may emphasize various aspects of daily living, including social services, rehabilitation options, and mental health assistance (Hardman et al., 2008).

Conclusion

In the position statement entitled *The Professional School Counselor and Students with Disabilities*, the ASCA notes that among the activities for school counselors to engage with students with disabilities is the activity of "providing assistance with developing academic and transition plans for students in the IEP as appropriate" (ASCA, 2013, p. 49). This chapter addressed a number of pertinent issues in this regard, both for the transition from preschool to kindergarten and from high school to post-secondary life. School counselors may play an invaluable role in the transition process by focusing on the concepts, activities, and areas of emphasis discussed herein. Their educational background and expertise provide a strong foundation for fulfilling the role functions of: (a) resource for information and contacts; (b) coordinator of services and educational options for the students to assist in the preparation for the transition to the next phase of their lives; (c) liaison between the school and greater community to assist the students in the realization of their goals; (d) advocate for the students in pursuing and achieving their transition goals; and (e) facilitator to the students with disabilities in acquiring and maintaining essential skills such as self-advocacy and self-determination.

References

Akos, P. (2003). Transition programming. *ASCA School Counselor*, 15–19.

Annual Disability Statistics Compendium (2013). Table 11.8: Special education-change in graduation rate among students serviced under IDEA. Retrieved from http://disabilitycompendium.org/compendium-statistics/special-education/11-8-special-education-change-in-graduation-rate-among-students-ages-14-21-served-under-idea-part-b.

ASCA (2013). *The Professional School Counselor and Students with Disabilities.* Retrieved from www.schoolcounselor.org/asca/media/asca/PositionStatements/PS_Disabilities.pdf.

Baditoi, B. E. & Brott, P. E. (2011). *What School Counselors Need to Know About Special Education and Students with Disabilities.* Arlington, VA: Council for Exceptional Children.

Carter, E. W., Brock, M. E., & Trainor, A. A. (2014). Transition assessment and planning for youth with severe intellectual and developmental disabilities. *Journal of Special Education, 47*, 245–255.

Chiang, H., Cheung, Y. K., Li, H., & Tsai, L. Y. (2013). Factors associated with participation in employment for high school leavers with autism. *Journal of Autism Developmental Disorder, 43*, 832–1842.

Cook, A. L., Hayden, L. A., & Wilczenski, F. L. (2014). Focusing on ability, not disability. *Counseling Today*, May, 57–61.

Division for Early Childhood (2014). *DEC Recommended Practices in Early Intervention/Early Childhood Special Education 2014.* Retrieved from www.dec-sped.org/recommendedpractices.

Fenlon, A. (2011). Road map for a dream, how can schools and families ease the transition into kindergarten for children with disabilities? *Educational Leadership, 68*(7), 23–26.

Fleming, A. R. & Fairweather, J. S. (2012). The role of postsecondary education in the path from high school to work for youth with disabilities. *Rehabilitation Counseling Bulletin, 55*, 54–81.

Florez, I. R. (2011). *Developing Young Children's Regulation Through Everyday Experiences.* Retrieved from www.naeyc.org/files/yc/file/201107/Self-Regulation_Florez_OnlineJuly2011.pdf.

Gargiulo, R. & Kilgo, J. (2005). *Young Children with Special Needs*, 2nd edn. Clifton Park, NY: Thomson Delmar Learning.

Hallahan, D. P., Kauffman, J. M., & Pullen, P. C. (2009). *Exceptional Learners: An Introduction to Special Education*, 11th edn. Boston, MA: Pearson Education, Inc.

Hamblet, E. C. (2014). Dispel the myths. *ASCA School Counselor*, 13–17.

Hardman, M. L., Drew, C. J., & Egan, M. W. (2008). *Human Exceptionality: School, Community, and Family*, 9th edn. Boston, MA: Houghton Mifflin Company.

Heward, W. M. (2013). *Exceptional Children: An Introduction to Special Education*, 10th edn. Upper Saddle River, NJ: Pearson Education, Inc.

Individuals with Disabilities Education Improvement Act, Public Law 108–446 (2004). *An Act to Reauthorize the Individuals with Disabilities Education Act, and for Other Purposes. Title I: Amendments to the Individuals with Disabilities Education Act.* Retrieved from www.copyright.gov/legislation/pl108446.pdf.

IRIS Center (n.d.a). What is the school counselor's responsibility in the transition planning process? Page 6: Post-secondary preparation: education/ training. In *School Counselors: Facilitating Transitions for Students with Disabilities from High School to Post-School Settings (Module)*, IRIS Center, Peabody College, Vanderbilt University. Retrieved from http://iris.peabody.vanderbilt.edu/module/cou2/cresource/what-is-the-school-counselors-responsibility-in-the-transition-planning-process/cou2_06/#content.

IRIS Center (n.d.b). What is the school counselor's responsibility in the transition planning process? Page 7: Post-secondary preparation: employment. In *School Counselors: Facilitating Transitions for Students with Disabilities from High School to Post-School Settings (Module)*, IRIS Center, Peabody College, Vanderbilt University. Retrieved from http://iris.peabody.vanderbilt.edu/module/cou2/cresource/what-is-the-school-counselors-responsibility-in-the-transition-planning-process/cou2_07/#content.

IRIS Center (n.d.c). What is the school counselor's responsibility in the transition planning process? Page 8: Post-secondary preparation: independent living. In *School Counselors: Facilitating Transitions for Students with Disabilities from High School to Post-School Settings (Module)*, IRIS Center, Peabody College, Vanderbilt University. Retrieved from http://iris.peabody.vanderbilt.edu/module/cou2/cresource/what-is-the-school-counselors-responsibility-in-the-transition-planning-process/cou2_08/#content.

Kochhar-Bryant, C. A. (2008). *Collaboration and System Coordination for Students with Special Needs, from Early Childhood to the Postsecondary Years.* Upper Saddle River, NJ: Pearson Education, Inc.

La Paro, K. M., Pianta, R. C., & Cox, M. J. (2000). Teachers' reported transition practices for children transitioning into kindergarten and first grade. *Exceptional Children*, 67(1), 7–20.

Luckner, J. L. & Sebald, A. M. (2013). Promoting self-determination of students who are deaf or hard of hearing. *American Annals of the Deaf*, 158, 377–386.

Marshak, L. E., Dandeneau, C. J., Prezant, F. P., & L'Amoreaux, N. A. (2010). *The School Counselor's Guide to Helping Students with Disabilities*. San Francisco, CA: Jossey-Bass.

Milsom, A. & Akos, P. (2003). Students with disabilities: school counselor involvement and preparation. *Professional School Counseling*, 5, 331–338.

Milsom, A. & Hartley, M. T. (2005). Assisting students with learning disabilities transitioning to college: what school counselors should know. *Professional School Counseling*, 8(5), 436–441.

National Center for Learning Disabilities (2006). *Transition to College: Strategic Planning to Ensure Success for Students with Learning Disabilities*. Retrieved from www.lausd.net/lausd/offices/spec_ed/_dots/Options_While_In_School/Parent_Advocacy_Brief_Transition_to_College.pdf.

National Center for Learning Disabilities (2013). *Diplomas at Risk: A Critical Look at the Graduation Rate of Students with Learning Disabilities*. Retrieved from www.ncld.org/images/content/files/diplomas-at-risk/DiplomasatRisk.pdf.

National Joint Committee on Learning Disabilities (2007). *The Documentation Disconnect for Students with Learning Disabilities: Improving Access to Postsecondary Disability Services*. Retrieved from www.council-for-learning-disabilities.org/wp-content/uploads/2013/11/NJCLDDisconnect2007.pdf.

Ohio Department of Education (2012). *IEP Individualized Education Program, PR-07 IEP FORM*. Retrieved from http://education.ohio.gov/getattachment/Topics/Special-Education/Federal-and-State-Requirements/Procedures-and-Guidance/Individualized-Education-Program-IEP/Development-of-IEP/iep_form_09_static.pdf.aspx.

Palmer, S. B., Summers, J. A., Brotherson, M. J., Erwin, E. J., Maude, S. P., Stroup-Rentier, V., Wu, H., Peck, N. F., Zheng, Y., Weigel, C., Chu, S., McGrath, G. S., & Haines, S. J. (2013). Foundations for self-determination in early childhood: an inclusive model for children with disabilities. *Topics in Early Childhood Special Education*, 33, 38–47.

Pierangelo, R. & Giuliani, G. A. (2004). *Transition Services in Special Education: A Practical Approach*. Boston, MA: Pearson Education, Inc.

Rosenberg M. S., Westling, D. L., & McLeskey, J. (2011). *Special Education for Today's Teachers: An Introduction*, 2nd edn. Upper Saddle River, NJ: Pearson Education, Inc.

Santrock, J. W. (2012). *A Topical Approach to Life-Span Development*, 6th edn. New York: McGraw-Hill.

Simonsen, M. L. & Neubert, D. A. (2013). Transitioning youth with intellectual and other developmental disabilities: predicting community employment outcomes. *Career Development for Exceptional Individuals*, 36, 188–198.

Test, D. W., Fowler, C. H., Wood, W. M., Brewer, D. M., & Eddy, S. (2005). A conceptual framework of self-advocacy for students with disabilities. *Remedial and Special Education*, 26, 43–54.

Trainor, A. A. (2005). Self-determination perceptions and behaviors of diverse students with LD during the transition planning process. *Journal of Learning Disabilities*, 38, 233–248.

US Department of Education (n.d.). *Building the Legacy: IDEA 2004*. P. L. 108–446, Part B, Section 614 [c] [5] [B] [ii]. Retrieved from http://idea.ed.gov/explore/view/p/%2Croot%2Cstatute%2CI%2CB%2C614%2C.

US Department of Education (2007). *Parents/My Child's Special Needs: A Guide to the Individualized Education Program*. Retrieved from www2.ed.gov/parents/needs/speced/iepguide/index.html?exp=3.

US Department of Education, Office for Civil Rights (2011). *Transition of Students with Disabilities to Postsecondary Education: A Guide for High School Educators*. Retrieved from www2.ed.gov/about/offices/list/ocr/transitionguide.html.

Vicker, B. (2009). *Moving from Preschool to Kindergarten: Planning for a Successful Transition and New Relationships*. Bloomington, IN: Indiana Resource Center for Autism. Retrieved from http://iidc.indiana.edu/?pageId=415.

Wehmeyer, M. E., Palmer, S. B., Shogren, K., Williams-Diehm, K., & Soukup, J. H. (2013). Establishing a causal relationship between intervention to promote self-determination and enhanced student self-determination. *The Journal of Special Education*, 46, 195–210.

Wilmshurst, L. & Brue, A. W. (2010). *The Complete Guide to Special Education: Proven Advice on Evaluation, IEPs, and Helping Kids Succeed*, 2nd edn. San Francisco, CA: Jossey-Bass, John Wiley & Sons, Inc.

Wrightslaw (2013). *Transition, Transition Services, Transition Planning*. Retrieved from www. wrightslaw.com/info/trans.index.htm.

10 Support for Teachers and Educational Personnel Working with Students with Disabilities

The following CACREP standards are addressed in this chapter:

PROFESSIONAL COUNSELING ORIENTATION AND ETHICAL PRACTICE
c. counselors' roles and responsibilities as members of interdisciplinary community outreach and emergency management response teams
e. advocacy processes needed to address institutional and social barriers that impede access, equity, and success for clients
j. technology's impact on the counseling profession

COUNSELING AND HELPING RELATIONSHIPS
k. strategies to promote client understanding of and access to a variety of community-based resources

ENTRY-LEVEL SPECIALTY AREAS: SCHOOL COUNSELING FOUNDATIONS
d. models of school-based collaboration and consultation

CONTEXTUAL DIMENSIONS
d. school counselor roles in school leadership and multidisciplinary teams

3. PRACTICE
l. techniques to foster collaboration and teamwork within schools

Chapter Objectives

After you have completed this chapter you should be able to:

- Identify the impact of school culture and climate on academic achievement.
- Discuss the role of the school counselor in Response to Intervention.
- Recognize the role of the school counselor in School-Wide Positive Behavior Intervention and Support.
- Name individuals who are able to assist with students with disabilities.
- Identify collaboration strategies.

Imagine entering a well-lit, clean school building, and as you check in at the front office, where a welcoming secretary assists you in signing in, you notice the school principal having a friendly conversation with one of the teachers. As you walk down the hall, you notice a poster that describes the attitudes and behaviors that are expected of all students, and you observe students from different ethnicities and racial groups heading to class engaged in friendly laughter and joking.

Now, compare this scene with the description of the next school.

As you enter the school building you notice garbage overflowing from the trash can placed outside the school entrance. In trying to locate the front office, you ask directions from a teacher dressed in jeans and a T-shirt, who is berating a student for missing a homework assignment. She barely looks up to see who is addressing her, and unconcernedly points in the direction of the office. Once you enter the main office you notice that chairs with broken rungs and torn vinyl are carelessly placed in the office area. The secretary looks up from her desk when you approach, yet continues to complete what she was working on without acknowledging your presence.

As you are able to recognize, each of these schools displays a different climate and culture; related terms in that both influence students' academic, career, and social/emotional development. But, there are differences. *School culture* is the shared beliefs and attitudes that teachers and administrators hold about teaching and learning, and give the school a standard for behavior. The culture also includes fundamental expectations regarding meetings, professional development opportunities, attitudes toward change, the way the building is decorated and maintained, and how administrators and other educators interact (Best Practice Briefs, 2004). These underlying assumptions and attitudes influence the school structure and organization.

However, *school climate* refers to the "feel" of the school including the physical, social, academic, and affective dimensions, as shown in Table 10.1.

Stakeholder perceptions of the school climate influence their attitudes, behaviors, and standards, and impact interactions and achievement. For instance, if an individual feels disrespected, it is likely this belief will adversely influence his/her behavior. An angry student who repeatedly gets into trouble may view his/her school climate as more negative than peers who feel supported and positively regarded (Loukas, 2007). Or, a teacher who is targeted for not making the expected adequate yearly progress may feel affronted and disgruntled with the school system.

School connectedness is related to feelings of belonging and friendships, and associated with student outcomes. The Search Institute (Best Practice Briefs, 2004), revealed that an attentive school environment is connected with higher grades and better attendance, higher self-esteem and self-concept, less anxiety and depression, and reduced substance abuse among students. Interdisciplinary collaborative relationships enhance the school climate and the corresponding concept of school culture. A discussion of collaborative partnerships is in the following section.

Table 10.1 Dimensions of School Climate

Physical dimension	Social dimension	Academic dimension	Affective dimension
Appearance of the classrooms and building	Quality of interpersonal relationships	Quality of instruction	Caring, responsive, and supportive
Student/teacher ratio	Equitable treatment of students	Educator expectations for student success	Feelings of safety and trust
School size	Degree of rivalry and social comparison among students	Monitoring and assessing student progress and providing immediate feedback	Feelings of belonging and openness to diversity
Classroom management	Collaborative decision-making among stakeholders		Sense of respect
Resource availability			Perception of warm, inviting environment

Collaboration for Student Success

It is unreasonable for any one person to address the wide range of difficulties presented by students (Bronstein, 2002), yet educators tend to work independently from one another, which often results in diminished or redundant student services. However, collaboration provides an opportunity to work in a partnership so that services can be shared among professionals. This distribution of services is increasingly important since student–provider ratios often far exceed the recommended ratios of professional organizations. For instance, the American School Counselor Association (ASCA) recommends a student/counselor ratio of 250:1, whereas most states far exceed this standard, with California having the highest ratio of more than 1,000:1. With the numerous social/emotional, career, and academic concerns our students bring into the school setting, the need for collaboration on behalf of all students—particularly those with disabilities—has never been greater (Bronstein, 2002).

School counselors are uniquely trained in collaboration skills, yet trying to get faculty to commit to a partnership is one of the most difficult jobs a school counselor encounters (Ryan et al., 2011). Educators are already faced with increasing demands, and are often resentful when asked to engage in one more responsibility, such as an additional meeting. A few of the educational interdisciplinary professionals and their role in supporting students with disabilities are listed in Table 10.2.

Effective collaboration involves flexibility in looking at issues from multiple perspectives and blending resources to support the academic and wellness needs of youth. When concerns are coordinated multiple advantages include: (a) knowledge about the skills and aptitude of other team members (Mellin et al., 2011); (b) a decrease in fragmented services and increased treatment protocol (Conoley & Conoley, 1991); (c) a greater acceptance of strategies that are determined cooperatively rather than prescribed; and (d) a reliable strategy for general education teachers who work with students with disabilities.

Table 10.2 List of Collaborative Team Members

Team member	Professional role
Professional school counselor	Professional school counselors support the academic, career, and post-secondary education, and social/emotional growth of all students (ASCA, 2013, para. 1).
General education teacher	Educators teach students in the general curriculum and students with disabilities are often placed in these classes as stipulated in the individualized education program (IEP).
School psychologist	School psychologists collaborate with educators, parents, and other professionals to strengthen connections for all students.
School nurse	School nurses advance students' personal wellness, academic achievement, and safety.
Occupational therapist	Occupational therapists promote well-being and health and help children with disabilities to participate in school and social situations.
Physical therapist	Physical therapists teach others how to prevent or manage their physical conditions by developing programs for healthy living.
Speech therapist	Speech therapists work with students on conversational skills, appropriate body language, and recognition of affect.
Adapted physical educator	Trained to understand disabilities and characteristics, and improve physical activity and health outcomes through physical education through an understanding of individual needs.
Special education teacher	Special education teachers ensure that students with disabilities receive the best possible education and educate others to promote this goal.
School resource officer	School resource officers (SROs) partner with school professionals to provide safer schools.
School social worker	School social workers work with others in the school to assist with youth with specific social, psychological, emotional, or physical problems that contribute to academic difficulties.
School administrators	School administrators enforce policies, collaborate with parents and faculty, evaluate teachers, and supervise programs.
Vocational rehabilitation counselor	Assists with individuals with disabilities on social/emotional issues and post-secondary plans.

School counselors are able to teach strategies to team members about characteristics of students with various disabilities. A few qualities of students with disabilities and strategies for assisting these students are listed below:

- *Inability to recognize personal space.* Students with autism spectrum disorder (ASD) and other disabilities have difficulty understanding personal boundaries, which may make people uncomfortable when personal distance is too close or too far away from them. Significant adults can use concrete props to teach personal space such as a hula-hoop around the student to concretely demonstrate appropriate distance, or utilize puppets to validate appropriate space in various situations (McCalley, 2010).

- *Lack of recognition of facial expressions and body language.* For these students, visuals such as clipart that aren't copyright protected, or photographs of people expressing various emotions can be used to convey various feelings. Or, role-playing various postures and facial expressions are also methods of teaching affect (McCalley, 2010).
- *Lack of understanding of others' perspectives.* To teach others' views, social stories, comic strip conversations in which bubbles above the character's head are filled in with thoughts, can depict thoughts and feelings. Or, puppets made from popsicle sticks that represent the student and peers can be used in a role play to depict appropriate behaviors in various situations.
- *Difficulty with change.* Creating calendars that contain visual images on days that there is a change in the daily routine are reminders of a schedule variation (McCalley, 2010). Or one-sheet wonders (OSW), one-page reminders that either list or depict three strategies or images for handling a schedule change such as an assembly, serve as a quick reminder to manage change (Goodman-Scott & O'Rorke-Trigiani, 2013).
- *Frequent frustrations and acting-out behaviors.* For students that have uncontrollable outbursts of anger, locating a cool-down spot where they are able to choose an object that serves as a reminder to cool down assists in controlling outbursts. Or designing several cards in which the student is able to select a card with pictures of strategies for calming down may also remind the student to implement the strategy on the card (McCalley, 2010). These cards are made from heavy paper or card stock and cut into small cards by or for the student to serve as reminders for exhibiting appropriate behaviors (Goodman-Scott & O'Rorke-Trigiani, 2013). On one side of the card is a reinforcing image chosen by the student, such as a football professional. An image of the desired behavior is on the other side of the card, such as staying seated at the desk. The football player image is placed face side up on the student's desk to serve as a reminder of the behavior that is desired. The teacher or other significant individual could unobtrusively point to the reinforcing image as a reminder as he/she walks by the student's desk.
- *Difficulty with interpersonal conversations.* Puppets could be used to practice conversational skills with guidance from the school counselor. Or, tossing a beanbag back and forth with the directive that only the person holding the beanbag can speak teaches appropriate interpersonal communication (McCalley, 2010).

Professional roles, structural characteristics, collaborators' personal characteristics, and history of interdisciplinary collaboration are additional factors that support or impede interdisciplinary efforts.

Professional Roles

Too often professionals take a territorial stance that precludes their ability to share tasks, yet when skills and knowledge are shared, a more robust, unique outcome results. At times, mutual reliance involves a balancing act in which individual members have to relinquish a share of their personal autonomy while relying upon the expertise of others. Effective collaboration includes a clear understanding of one another's role, professional jargon, role perceptions, limits of confidentiality, and available time (Mellin et al., 2011). Most individuals on a collaborative team are not bound by the ethics of confidentiality, and therefore have the mistaken notion that school counselors are withholding valuable information. To assuage these beliefs, the school counselor has a responsibility to explain his/her ethical obligation in regard to confidentiality.

Attention to cultural differences also contributes to how well collaboration will occur. For instance, some cultures resolve conflicts differently from others, and recognizing these differences may impact the final outcome (Worchel, 2005, cited in Murawski & Spencer, 2011). In Korea and other Asian countries, it is considered rude to question a person during a lecture, whereas in Western societies questions are expected and encouraged. Case Study 10.1 emphasizes the importance of a team effort to maximize the assistance students receive.

Case Study 10.1

As a school counselor, I am involved with many aspects of special education, and all are important. For instance, I ensure students receive their IEP accommodations during testing and that the students are scheduled for the correct classes for graduation. Yet, my greatest impact is when I identify and advocate for students who need additional supports and services. For example, I worked with a student with whom I formed a good relationship. One day she expressed suicidal thoughts, and due to the severity of these thoughts, she was hospitalized for over a week. During that week, I worked with my principal to set up a support team meeting, and upon her return to school, we met with the school psychologist, her parents, and special teacher. During this meeting I shared the student's strengths and areas of concern based on my observations. Other team members provided additional views and we decided to pursue further testing. Based on the tests she qualified as "emotionally disturbed" and eligible for special services, which were included on her IEP in addition to supplemental supports and services. I continue to be part of the IEP team to determine the best supports and services for this student.

High school counselor

Structural Characteristics

Structural characteristics refer to the provision of administrative support, professional autonomy, an allowance for space and time, and encouragement (Bronstein, 2003, cited in Mellin et al., 2011). Administrators who support collaborative efforts by providing sufficient time and space for meetings to occur, sufficient funding, or even serving as a member of the collaborative team impart the importance of these relationships. In addition for time to conduct meetings, time is also necessary for all members to share perceptions, feelings, and assessments (Mellin et al., 2011) to reflect on the process during each meeting and again at the conclusion of the group. In a study by Mellin et al. (2011), professionals noted that when they spent time reflecting on meeting dynamics including *how* they work together, *what* could be improved, and *how* the process could be strengthened, collaboration was improved.

Figure 10.1 Collaboration provides an opportunity to work in a partnership so that services can be shared among professionals.

Source: ©*iStockphoto.com, www.istockphoto.com/photo/middle-school-43033480.*

Personal Characteristics

Personal characteristics of individual members also influence the process. Trust among members grows when there is a belief and expectation that all collaborators will fulfill their responsibilities. Effective communication between members, between members and their organizations, and between the members and the greater community is integral to the development of trust.

Moreover, optimistic personalities construct a positive perspective for educators engaged in the demanding work of instructing students with disabilities. These personalities aid in reframing negative attributes such as "lazy" or "manipulative" that some teachers ascribe to students. These adverse labels may be altered when the characteristic is relabeled, such as "laid back" or "cautious," with a focus on what the student does well rather than concentrating on the negative label (Conoley & Conoley, 2010).

History of Collaboration

Finally, experiences members have had with previous collaborative processes impact how well collaborators are willing to invest their time and expertise in future partnerships (Bronstein, 2003, cited in Mellin et al., 2011). If there is a perception that personal goals did not integrate with the collective ownership of goals from previous partnerships, potential members will have difficulty agreeing to participate in future collaborative measures.

Collaboration between professionals and parents/guardians contributes to resources for teaching and reinforcing academic, vocational, and social/emotional growth. Some students with disabilities may not receive services for special education if the disability does not negatively affect academics. For instance, some students may not qualify for school-based services, and therefore it may be important to seek out community resources and people to support continuing academic achievement (McCalley, 2010) for students who need services but do not qualify.

Schools are primary institutions for assisting youth with disabilities, and several legislative mandates have been initiated to improve the academic growth of students. In addition to the individualized education plan (IEP) that was discussed in previous chapters, Response to Intervention (RTI) and School-Wide Positive Behavioral Interventions and Supports (SW-PBIS) are two additional federal mandates that require interdisciplinary collaboration. An overview of these approaches was previously addressed in Chapter 4; however, the information provided in that chapter was discussed more in relation to the identification of a suspected disability, in particular specific learning disabilities (SLD). The information presented in this chapter addresses more specifically the role of school counselors as they contribute to these initiatives.

The School Counselor and Response to Intervention

As you are aware from the discussion in Chapter 4, in 2004 the Individuals with Disabilities Educational Improvement Act (IDEIA) mandated that schools implement a systematic method to identify and institute interventions with students who are struggling academically. Response to Intervention (RTI), also known as Response to Instruction or Responsiveness to Instruction (Murawski & Spencer, 2011), was developed to address this requirement. The intention behind RTI is to identify and provide support services to students early before they lag so far behind that they are eventually identified with a disability. Rather than focusing on student deficiencies, this initiative emphasizes students' abilities and strengths (Fletcher & Vaughn, 2009, cited in Shepard et al., 2013).

RTI consists of three levels of intervention, with each level embodying one or more tiers of intervention (Shepard et al., 2013). (Formerly, "tiers" were used to describe each of the different interventions. However, the Center on Response to Intervention (n.d.) now uses the term "level" with different tiers of intervention within each level, see Figure 10.2.)

To review from Chapter 4, RTI is a data-driven framework in which students at risk for emotional or behavioral problems receive the attention and assistance that they need based on empirically based individualized instruction and systemic interventions (Murawski & Spencer, 2011). The framework is created with the premise that all educational personnel are involved in the implementation of RTI, including school counselors. As stated by the ASCA position statement (ASCA, 2014, para. 1), "professional school counselors are stakeholders in the development and implementation of multi-tiered systems of support (MTSS) … Professional school counselors align their work with MTSS through the implementation of a comprehensive school counseling program designed to improve student achievement and behavior."

The effectiveness of RTI is evident in that there has recently been a decline in referrals to special education programs from approximately 4.5 percent to 2.5 percent (Dunn,

2010, cited in Grant & Ray, 2013). Furthermore, in a study by Cheney et al. (2008, cited in Froiland, 2011), elementary students deemed to be "at risk" responded well to RTI interventions and, as a result, learned appropriate ways of responding that prevented them from developing problems (Froiland, 2011). Students who are unable to respond to preventive measures and interventions within each level are given increased support and individualized instruction.

Level 1: Primary Prevention Services

Curricular, preventive, research-based programs such as *Second Step: A Violence Prevention Curriculum* are provided to all students in the general education classroom (Gruman & Hoelzen, 2011). This curriculum addresses topics such as empathy, impulse control, problem-solving, and anger management with activities designed for students to generalize skills outside of the classroom (Mindess et al., 2008). In a study by Bogdan et al. (1996), identified students in the second, fourth, and fifth grades participated in the Second Step Curriculum, and at the end of the intervention, students showed marked improvements in discipline issues, ability to mediate conflicts, and cooperation. In another study, Durlak et al. (2011, cited in Shepard et al., 2013) analyzed various RTI programs that were designed to improve students' social skills, and as a result of these programs significant gains in skills were revealed with a decline in troublesome behavior and emotional anxiety.

Through RTI interventions, all students are monitored by universal screening, and approximately 80–95 percent of the students respond to interventions at this level (Shepard et al., 2013). Students who are not responding to this level of intervention are given additional support, and if an identified student still does not meet the established standards then he/she will be provided more concentrated intervention at level 2.

Level 2: Secondary Prevention Services

Approximately 5–15 percent of the student population is identified as needing the more intense interventions found at level 2 and receive these services in tandem with level 1 interventions. Level 2 interventions are individually targeted to the specific needs of each student, and include such strategies as small-group instruction, tutoring, speech, physical therapy, and/or individual or group counseling. If the student responds appropriately at this level, he/she will return to level 1 interventions (Shepard et al., 2013). *The First Step to Success* program is a successful level 2 approach designed to improve anti-social behaviors (Frey et al., 2013) such as oppositional defiant disorder, temper tantrums, and confrontations with their peers. Frequent assessments monitor the extent to which students are responding to interventions (Gruman & Hoelzen, 2011), and parents are informed of their child's progress within this level. However, if these supports are not effective, the student may move to the third level of intervention (Ryan et al., 2011).

Level 3: Tertiary Prevention Services

Level 3 is marked by more intense individualized interventions. Approximately 5 percent of the students who did not respond to interventions at the previous levels will need the more in-depth interventions that have proven to be effective at this level. And it is possible that behavior management plans, and coordination with community and

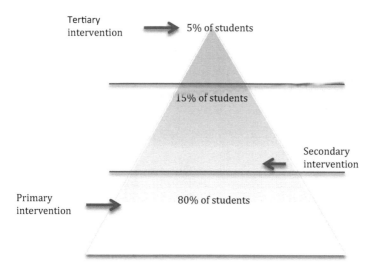

Figure 10.2 Depiction of students served through Response to Intervention. Note that the term "tier" was originally used to describe the various phases of intervention and screening. The National Center on Response to Intervention (NCRTI) now uses the term "level" with different tiers of intervention within each level.

mental health facilities that are able to provide services above and beyond the scope of the school may be necessary (Gruman & Hoelzen, 2011). If the student responds well to the intervention, this intercession may be discontinued. However, students who do not respond may be referred for special education (Murawski & Spencer, 2011; Shepard et al., 2013). Figure 10.2 illustrates the various levels.

School counselors are often involved in the following strategies to address individual needs at the different levels and tiers of intervention:

- Providing group and individual counseling regarding the influence of the disability on academic performance.
- Conducting family counseling and parenting skills.
- Teaching and practicing anger management skills.
- Demonstrating and practicing relaxation skills.
- Teaching social skills.
- Using social stories and comic strip conversations.
- Engaging in role play exercises.
- Video-recording appropriate behaviors and emotion recognition.

In addition to the strategies above, school counselors also assist in creating self-management plans to replace an undesirable behavior with one that is desired. Self-management includes encouraging students to establish their own goals, self-observe behavior, and reinforce self when progress is made toward the goal. One self-management plan is to identify a desired target behavior. The student identifies possible reinforcers (e.g., stickers, extra recess minutes, etc.) when the target behavior is demonstrated, and a simple, easy recording form is developed for the student to use. Time is spent to ensure that the student understands how to record on the form, to assess the student's ability to accurately record time on-task, and to monitor appropriate reinforcers. Successes are celebrated on a regular basis. Making decisions and setting goals based on personal values and consequences influences personal goals. Student Activity 10.1 is an example of a goal-setting worksheet that can be adopted for students.

Student Activity 10.1

My Goals

Directions: Adopt the following worksheet to match the developmental level of the student, and either ask the student to write down his/her goals, or if the student is unable to do so, you can write down the answers provided by the student. Or, as an alternative, the student can draw pictures or cut suitable pictures out of magazines and place them in the appropriate spaces.

	Goals	Short-term	Long-term	Obstacles to overcome in reaching goals	Completion date
Academic					
Family					
Social/ emotional					
Career					

As previously indicated in Chapter 4, SW-PBIS is similar to RTI in that a range of interventions are systematically provided as preventive strategies to teach appropriate behaviors based on individual levels of need (PBIS World, 2014).

School-Wide Positive Behavioral Interventions and Supports

This multilevel approach emphasizes a positive school culture with a focus on prevention. SW-PBIS (sometimes called Positive Behavioral Supports, PBS) is structured to meet the culture and climate of each individual school, yet regardless of the program that is implemented in the school, there are five comprehensively accepted components (Curtis et al., 2010) that are found in every program, which include:

- A leadership team.
- An accepted school philosophy.
- Behavioral guidelines that apply to specific school areas.
- Specific classroom rules.
- Identified strategies for students who require additional interventions.

Keeping students in school is an essential academic goal (Flannery et al., 2014). This aim is even more complex as we are apprised of the increasing reports of bullying and

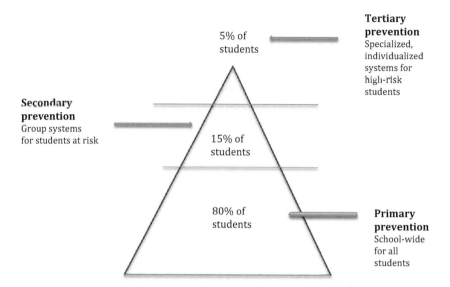

Figure 10.3 Illustration of levels within SW-PBIB.

violence, and school dropout rates that approach 20 percent among the general school population (National Dropout Prevention Center/Network, 2014), but exceed 39 percent among students with disabilities (National Dropout Prevention Center/Network, 2014). The goal of the SW-PBIS model is to prevent academic and social/emotional problems through a preventive approach for addressing behavioral problems rather than the traditional punitive method of addressing these problems, such as through suspensions (Debnam et al., 2012). Through the creation of a predictable, positive school climate, students learn appropriate behaviors and receive support for their successes. Data are then collected and decisions are made based on these results. Similar to RTI, there are three levels of support with a team of individuals from different disciplines who monitor students' progress (Shepard et al., 2013) across all levels (see Figure 10.3).

At the first level, all students receive classroom information through common programs and strategies that are often implemented with the assistance of the school counselor (Elementary & Middle Schools Technical Assistance Center, n.d.; Gruman & Holzen, 2011). Some of the more successful, empirically based programs include:

- *Character Education*, a program designed for all ages and grades to foster the values of caring, honesty, fairness, responsibility, and respect.
- *Project ACHIEVE* is designed for all students in elementary and middle school with the goal of enhancing the development of academically at-risk students.
- *Project Pathe* is designed for middle and high school students to strengthen students' self-concepts and attitudes toward school.
- *Second Step* is available for preschool through ninth-grade students. Empathy, impulse control, and anger management are introduced and developed through a five-step problem-solving strategy.

As in RTI, more intensive aid is provided at the secondary level such as small-group counseling and/or more focused individualized support (Shepard et al., 2013). Through monitored assessments, students who are not progressing as expected at this level are provided more robust interventions at the tertiary level. Supports at the third level may include assistance from specialized individuals, behavioral interventions, progress monitoring, and possibly special education services.

Elementary and middle schools that have implemented SW-PBIS revealed improved school climate, enhanced academic achievement, and fewer discipline problems (Horner et al., 2010, as cited in Flannery et al., 2014). Although evidence supports the benefits of SW-PBIS at the lower school levels, less is known about its influence at the high school level. To assuage this gap in research, Flannery et al. (2014) examined the effectiveness of SW-PBIS at the secondary school level, and found that when PBIS was implemented over a period of time, problematic student behavior decreased significantly in comparison to high schools in which this strategy was not implemented. Although this study reveals positive outcomes at the higher grades, further information is needed.

Implications for School Counselors

The school counselor has the skills to work with their school principal on creating a safe, welcoming school climate. Curtis et al. (2010) investigated an elementary school in North Carolina that implemented a SW-PBIS program. Throughout this program, the school counselor and principal worked with students and faculty on a continual basis, and outcome data were collected to understand effective methods for working with students who needed additional assistance. Data revealed a significant decrease of behavioral referrals and suspensions, which was attributed to the consistency among faculty in attending to the program structure. School counselors are also able to intervene by developing and leading groups, attending to mental health issues, facilitating the creation of caring school communities, and creating and implementing social stories. Each of these interventions is discussed below.

Groups as an Intervention

School counselors are trained to lead groups, yet selecting participants for a group designed to decrease inappropriate behavior is often difficult as students frequently use this venue for bragging about some of their exploits. This issue can be addressed by selecting peers who are able to display positive behaviors, serve as role models (Shepard et al., 2013), and aid as powerful group members to dissuade peers from boasting about their undesirable behaviors (Sherrod et al., 2009). Moreover, when school counselors collect data to provide evidence as to the impact of groups and their influence in the school environment, there is greater support and understanding of the school counselor's role in enhancing student growth. Chapter 8 provides a more extensive discussion on group work in the school environment.

Mental Health Issues

Social and emotional problems, in addition to family difficulties, are the greatest mental health issues that school-aged youth experience (Substance Abuse and Mental Health

Services Administration, 2005, as cited in Shepard et al., 2013), and the school counselor is often the only mental health professional in the school with the training and skills to assist these individuals with their mental health concerns. School counselors commonly implement social skill interventions for all students, but particularly those with attention deficit hyperactivity disorder (ADHD) or ASD at levels 2 and 3. For instance, those with ADHD may have difficulty talking out of turn, identifying social cues, taking turns, or having a propensity for interrupting peers. Furthermore, those with ASD may also have difficulty picking up on social cues, understanding non-verbal communication, showing awareness of others, and carrying on a conversation. Teaching social skills includes four primary standards (Gresham, 2002, as cited in Kampwirth, 2006):

1. Teaching skill acquisition
2. Improving skill performance
3. Reducing or eliminating behaviors that interfere with social abilities
4. Promoting generalization and maintenance of skills

Teaching students to transfer newly acquired social skills across various situations is often the most difficult step in skill instruction. An analysis of studies revealed that students with autism showed positive results across various conditions when they were provided social skills through video modeling. This intervention is even more effective when school counselors are able to identify and address students' emotional reactions regarding their lack of social skills (Shepard et al., 2013).

Creating a Caring Community

The creation of a school community that provides a sense of connection and belonging contributes to school success (Lindwall & Coleman, 2008). And, when the school counseling curriculum is developmentally appropriate, with a focus on strengths rather than deficits, students may be more engaged in the school community. In a study by Lindwall and Coleman (2008), elementary school counselors were asked how they contributed to a caring school environment. Participants revealed that it was their range of experiences in the school that had the most impact on connectedness and empowerment; elements that fostered a caring school community. Moreover, participants in this study reported that when they took the time to build relationships, faculty and staff were more cooperative, especially when they felt that their needs were considered in making program changes (Lindwall & Coleman, 2008).

Finally, when school counselors assess the school climate at the beginning of the school year and compare this information with the data at the end of the school year, concrete information is available to determine students' attitudes toward school as a safe environment (Sherrod et al., 2009). Other strategies include:

1. Increasing school safety by developing violence-prevention programs.
2. Increasing awareness of diversity.
3. Treating all students equitably.
4. Teaching decision-making skills.
5. Diminishing student competitiveness (Loukas, 2007).

Case Study 10.2

I sometimes provide an in-service workshop for teachers who have difficulty modifying instruction and assignments. I discuss how some students need to have tests read orally, and that some students who have difficulty with note-taking could be given a copy of PowerPoints that are presented in class. Unfortunately, many times teachers who do not understand the concepts of accommodations and modifications believed that they do not need to change their instruction for some students.

Middle school counselor

Social Stories

Social stories are used with students with ASD, those who display behavioral disorders, communicative disorders such as echolalia, apraxia, or youth with social deficits. The purpose of these stories is to assist individuals in understanding interpersonal situations by describing people, skills, and events in a social situation (Gray, 1998, cited in Hutchins & Prelock, 2013). In addition, social skills such as getting the attention of another, decision-making, and interactions with peers (Soenksen & Alper, 2006, cited in Hutchins & Prelock, 2013) can be taught, or may also be used to describe a troublesome situation while providing direction, affirmation, and concepts to teach an identified skill. Counselors, parents, and teachers write a narrative to target specific skills that relate to the needs of each individual using the first or third person (Schwartzberg & Silverman, 2013). For example, a four-year-old preschool boy diagnosed with ASD had difficulty communicating and deferring his needs, which resulted in temper tantrums. This young student was able to use three signs to communicate with his caregivers, but had difficulty indicating specific needs such as "eat" or "drink." Social stories were created and read to the young boy, and his mother assessed his progress on a daily basis by answering the questions, "Based on my observations today, my son is able to use his signs for 'eat' and 'drink.'" After the end of the intervention, his mother reported that her son was making excellent progress as a result of this strategy (Hutchins & Prelock, 2013).

Conclusion

Each school building has a unique climate and culture that influences how students learn, the school appearance, beliefs and attitudes of stakeholders, and interactions among personnel. The school counselor is trained in interpersonal communication and group facilitation that contribute to a positive school environment with a sense of belonging. Furthermore, when school professionals collaborate and work together to reach shared goals, students are able to receive improved services without redundancies. Numerous school personnel, as well as individuals from the community, contribute to the success of all students, including those with disabilities, particularly when roles are clarified, structural characteristics support collaboration, collaborator personalities encourage the process, collaboration has been successful in the past, and members' cultures are considered.

RTI and School-Wide SW-PBIS are two collaborative initiatives that have proven successful in the school environment. Each of these models consists of three levels designed to support students who are struggling academically and behaviorally. At each level, students who continue to struggle are moved to more intense interventions to improve identified skills. School counselors are able to address student needs through the provision of groups, addressing mental health issues, creating a caring community, and the use of social stories.

References

ASCA (2013). *The Professional School Counselor and Students with Disabilities.* Retrieved from www.schoolcounselor.org/asca/media/asca/PositionStatements/PS_Disabilities.pdf.

ASCA (2014). *The Professional School Counselor and Multi-Tiered Systems of Support.* Retrieved from www.schoolcounselor.org/asca/media/asca/PositionStatements/PS_MultitieredSupport Systems.pdf.

Best Practice Briefs (2004). *School Climate and Learning.* Retrieved from http://outreach.msu.edu/bpbriefs/issues/brief31.pdf.

Bogdan, J., Dye, J., Leitner, B., & Meersman, R. (1996). *Promoting Appropriate Behavior Through Social Skill Instruction.* Retrieved from ERIC database, ED412008.

Bronstein, L. R. (2002). Index of interdisciplinary collaboration. *Social Work Research,* 26, 113–123.

Center on Response to Intervention (n.d.). *Multi-Level Prevention System.* Retrieved from www.rti4success.org/essential-components-rti/multi-level-prevention-system.

Conoley, J. C. & Conoley, C. W. (1991). Collaboration for child adjustment: issues for school and clinic-based child psychologists. *Journal of Consulting and Clinical Psychology,* 59, 821–829.

Conoley, J. C., & Conoley, C. W. (2010). Why does collaboration work? Linking positive psychology and collaboration. *Journal of Educational and Psychological Consultation,* 20, 75–82.

Curtis, R., Van Horne, J. W., Robertson, P., & Karvonen, M. (2010). Outcome of a school-wide positive behavioral support program. *Professional School Counseling,* 13, 159–164.

Debnam, K. J., Pas, E. T., & Bradshaw, C. P. (2012). Secondary and tertiary support systems in schools implementing School-Wide Positive Behavioral Interventions and Supports: a preliminary descriptive analysis. *Positive Behavior Interventions,* 14, 142–152.

Elementary & Middle Schools Technical Assistance Center (n.d.). *Behavior.* Retrieved from www.emstac.org/registered/topics/posbehavior/programs.htm.

Flannery, K. M., Fenning, P., Kato, M. M., & McIntosh, K. (2014). Effects of School-Wide Positive Behavioral Interventions and Supports and fidelity of implementation on problem behaviors in high schools. *School Psychology Quarterly,* 29, 111–124.

Frey, A. J., Lee, J., Small, J. W., Seeley, J. R., Walker, H. M., & Feil, E. G. (2013). Transporting motivational interviewing to school settings to improve the engagement and fidelity of tier 2 interventions. *Journal of Applied School Psychology,* 29, 183–202.

Froiland, J. M. (2011). Response to Intervention as a vehicle for powerful mental health interventions in the schools. *Contemporary School Psychology,* 15, 35–42.

Goodman-Scott, E. & O'Rorke-Trigiani, J. (2013). 1 picture = 1,000 words. *ASCA School Counselor,* 51, 31–38.

Grant, K. B. & Ray, J. A. (2013). *Home, School, and Community Collaboration: Culturally Responsive Family Engagement.* Thousand Oaks, CA: Sage.

Gruman, D. H. & Hoelzen, B. (2011). Determining responsiveness to school counseling interventions using behavioral observations. *Professional School Counseling,* 14, 183–190.

Hutchins, T. L. & Prelock, P. A. (2013). The social validity of social stories for supporting the behavioral and communicative functioning of children with autism spectrum disorder. *International Journal of Speech-Language Pathology,* 15, 383–395.

Kampwirth, T. J. (2006). *Collaborative Consultation in the Schools.* Upper Saddle River, NJ: Pearson.

Lindwall, J. J. & Coleman, H. L. K. (2008). The elementary school counselor's role in fostering caring school communities. *Professional School Counseling,* 12, 144–148.

Loukas, A. (2007). What is school climate? *Leadership Compass*, 5. Retrieved from www.naesp. org/resources/2/Leadership_Compass/2007/LC2007v5n1a4.pdf.

McCalley, C. (2010). Social deficits. *ASCA School Counselor*, October, 23–25.

Mellin E. A., Anderson-Butcher, D., & Bronstein, L. (2011). Strengthening interprofessional team collaboration: potential roles for school mental health professionals. *Advances in School Mental Health Promotion*, 4, 51–60.

Mindess, M., Chen, M., & Brenner, R. (2008). Social-emotional learning in the primary curriculum, *Young Children*, 63, 56–60.

Murawski, W. W. & Spencer, S. (2011). *Collaborate, Communicate, & Differentiate! How to Increase Student Learning in Today's Diverse Schools*. Thousand Oaks, CA: Corwin.

National Dropout Prevention Center/Network (2014). *Statistics and Facts*. Retrieved from www. dropoutprevention.org/statistics.

PBIS World (2014). *Social Stories*. Retrieved from www.pbisworld.com/tier-2/social-stories.

Ryan, T., Kaffenberger, C. J., & Carroll, A. G. (2011). Feature article: Response to Intervention: an opportunity for school counselor leadership. *Professional School Counselor*, 14, 211–221.

Schwartzberg, E. T. & Silverman, J. J. (2013). The effects of music-based social stories on comprehension and generalization of social skills in children with autism spectrum disorders: a randomized effectiveness study. *The Arts in Psychotherapy*, 40, 331–337.

Shepard, J. M., Shahidullah, J. D., & Carlson, J. S. (2013). *Counseling Students in Levels 2 and 3: A PBIS/RTI Guide*. Thousand Oaks, CA: Corwin.

Sherrod, M. D., Getch, Y. Q., & Ziomek-Daigle, J. (2009). The impact of positive behavior support to decrease discipline referrals with elementary students. *Professional School Counseling*, 12, 421–427.

11 Collaboration and Consultation with Parents/Families of Students with Disabilities and Members of the Community

The following CACREP Standards are addressed in this chapter:

PROFESSIONAL COUNSELING ORIENTATION AND ETHICAL PRACTICE
b. the multiple professional roles and functions of counselors across specialty areas, and their relationships with human service and integrated behavioral health care systems, including interagency and interorganizational collaboration and consultation

ENTRY-LEVEL SPECIALTY AREAS: SCHOOL COUNSELING FOUNDATIONS
d. models of school-based collaboration and consultation

CONTEXTUAL DIMENSIONS
b. school counselor roles in consultation with families, P-12 and postsecondary school personnel, and community agencies
k. community resources and referral sources

Chapter Objectives

After you have completed this chapter you should be able to:

*   Identify methods for creating a family, school, community partnership.
*   Demonstrate knowledge of collaboration models.
*   Be familiar with community/school asset mapping strategies.
*   Discuss methods for engaging parents in school activities.

Throughout the ages, educational personnel have lamented the lack of parental involvement in their child's learning. Although many parents want to be involved with their child's teachers, many do not know how to engage in this process (Serres & Simpson, 2013), or have negative attitudes toward the educational environment based on their own experiences in the school setting.

> ### Case Study 11.1
>
> *The paternal grandparents had custody of their seven-year-old grandson, who displayed extreme behavioral issues and as a result this young student was seeing*

an outside caseworker, and the Department of Children Services (DCS) were also involved in the home. The grandmother suffers from depression and did not follow through on discipline in the home due to this mental state. At school, the student displayed severe, aggressive behaviors and frequently needed to be sent home. The administration contacted the grandmother to attend a meeting to develop a behavior plan for home and school, but she was very hostile about meeting and asked the caseworker to attend as her advocate. Throughout the meeting the school counselor was able to discover that the grandmother attended school in the same building as her grandson and had a very poor school experience that triggered her anger and anxiety. Once this information was understood, a plan was developed that provided an opportunity to work collaboratively. If an IEP meeting or a signature was needed, the team would travel to the home and hold the meeting there. School personnel also allowed another family member to pick the student up from school if he needed to be sent home. Within a month there was improved academic performance and a collaborative relationship between home and school resulted.

Elementary school counselor

Parents of children with special needs are even more reticent to engage with school personnel due to such reasons as: (a) feeling responsible for causing their child's disability; (b) embarrassment and confusion about their child's diagnosis; (c) navigating the referral system; and (d) feeling like an outsider in the process (Serres & Simpson, 2013). For example, consider Case Study 11.2.

Case Study 11.2

A female fifth-grader was difficult to be around in that she was quick to insult and criticize others, yet her parents viewed this behavior as normal reactions to remarks other students made to her. In fact, her mother insisted that her daughter be switched to a different class because of the poor treatment she believed her daughter was receiving from her peers, and from what she perceived as the school personnel not properly addressing this issue. The school counselor was finally able to convince the mother that there were patterns to her daughter's behavior across settings, and convinced the mother to allow her daughter to be tested. Testing results indicated Asperger's Syndrome, which the mother was not able to accept, and even more devastating to her was that her daughter would be placed in special education classes. She insisted that this diagnosis was not to be shared with anyone due to the label placed on her daughter, and refused for her daughter to be placed in this class. If the mother had been able to accept this diagnosis, the daughter would have been able to receive the services that were so desperately needed.

Intermediate school counselor

The family is the child's most essential support system, with the school environment often considered as the next most influential institution impacting the child's growth and development. And, it is frequently the only place in which mental health assistance is available for the student (Paylo, 2011).

Although school counselors recognize the importance of collaboration with families, and how these relationships are crucial to the academic success of youth (Manz et al., 2009), many school counselors acknowledge that they are not actively involved in these partnerships (Griffin & Steen, 2010) for several reasons: (a) school personnel often hold the belief that parents/guardians of children from lower socioeconomic homes are not interested in their child's academic performance—this belief often creates lowered expectations, resulting in limiting students' abilities to perform and parents'/guardians' opportunities for involvement; (b) school professionals often regard parents as being too emotionally involved with their child's disability, believe that parents/guardians do not acknowledge their child's limitations, and think that they are unaware of the individualized education program (IEP) process; (c) school counselors do not have adequate time to contribute to quality parent/guardian interactions; and (d) the student's age and specific disability may preclude continual involvement (Manz et al., 2009).

Interestingly, families report being excluded from their child's IEP meetings, express that they do not feel heard, and feel as if they are denied opportunities to contribute during these meetings (Mpofu & Wilson, 2004). Furthermore, low-income and/or single parents often have limited resources and opportunities, which increase parents' perceptions that they are not able to contribute to their child's education (Bryan & Henry, 2008).

When school personnel have high expectations, believe that success is attainable for all students, respect the culture and language of the student and family, and strive to create a nurturing, positive climate for students, successful partnering is attainable (Bryan & Henry, 2008). Partnerships between the family and educational personnel serve as an asset in enhancing academic achievement, promoting resiliency, and lessening inequalities (Moore-Thomas & Day-Vines, 2010). For example, there is plenty of documentation that supports the high dropout rate of student subpopulations, such as those with disabilities (Mitchell & Bryan, 2007). Cooperative relationships between individuals who have a vested interest in the student's well-being contribute to successful academic achievement.

Self-efficacy and perceptions of the school climate are two concepts that are related to successful collaboration between school personnel and families (Caprara, 2003, as cited in Manz et al., 2009). For example, when school personnel feel more confident in their ability to involve parents/guardians with the school, greater involvement is an outcome in the form of parent/guardian volunteers, enhanced home-based instruction, and superior participation in school activities (Manz et al., 2009). School climate also influences educators' assessment of personal competence and their ability to engage families in the school agenda (Epstein, 1982, as cited in Manz et al., 2009). Educators who have a more optimistic view of the school climate, which includes a more positive view of administrator support and appreciation, are more likely to invite and involve parents and guardians in collaborative efforts (Manz et al., 2009).

Conceptual Application Activity 11.1

Interview a school counselor about his/her experiences with family consultations, particularly with families of students with disabilities. What are some of the helpful strategies this individual uses to engage the family in the school? What were some of the frustrations that were encountered in family/school partnerships and how were they overcome? Share your answers with your peers.

No one individual is able to undertake collaborative tasks without the assistance and support of those within and outside of the school. As school administrators attempt to make difficult decisions with fewer monetary resources, school counselors are often the targets of staff reduction. As a result, students such as those with disabilities, those who are homeless, or students with suicidal ideation and depression are often shortchanged by not receiving the services they desperately need. In these instances, identifying community, school, and family resources for these individuals is vital. These partnerships lead to enhanced educational outcomes for students, future career success, and social/ emotional growth (Mitchell & Bryan, 2007).

Recognition of the various resources in a community is a large task that cannot be undertaken by a single individual, but rather one that could be undertaken with the help of an advisory board or community members, and provides an opportunity for the school and community to work together to identify assets that already exist. Community asset mapping is one method in which resources can be identified.

Community Asset Mapping

Reduced funding for educational systems forces difficult decisions, and school counselors are often targets for cuts despite the fact that these professionals are working more frequently with students such as those with disabilities, those who are homeless, students with suicidal ideation and depression, and so on. These events create a need for school counselors to seek additional assistance outside of the school, and to coordinate activities that provide a foundation for school–family–community collaboration (Griffin & Farris, 2010). Cultural brokers (individuals who are familiar with the community as well as the culture of the families represented in the schools) are ideal resources to serve as members on the collaborative team (Griffin & Farris, 2010) to ensure that groups of students are not overlooked.

Mapping the assets within the community is a proactive approach for recognizing the people, resources, agencies, and so on that exist to provide services and support. Community mapping is often paired with a needs assessments, yet a major difference between these two techniques is that community mapping is used to focus on strengths and assets within the community, whereas the needs assessment is often used to identify deficits or weaknesses within a system (Griffin & Farris, 2010).

Community mapping is a relatively economical means that identifies locations of resources and programs without relying on the school to fund programs, assists school counselors with people and resources to which students may be referred, and strengthens community and school relationships (Griffin & Farris, 2010). Table 11.1 is an example of some of the institutions and resources that may be identified through community mapping.

Lexington, Kentucky, conducted community mapping for the purpose of linking students with disabilities to community resources to: (a) assist students with disabilities with the transition from high school to career or work opportunities; (b) improve school and post-secondary options; and (c) to make resources more available to youth (Griffin & Farris, 2010). The results of this endeavor provided a results-based outcome that improved services to youth with disabilities and created a collaborative partnership with an emphasis on the needs of students with disabilities.

Table 11.1. Community/School Asset Map

Individual	Institution	Government
Skills	Churches	State/local
Talents	Colleges/universities	Federal
Experiences	Senior care facilities	Military
Personal	Police/fire departments	Small businesses
Professional	Hospitals/clinics	State education agency
Leadership	Libraries	Telecommunications
Networks	Schools	Vocational rehabilitation
Vocational Rehabilitation Counselor	Transportation	Services
	Banks	Social security offices
	Group homes	
Organization	*Physical/Land*	*Culture*
Small and large businesses	Parks and recreation	Museums
Citizen groups/clubs	Utility companies	Center for cultural affairs
Community centers	Real estate agencies	Tourism
Home-based initiatives	Waste management	Arts/historic groups
Non-profit organizations	facilities	
Radio/TV stations	Chamber of commerce	
Professional and/or family advocacy groups		

Families, particularly those who are lower socioeconomic, are often unaware of the availability of rehabilitation agencies and services that are accessible in the community (Mpofu & Wilson, 2004). Identifying these resources and informing families of various community assets is instrumental in engaging families with the school and community. Although asset mapping is a useful, beneficial strategy with a valuable outcome, additional collaborative approaches that connect community, family, and school are required for optimal assistance to students with disabilities and their families. The *Epstein Typology of Collaboration* and *Ferguson's Developmental Model of Community Involvement* are two collaboration models that depict strategies applicable to families of students with disabilities.

Epstein Typology of Collaboration

The Epstein Typology of Collaboration categorizes six types of parent–school–community interactions that include: parenting, communicating, volunteering, learning at home, decision-making, and community collaboration (Epstein, 1995, as cited in Griffin & Steen, 2010). Each type is discussed below.

Parenting

Parents/guardians generally identify problematic behavior exhibited by their child much earlier than when it is formally diagnosed. Early identification of students with disabilities, particularly those with autism spectrum disorder (ASD), is critical as this diagnosis opens up myriad resources to parents/guardians (Robinson et al., 2014) that results in greater assistance and resources while the child is still young.

It is not uncommon for parents/guardians of students with disabilities to report considerable stress, feelings of rejection, and being chastised by others for their parenting style (Conner & White, 2014; Gray, 2002, as cited in Robinson et al., 2014). School personnel, particularly the professional school counselor, can lessen the stress by listening and taking parents' concerns seriously by initiating support services and resources (Robinson et al., 2014). For instance, the provision of classes for parents/guardians could assist in their understanding of their child's disability, and inform them of policies surrounding students with disabilities, including the IEP and transitions (Mitchell & Bryan, 2007). An added benefit of these educational sessions may be a boost in parental confidence in their childrearing ability, and might also possibly promote more realistic expectations for their child. In addition, school counselors could garner support for the creation of parent/guardian support groups that would include learning advocacy skills to aid their child, and/or supporting one another when a break is necessary (Robinson et al., 2014). Furthermore, workshops designed to help parents/guardians understand child development issues, parenting styles, and how to help their child with homework are additional topics that school counselors could promote so that parents/guardians feel empowered in their interactions with the school personnel. In a study by Lee et al. (2003), children diagnosed with an emotional disturbance (ED) had an increased level of functioning when various systems collaborated with schools, and parents were taught skills to address their child's issues. However, rather than assuming that families would benefit from a particular workshop or topic, it is critical that the school counselor conducts a needs assessment to glean a better understanding of the topics that are most desired, and includes cultural brokers into the planning (Mitchell & Bryan, 2007).

Communicating

Creating a consistent method for communicating school events and contacting parents/guardians about student progress creates a venue for two-way communications. Some types of communication include parent/teacher conferences, fliers, newsletters, and calendars (Mitchell & Bryan, 2007). Although electronic communications are a common method of connecting, not all families have access to technology, which necessitates exploring alternative approaches for notifying families. Unfortunately, although communication is an essential means to reduce mistrust between the school and parents, Griffin and Steen (2010), revealed that only 13 percent of the school counselor participants indicated that they engaged in communication activities (Griffin & Steen, 2010), partly due to issues of confidentiality. However, communicating that students are a top priority and indicating the guidelines of privacy, confidentiality, and privileged communication—including the importance of keeping students' information private unless there is "serious and foreseeable harm to the student" (ASCA, 2010)—is a proactive method for creating a trusting relationship with families (Huss et al., 2008).

Delivering bad news to parents/guardians is difficult, and school counselors are often put in positions where they are the designated individual to speak to parents/guardians about issues that could negatively impact their child's achievement. When parents are informed that their child has a disability, reactions range from anger, shock, self-blame, and disbelief (Heiman, 2002, as cited in Auger, 2006). And parents who have received this type of news report that they were dissatisfied with the way in which they were provided information about their child (Nissenbaum et al., 2002, as cited in Auger, 2006). Delivering news that could be perceived negatively is generally a process that includes: (a) preparing to deliver the news; (b) news delivery; (c) responses to the news; and (d) follow-up.

PREPARING TO DELIVER THE NEWS

When parents/guardians are first contacted, the school counselor can either share general information regarding the purpose of the meeting such as, "I am hoping that you can come in for a parent conference to talk about your daughter." Or they can be specific such as, "I would like you to come in and meet with a group of school personnel to speak with you about your daughter's academic achievement." School counselors need to be prepared to respond to a parent/guardian's request for more specific information in either of these approaches. When a meeting is scheduled regarding special education eligibility, a designated list of participants must attend the meeting. The school counselor should take time to introduce the parents/guardians to all the members present at the meeting, and make an effort to create a comfortable and friendly environment by examining the seating arrangements, and providing time for questions (Auger, 2006).

NEWS DELIVERY

Difficult information is challenging to process. Therefore, delivering bad news in small portions, rather than relaying the information as a whole, gives parents/guardians an opportunity for processing the information better. Moreover, offering time for checking with the parent/guardian as to what they have heard, inviting parents to ask any questions about terms that are unclear, conveying compassion, and giving the news in an empathic manner facilitates communication and an opportunity for offering support (Auger, 2006).

RESPONSES TO THE NEWS

As noted above, parents/guardians react differently to troublesome news. Whereas some respond with anger, distress, or disbelief, others may express relief because their observations are now officially validated. Awareness of the meaning behind different reactions facilitates how the school counselor is able to ease news delivery. For example, fear or hurt are often the genuine feelings behind the anger that parents may express. Parents/guardians who express disbelief could have difficulty understanding how this news will affect them and their child, whereas distressed parents/guardians may need support and encouragement (Auger, 2006).

FOLLOW-UP STRATEGIES

Scheduling a future meeting facilitates a means to answer any additional questions parents/guardians may have, and allows time to accrue resources that may assist the child and his/her family. Or if scheduling an appointment is not feasible, a follow-up phone call after the meeting to check on how well the parents/guardians are accepting the news or to answer additional questions may be more practical (Auger, 2006).

As previously discussed, a solid partnership between the school personnel and family with honest, direct communication as the backbone of the relationship encourages student growth. Yet, volunteering, learning at home, decision-making, and community collaboration are additional opportunities for families to become involved and generate positive affiliations.

Volunteering

As previously noted, there is an association between parent involvement in their child's education and their achievement (Reece et al., 2013), particularly when attention is given to potential barriers to collaboration such as transportation and child care, available time, feelings of intimidation, or fear of speaking with school personnel. These barriers are particularly evident among low-income families (Reece et al., 2013). A project entitled Neighboring Project Parent Empowerment and Volunteer Readiness Program was developed to: (a) involve parents and schools to increase student academic achievement; (b) provide opportunities for volunteering; and (c) offer knowledge on methods to connect with the community and school. Needs of community participants were addressed through a workshop that presented information on such topics as facilitating a learning community in the home, connecting math to the home and school, goal-setting, and how to respond if your child is bullied. Focus groups were held to gain information on participants' satisfaction with this initiative, and results revealed that parents felt better prepared to communicate with school personnel, and as a result of this project there was an increase in parental volunteerism.

Understanding the types of clubs, organizations, or activities that need assistance provides an opportunity to solicit the help of parents to lead, support, or monitor events. For instance, in one high school there were problems with students roaming through the hallways when classes were in session. In this instance a "parent patrol" was established, in which parents volunteered their time to monitor the hallways, cafeteria, or parking lot. This enterprise influenced student misbehavior in that it was difficult for students to break a rule when a known parent/guardian was present and watching. Parents are also able to volunteer in other programs such as designing and leading workshops for other parents, tutoring or assisting in the inclusive classroom, or participating in a career fair. Other types of volunteer experiences include:

- reading stories to students or listening to them read;
- engaging in clerical tasks such as contacting parents about upcoming school activities, or preparing assistive materials;
- preparing learning center materials;
- working one-on-one with students with special needs.

Learning at Home

Support is provided for parents/guardians to assist their child at home through such means as interactive homework assignments and holding workshops on skills and information

Figure 11.1 Families are able to reinforce educational concepts such as fractions through activities such as cooking.

Source: ©iStockphoto.com, www.istockphoto.com/photo/photo-of-a-happy-famil y-preparing-food-together-36573130.

to assist student success (Mitchell & Bryan, 2007). Parents/guardians sometimes have difficulty knowing how to help their child with homework, particularly when their child enters the more advanced grades and brings home assignments that are beyond the parents' ability. Parents/guardians sometimes lack knowledge of the types of assistive devices or accommodations that are available to help their child learn more effectively. In a study by Sanders et al. (1999, as cited in Griffin & Steen, 2010), parents who had lower levels of education engaged in their child's learning less frequently than did those parents with higher levels of education. Yet school counselors can facilitate parent meetings designed to keep parents/guardians aware of the school expectations and equip them with concrete strategies for helping their student, or demonstrating teaching methods to accommodate their child's disability. Barbor (2010, as cited in Grant & Ray, 2010) described interactive home learning activities that encourage authentic experiences to integrate classroom concepts such as:

- individualizing assignments designed at the child's reading level and learning style;
- cooking activities in which fractions in a recipe are reviewed while following directions;
- learning turn-taking while playing a family game;
- decision-making in choosing activities for the day.

Decision-making

Involving parents/guardians and community members on various committees such as advisory boards provides an opportunity to share insights, collaborate on essential school topics, and serve as community cultural brokers. Surprisingly, parents who are chronic complainers or are verbally negative towards school and programs are often the ideal people to serve on these committees. Their membership on the committee provides an opportunity for them to understand the rationale behind policies and procedures, and their comments may also offer opportunities to re-evaluate existing decisions and strategies. In addition, they can serve as ambassadors for parents who have difficulty understanding the reason certain procedures and policies exist.

Collaborating with the Community

As discussed in the section on community mapping, identifying individuals, resources, and services provides a comprehensive understanding of what is available in the community to assist students and their families. School counselors are able to use their extensive interpersonal communication skills to close the gap of inequality and marginalization that may exist between diverse families and the school system through knowledge of community services. Just as there are different responses from parents/guardians when they learn about their child's diagnosis of a special need, awareness of cultural variations in communication styles invites partnerships. Examples of an effective affiliation include inviting culturally diverse parents/guardians to school to listen to children read, tutor students in difficult subjects, or assist with homework completion. This connection also has the potential to more critically examine and challenge personal beliefs. For example, investigators looked at cultural beliefs in regard to disabilities (Nichols & Keltner, 2005, as cited in Grant & Ray, 2010) and in this inquiry, some Mexican American parents who had children diagnosed with a disability believed this disability was due to supernatural intervention or a sociocultural factor. Similarly, some Korean American parents who had children with a disability believed that this was due to a divine plan or previous mistakes they made. Understanding these beliefs provides an opportunity to discuss the empirical evidence surrounding child development and disabilities.

Ferguson's Developmental Model of Community Involvement

Ferguson's Developmental Model of Community Involvement posits that in any partnership, a crisis or challenge emerges at various stages that must be confronted before the relationship is able to progress (Ferguson, 1999, as cited in Moore-Thomas & Day-Vines, 2010) to accomplish identified goals. These stages and critical tasks that need to be accomplished are outlined in Figure 11.2.

A successful partnership that embraces the tenets of both the Epstein and Ferguson collaborative models was implemented in An Achievable Dream Academy, a K-12 school located in Virginia, in which all students are on free and reduced lunch. This program provides intensive education in basic skills, and offers a lengthened school day and calendar year, along with other efforts that included parental involvement opportunities. This program was implemented with clearly stated goals, agreed-upon expectations, a positive school culture and climate, and parental/guardian volunteer opportunities.

Figure 11.2 Ferguson's collaboration stages and tasks.

Stage	Task
Trust and interest vs. mistrust and disinterest	This stage involves articulating a need for partnership and identifying the talents of individuals and social resources people can bring into the collaboration. In working with families with disabilities, the worldview of the family needs to be understood including struggles, social realities, and economic difficulties the family experiences due to the child's disability. The school counselor has a responsibility to acknowledge the realities of the family members despite contradictions in experiences or values (Farquahar et al., 2005, as cited in Moore-Thomas & Day-Vines, 2010).
Compromise vs. conflict or exit	At times, school personnel make the faulty assumption that the beliefs and culture of the educational environment represent the norm for behaving and making decisions. This belief does not take into account other ways of thinking or behaving, which often leads to mistrust and frustration. Without a high level of trust in which standards are established that reflect shared commitment to agreed-upon goals, families could choose to withdraw from the partnership with a reluctance to participate in present or future collaborations. This includes agreed-upon goals for students with disabilities.
Commitment vs. ambivalence	As the parties recognize various factors that negatively impact families and students with disabilities, greater dedication to achieving the purpose of the partnership will result. For instance, without an understanding of how attitudes, school policies, or lack of available resources for these students adversely influence their academic, vocational, and/or social/emotional growth, there could be a lack of allegiance to the process.
Industrious vs. discouragement	As roles are more clearly articulated and an effort is made to create an equalitarian relationship, the partnership grows with deeper respect for each member. This phase includes sharing genuine feelings, thoughts, and beliefs so that each participant is able to have a clear perspective of one another's views.
Transition vs. stagnation	As each member feels empowered with the skills to work independently and collaboratively to achieve goals, the result could be greater networking opportunities and the ability to transition to other educational goals for the benefit of students with disabilities.

Program evaluations revealed that student were able to surpass academic expectations, and discipline and absentee levels decreased (Moore-Thomas & Day-Vines, 2010).

Conceptual Application Activity 11.2

Interview a school counselor and ask this individual the strategies that are used to engage parents/guardians and families in the school. Discuss your answers with your peers.

As school counselors become more cognizant of elements that create favorable partnerships, it is possible that future efforts will be realized on behalf of students with special needs and their families. It is clear that school counselors have a responsibility to move beyond the traditional means of working with families and to look at new ways for creating partnerships that will benefit all students, including those with disabilities.

Conclusion

Partnerships between the family and school serve as factors that enhance student resiliency and self-concept. Unfortunately, many parents/guardians do not feel welcome in schools and believe that their contributions are unappreciated, and it is the school counselor who is able to serve as a catalyst for creating positive relationships between the school personnel, community, and parents/guardians of students with disabilities.

Awareness of community resources and services through community/school asset mapping, and organizing various types of school/parent interactions with attention to cultural factors promote collaborative relationships. The Epstein Typology of Collaboration includes six types of involvement between the school and community: parenting, communicating, volunteering, learning at home, decision-making, and collaboration. In addition, Ferguson identifies various collaborative stages and tasks—trust and interest vs. mistrust and disinterest; compromise vs. conflict or exit; commitment vs. ambivalence; industrious vs. discouragement; and transition vs. stagnation—that need to be successfully negotiated to benefit families and students with disabilities. When collaborative efforts between the school, family, and community are created, all students, particularly students with disabilities, benefit.

References

ASCA (2010). *Ethical Standards for School Counselors*. Retrieved from www.schoolcounselor. org/asca/media/asca/Resource%20Center/Legal%20and%20Ethical%20Issues/Sample%20 Documents/EthicalStandards2010.pdf.

Auger, R. W. (2006). Delivering difficult news to parents: guidelines for school counselors. *Professional School Counseling*, 10, 139–145.

Bryan, J. & Henry, L. (2008). Strengths-based partnerships: a school–family–community partnership approach to empowering students. *Professional School Counseling*, 12, 149–156.

Conner, C. M. & White, S. W. (2014). Stress in mothers of children with autism: trait mindfulness as a protective factor. *Research in Autism Spectrum Disorders*, 8, 617–624.

Grant, K. & Ray, J. A. (2010). *Home, School, and Community Collaboration: Culturally Responsive Family Involvement*. Thousand Oaks, CA: Sage.

Griffin, D. & Farris, A. (2010). School counselors and collaboration: finding resources through community asset mapping. *Professional School Counseling*, 13, 248–256.

Griffin, D. & Steen, S. (2010). School–family–community partnerships: applying Epstein's theory of the six types of involvement to school counselor practice. *Professional School Counseling*, 13, 218–226.

Huss, S. N., Bryant, A., & Mulet, S. (2008). Managing the quagmire of counseling in a school: bring the parents onboard. *Professional School Counseling*, 11, 362–267.

Lee, M. Y., Teater, B., Hsu, K. S., Green, G. J., Fraser, J. S., Solovey, A. D., & Grove, D. (2003). Systems collaboration with schools and treatment of severely emotionally disturbed children or adolescents. *Children & Schools*, 35, 155–168.

Manz, P. H., Mautone, J. A., & Martin S. D. (2009). School psychologists' collaborations with families: an exploratory study of the interrelationships of their perceptions of professional efficacy and school climate, and demographic and training variables. *Journal of Applied School Psychology*, 25, 47–70.

Mitchell, N. A. & Bryan, J. A. (2007). School–family–community partnerships: Strategies for school counselors working with Caribbean immigrant families. *Professional School Counseling,* 10(4), 399–409.

Moore-Thomas, C. & Day-Vines, N. L. (2010). Culturally competent collaboration: school counselor collaboration with African American families and communities. *Professional School Counseling,* 14, 53–63.

Mpofu, E. & Wilson, K. B. (2004). Opportunity structure and transition practices with students with disabilities: the role of family, culture, and community. *Journal of Applied Rehabilitation Counseling,* 35, 9–16.

Paylo, M. J. (2011). Preparing school counseling students to aid families: integrating a family systems perspective. *The Family Journal,* 19, 140–146.

Reece, C. A., Staudt, M., & Ogle, A. (2013). Lessons learned from a neighborhood-based collaboration to increase parent engagement. *School Community Journal,* 23, 207–225.

Robinson, C. A., York, K., Rothenberg, A., & Bissell, L. J. L. (2014). Parenting a child with Asperger's Syndrome: a balancing act. *Journal of Child & Family Studies,* 24(8), 2310–2321.

Serres, S. A. & Simpson, C. (2013). Serving educational pie: a multidisciplinary approach to collaborating with families. *Children & Schools,* 35, 189–191.

Part III

Issues of an Ever-Evolving Field

12 Current and Evolving Issues in Regard to Students with Disabilities

The following CACREP standards are addressed in this chapter:

PROFESSIONAL COUNSELING ORIENTATION AND ETHICAL PRACTICE
k. strategies for personal and professional self-evaluation and implications for practice

HUMAN GROWTH AND DEVELOPMENT
e. biological, neurological, and physiological factors that affect human development, functioning, and behavior

ASSESSMENT AND TESTING
e. use of assessments for diagnostic and intervention planning purposes

Chapter Objectives

After you have completed this chapter, you should be able to:

- Discuss current issues of concern for school counselors as they work with students with disabilities.
- Self-reflect on the role of school counselors in assisting the students with disabilities to successfully navigate particular issues and situations of concern.
- Appreciate the benefit of keeping current and being lifelong learners in an ever-evolving field.
- Acknowledge the importance of school counselors taking a leadership role in the education of students with disabilities.

Current Issues of Importance in Special Education to School Counselors

Special education is an ever-evolving field. Changing diagnostic procedures, innovative medical discoveries, and the increase and improvement of scientifically based knowledge and evidence-based techniques are circumstances that individuals working with students with disabilities confront as part of their professional responsibilities. To be effective in their special education-related role, school counselors should keep current on issues of relevance. This chapter will provide an overview of four of the most pertinent current issues in special education to both expand the knowledge base of school counselors and provide the opportunity to apply the information to their roles in working with students with disabilities and related personnel.

There are numerous possibilities that could be addressed as pertinent issues in special education for school counselors. Some of these issues have already been addressed to some extent in the preceding chapters, such as the increase in recent years of students identified with autism spectrum disorder (ASD) and the expansion of options for post-secondary education for students with disabilities. Other vital issues may relate more to accountability concerns in regard to high stakes assessment for the students with disabilities or the increasing of partnership opportunities between families and school personnel. Clearly, an entire book could focus on crucial issues in regard to working with students with disabilities. As this is but one chapter, the discussion will be focusing on four critical issues: (a) neuroscience and special education; (b) the multicultural considerations of students with disabilities for whom English is not the first language; (c) the increased vulnerability of some students with disabilities in regard to bullying; and (d) the issue of graduation rates for students with disabilities.

Neuroscience and Special Education

"The neurosciences are the cluster of disciplines that investigate the structure and functions of the brain and the central nervous system" (Lerner & Johns, 2012, p. 301). Neuroscience draws from various fields, such as neurology, biology, physiology, and psychology (Goswami, 2004). An area of particular interest to school counselors and other educational personnel is that of neuropsychology, which is a combination of neurology and psychology in the investigation of behavior and brain function (Lerner & Johns, 2012).

The field is clearly interdisciplinary in nature and may involve the collaboration of such professionals as neuroscientists, biologists, geneticists, cognitive scientists, and educational personnel (Willis, 2008). As various disciplines may be involved in neuroscience as it relates to educational issues, there are also various terms that have been associated with this field, among them "brain-based education" (Jensen, 2008) and "cognitive neuroscience" (Goswami, 2008). Jensen (2008, para. 7) makes a direct association between neuroscience and education through his description of brain-based education as an "engagement of strategies based on principles derived from an understanding of the brain."

As learning is affected by brain functioning and the workings of the central nervous system (Lerner & Johns, 2012), educational professionals have a vested interest in the practice and outcomes of the neurosciences. Neuroscience can provide evidence-based information to add to the knowledge base of educational practice in regard to the components and processes associated with learning (Goswami, 2008). One would expect this field and its relevance to education in general, and learning and learning difficulties specifically, to continue to grow as technological advancements are providing various opportunities for research to be conducted (Lerner & Johns, 2012).

Several practices have provided relevant information to the field of education, particularly imaging techniques for the brain, "including positron emission tomography (PET), functional magnetic resonance imaging (MRI) and electroencephalography (EEG)" (Müller, 2011, p. 1).

Müller (2011) emphasizes that these procedures may have particular relevance to detecting which portions of the brain may be involved during certain cognitive activities, as well as providing opportunities to compare and contrast typical patterns of neural activity with atypical ones. This option will obviously be of particular interest to school personnel who work with students with disabilities.

One specific area of disability that has been a focus in the activities of neuroscience is dyslexia. Lyon et al. (2003) note that there is a neurobiological aspect to dyslexia. The problems that individuals with dyslexia have with reading appear to be related to the function and structure of the brain (Lerner & Johns, 2012). Some brain imaging has exhibited that areas of the brain are activated when a person interprets words in print (Lerner & Johns, 2012). Yet studies of brain imaging have also revealed that individuals with dyslexia show noticeable differences in the functioning of the brain (Dehaene, 2009, cited in Lerner & Johns, 2012). Additional investigation will no doubt prove to be very informative. As Katzir and Paré-Blagoev (2006, p. 59) note: "Neuroscience holds the promise of differentiating among different etiologies that exhibit similar outcomes." These authors further remark that future investigations will have to discover whether individuals who have difficulty reading because of various challenges such as cognitive issues, can be distinguished from persons with dyslexia, based on the results of their brain activation during times when they are reading.

Research that connects neuroscience to outcomes in education and/or special education is still limited. In regard to research associated with educational neuroscience, results appear to have primarily assisted in the identification of the portions of the brain that are activated or fail to be activated during various types of activities (Müller, 2011). Clearly, more studies must be completed to add to the knowledge base of the association between neuroscience and education/special education, and more scientifically validated evidence must be gathered to distinguish the effect of this knowledge on instructional practice in authentic learning environments. There are authors, however, who call for caution in this area. Tommerdahl (2010, p. 97) notes that her paper takes the perspective that "neurosciences are an excellent source of knowledge regarding learning processes, but also provides a warning regarding the idea that findings from the laboratory can be directly transposed into the classroom." Particularly with the intensified interest in the field of neuroeducation, Hook and Farah (2013) also warn against the potential for misinformation. Müller (2011, p. 10) summarizes the promise of the association between neuroscience and education/special education as well as the care that should be taken in regard to the implementation of the results of this relationship to the educational environment: "It is … important to remember that while neuroscience holds much promise for the field of special education, the process of translating brain research into classroom practice must be handled methodically."

Multicultural Considerations of Students with Disabilities for Whom English is Not the First Language

The student population of the United States of America is becoming progressively more diverse (Smith et al., 2014) and the challenge for school personnel is to determine how to best provide educational services to these students (Gargiulo, 2015). A growing number of these students may not speak English as their primary language and may be limited in their English proficiency. These students are generally referred to as English language learners (ELLs) (Lerner & Johns, 2012). In addition, some ELL students have an identified disability, thereby requiring their specialized program and services to not only focus on their needs due to the disability, but also to their language concerns and how these language issues relate to the student's specialized programming (Lerner & Johns, 2012). In other words, regardless of which approach is implemented for the language instruction (e.g., bilingual instruction), the overall perspective should be the same for educational personnel who work with students who have both a disability and English language concerns: They must be supportive and sensitive not only to the students' cultural and linguistic characteristics but also to the challenges that result from the areas of disability (Gargiulo, 2015; Lerner & Johns, 2012).

Non-Discriminatory Evaluation and Identification of a Disability

It is important for school counselors to appreciate some of the concerns and issues that may present themselves as they work with students with disabilities who are also ELLs, as well as with their families. The first issue relates to the disability identification process. As you are already aware from Chapter 2 on the laws and Chapter 4 on the requirements of the evaluation process for a disability, the assessment for potential identification of a disability must be *non-discriminatory*. As has been discussed previously, non-discriminatory assessment is "one of the provisions of IDEA, which requires that testing be done in a child's native or primary language. Procedures to prevent cultural or racial discrimination are also stipulated" (Hardman et al., 2008, p. 119).

The issue of providing an appropriate and non-biased assessment for potential identification of a disability is not only a legal mandate, but clearly an ethical requirement. As you are aware from previous discussions, school counselors may be actively engaged in the identification procedures and discussions surrounding the determination of whether a disability exists for a particular student. The importance of this tenet of non-discriminatory assessment must be appreciated. It can lead to identification errors if not conscientiously implemented, particularly in cases where there are diversity issues, such as students who are not native speakers of English. In the case of ELLs, because of the language issue, the students may exhibit academic and/or social behaviors that may appear to be of concern, and are thus at risk for consideration for specialized services or special education (Blatchley & Lau, 2010). It is critical that students are not identified as having a disability when their educational concerns are based on their proficiency in the English language (Salend & Salinas, 2003).

Unfortunately, the overrepresentation of students with cultural and/or linguistic diversity has been a problem that has plagued special education (Smith et al., 2014) and is one that we must be vigilant to avoid. As Kapantzoglou et al. (2012, p. 81) note: "Bilingual children are often diagnosed with language impairment, although they may simply have fewer opportunities to learn English than English-speaking monolingual children." Clearly this is not always the case, but a disproportionate representation of students with cultural and linguistic diversity in special education is a critical issue that must be addressed by various educational personnel, including school counselors.

To assist toward eliminating this situation, a critical priority in regard to the procedures and assessment tools implemented in the assessment process for potential identification of a disability for a student who is also ELL, is that they not only be non-discriminatory as previously noted, but also be thorough, multifactored and multidisciplinary. This is particularly crucial since "inappropriate assessment measures and evaluation procedures are thought to be one of the primary reasons for the disproportionate representation of culturally and linguistically diverse students in various special education programs" (Gargiulo, 2015, p. 95). Moreover, the evaluation approaches must be appropriately rigorous to enable evaluators to distinguish between a language concern and a disability (Duarte et al., 2013). While the implementation and interpretation of valid and rigorous assessment instruments and the employment of appropriate assessment procedures should assist in moving toward resolution of misidentifications and inappropriate placements for ELLs, educational personnel may also want to consider a broader perspective such as that proposed by Gargiulo (2015, pp. 94–95): "Attention needs to be focused on the identification and referral process, assessment bias, instructional factors, and teacher attitudes, as well as environmental factors impinging on the student and the interrelationships among these variables."

While it is imperative that educators and counselors be aware of the problem of the overrepresentation of students with cultural and/or linguistic differences in special education as well as actively engage in its resolution, it is also critical to recognize and appreciate that there is a population of students who are ELLs and who, in fact, have a disability and may require specialized services, including special education. When the aforementioned type of disproportionality is coupled with the legal and ethical mandate of providing appropriate and effective programming for students who are ELLs and who, in fact, are in need of special education, it is easy to appreciate why assessment involving potential special education services for students who are ELLs is a major current issue of concern to educational personnel, including school counselors. As you are aware, Chapter 4 went into depth in regard to the assessment procedures for identifying a student with a disability. While that information is applicable, we would also like to emphasize a few of the recommendations to consider for the population of students who are ELLs and may have a disability:

- All of the data and evaluation results should be interpreted by the members of the assessment team to ensure a non-discriminatory analysis of the information and should be reviewed in the context of the student's cultural and linguistic background, including the results of the evidence-based interventions implemented (Blatchley & Lau, 2010).
- Along these same lines, if a student has participated in a Response to Intervention (RTI) approach, particularly if a disability is suspected, there should be evidence that the student has been involved with culturally and/or linguistically appropriate instruction at the various tiers of the RTI intervention process before being considered for more specialized services (Klingner & Harry, 2006).

Educational Considerations

As you are already aware from previous discussions, according to the American School Counselor Association's (ASCA) position paper, *The Professional School Counselor and*

Students with Disabilities, the responsibilities of school counselors in regard to students with disabilities include consultation and collaboration with stakeholders about adaptations and/or modifications for the student, as well as the provision of assistance with the development of plans for meeting their educational and transitional needs (ASCA, 2013). To enable school counselors in the attainment of these goals for students who have disabilities and who are ELLs, a brief discussion of issues related to the instructional needs of these students would be beneficial. The discussion will focus primarily on general concepts and practices instead of specific programming for ELLs (bilingual education, English as a second language, etc.), as a discussion of particular approaches is beyond the scope of this book.

CULTURALLY RESPONSIVE INSTRUCTION/COUNSELING AND EDUCATIONAL ENVIRONMENT

A recommendation for working with students who are ELLs and have a disability is to provide an environment of culturally responsive instruction. "Culturally responsive instruction teaches to the strengths of each student while validating and affirming their backgrounds, experiences, and cultural knowledge" (Smith et al., 2014, p. 76). A culturally responsive educator appreciates the role that culture plays in education and builds on the culture as a foundation for learning activities (Smith et al., 2014). This type of educator must also extend this practice to working with parents and families of the students and maintain open lines of communication and collaboration with them, as well as with the other stakeholders, including school counselors, in the process of providing an appropriate education to the students.

School environments, including classrooms, that are culturally responsive are ones in which cultural diversity is recognized and pertinent connections between the students and the subject matter and activities are encouraged. Particular needs and varying learning styles of the students are also acknowledged and instructional approaches correspond accordingly (Montgomery, 2001). It is also imperative that educators always focus on the fact that for these students who have a disability as well as being ELLs, a primary focus must also be on the academic and/or behavioral issues related to the disability. Educational personnel who work with students who are ELLs and have a disability must not lose sight of the fact that specialized instructional options must be based on the individual areas of need related to the disability, in addition to the focus on linguistic and cultural considerations (Hardman et al., 2008).

As noted previously, a discussion of various types of programming implemented for ELLs will not be addressed in this chapter. There are, however, some practices and techniques that have been discussed in the professional literature that provide us with some general options for meeting the needs of students with disabilities and who are ELLs. For example, Rosenberg et al. (2011) discuss the importance of implementing a curriculum that is culturally relevant, enabling the students to identify with the material and make a connection to it. Other authors have written about the technique of explicit instruction as an option (Echevarria, 2006; Montgomery, 2001), which is connected to meaningful learning activities (Rosenberg et al., 2011). Moreover, Montgomery (2001) focuses on the techniques of instruction through interdisciplinary units and instructional scaffolding, as well as the assignment of journal writing and open-ended projects where students may have variable completion dates. Further, peer teaching has also been discussed as being beneficial for students who are ELLs (Gerena & Keiler, 2012). These are but a few examples of techniques that may be considered when working with students with disabilities and who are ELLs.

THE IMPORTANCE OF SELF-ASSESSMENT

To be effective as a culturally responsive school counselor or to assist other educational personnel in their goal of becoming more culturally responsive, it is critical to evaluate your personal perceptions and beliefs and be open to the enhancement of your self-awareness. Self-examination of cultural attitudes should enable individuals to ascertain a clearer picture of how their perceptions may have an impact on their instruction or counseling, and how they may be influencing their interactions with the students and their parents and families (Rosenberg et al., 2011; Smith et al., 2014).

After self-assessment, school counselors and other educational personnel could build on this awareness to increase their knowledge base in regard to other cultures, which in turn could provide a more culturally responsive learning environment (Montgomery, 2001; Turnbull et al., 2013). As activities focused on self-awareness and critical reflections appear to fall into the natural domain of expertise for school counselors, this is a particularly appropriate and applicable aspect of the role of the school counselor when working with students who are ELLs and have disabilities.

Conceptual Application Activity 12.1

Leadership in Student Group Activities

Directions: As the school counselor, you have been requested to set up and lead/facilitate a series of five group sessions to enhance the students' awareness of cultural and linguistic diversity and English language learners (with and without disabilities), and to assist them in the self-evaluation of their own perspectives in this regard.

- Determine the age range of the students with whom you will be working in your example.
- Determine the specific topics to be covered, activities to be implemented, and scheduling factors. Provide particular focus on your leadership role as a school counselor in the identification of topics, research and delineation of content, and your engagement and facilitative activities with the students.

This activity may be completed individually, in dyads, small collaborative groups, or in a large group format.

Students with Disabilities and Bullying

A third issue of current importance for school counselors relates to bullying and students with disabilities. Bullying, including cyberbullying, has been the subject of intensive scrutiny recently across various populations of students in the schools. While it appears to be a major issue for many students, there appears to be an increased vulnerability of some students with disabilities in regard to bullying. To provide a common framework from which to build the discussion of students with disabilities and bullying, a brief overview of the topic of bullying in general will be provided.

A Description of Bullying Behavior

Although it can involve a myriad of unfortunate actions, there appears to be at least some degree of consensus as to what typifies bullying activities: (a) aggressive behavior; (b) imbalance of power; and (c) repetitive behavior or the potential for repetition of the behavior (Bullying and Children, n.d.; Bullying definition, n.d.; Limber, 2007; Shore, 2011). According to the Stopbullying.gov website (Bullying definition, n.d.):

> Bullying is unwanted, aggressive behavior among school aged children that involves a real or perceived power imbalance. The behavior is repeated, or has the potential to be repeated, over time. Both kids who are bullied and who bully others may have serious, lasting problems.

In order to be considered bullying, the behavior must be aggressive and include:

• An imbalance of power: kids who bully use their power—such as physical strength, access to embarrassing information, or popularity—to control or harm others. Power imbalances can change over time and in different situations, even if they involve the same people.
• Repetition: bullying behaviors happen more than once or have the potential to happen more than once (para. 1 and para. 2).

Bullying behavior may be exhibited in person or carried out in a more surreptitious manner, and may be carried out by a lone student or a group of students (Shore, 2011). It may include the making of threats, physically or verbally attacking someone, and other more direct types of actions (Bullying definition, n.d.; Limber, 2007). As Limber (2007, para. 2) notes, bullying can also be indirect and "can involve getting another person to bully someone for you, spreading rumors, deliberately excluding someone from a group, and cyberbullying."

On the Stopbullying.gov website (Bullying definition, n.d., para. 3) bullying behavior is delineated into three types:

• Verbal bullying is saying or writing mean things. Verbal bullying includes:
  • Teasing
  • Name-calling
  • Inappropriate sexual comments
  • Taunting
  • Threatening to cause harm.
• Social bullying, sometimes referred to as relational bullying, involves hurting someone's reputation or relationships. Social bullying includes:

- Leaving someone out on purpose
- Telling other children not to be friends with someone
- Spreading rumors about someone
- Embarrassing someone in public.
- Physical bullying involves hurting a person's body or possessions. Physical bullying includes:
- Hitting/kicking/pinching
- Spitting
- Tripping/pushing
- Taking or breaking someone's things
- Making mean or rude hand gestures.

The effects of bullying can include such serious issues as health difficulties, psychological concerns, problems with self-esteem, depression, and even suicidal thoughts or suicide, in addition to school absences and lowered academic performance (Bullying and Children, n.d.; National Center on Birth Defects and Developmental Disabilities, Centers for Disease Control and Prevention, 2014).

Cyberbullying

With the increasing technology and online media sources, the phenomenon of cyberbullying is also of concern. "Cyberbullying is bullying that takes place through the use of electronic media, such as email, text messages, phone calls, chat, social media and websites" (National Center for Learning Disabilities, n.d.a, p. 1). Cyberbullying can appear in various forms, such as rumors posted on social media sites, fake profiles, or embarrassing pictures (Bullying definition, n.d.; National Center for Learning Disabilities, n.d.a). Two particularly disturbing issues with cyberbullying are its ability to potentially provide anonymity to the person sending the information and its persistence. Cyberbullying images and messages can be posted anonymously, making the tracing of the sources difficult. Moreover, cyberbullying has no time limits. These actions can be taken day or night with no time constraints. As for the effects of cyberbullying, the effects already discussed previously in regard to bullying in general also have relevance to cyberbullying (Bullying definition, n.d; Shore, 2011).

Bullying and Its Particular Relevance to Students with Disabilities

As Limber (2007, para. 3) points out: "The research that has been conducted on bullying among children with disabilities and special needs indicates that these children may be at particular risk of being bullied by their peers." An example of one of these research studies is that of Little (2002) who, through a survey of a national sample of mothers of children with non-verbal learning disorders and Asperger's Syndrome, found a reported high incidence of peer victimization and shunning for these groups of students. Two other studies focused on students with attention deficit hyperactivity disorder (ADHD). The results from Unnever and Cornell (2003) identified ADHD as a possible risk factor for victimization and bullying, while Wiener and Mak (2009) noted that reports of victimization and/or bullying behavior were higher for students with ADHD than children without ADHD.

Additional research, however, should be a major priority, as according to Rose et al. (2012, p. 1), "research on bullying and victimization by and toward students with disabilities is in its relative infancy in the United States." As for what has been completed, it may be inadequate to attend to the seriousness of the issue (Young et al., 2011).

> While the existing literature has clearly established that students with disabilities face higher rates of bullying and victimization than the general student population, very little research on bullying prevention has focused on students with disabilities either in isolation or as an identified sub-category in broader bullying prevention initiatives.
>
> (Young et al., 2011, p. 3)

Although there is support in the research that has been completed thus far that some students with disabilities are at a high risk for bullying, it is difficult at times to obtain specific reliable statistics in regard to the incidence of bullying students with disabilities, not only because additional research is required, but also because the data can be inconsistent depending on the source of the data (National Center for Learning Disabilities, n.d.b). Despite the fact that hard statistical numbers may not always be available, "the message is clear: bullying is widespread, often goes unnoticed, and can have immediate and long-lasting consequences" (National Center for Learning Disabilities, n.d.b, p. 1).

Legal Implications of Bullying Students with Disabilities

As you are already aware, the provision of an appropriate education for students with disabilities is strongly influenced by educational law and tenets. The issue of bullying for these students has been addressed within the legal domain, in particular in relation to IDEA 2004, Section 504 of the Rehabilitation Act of 1973, and the Americans with Disabilities Act (ADA) (Eckes & Gibbs, 2012). Some of the bullying behaviors may be perceived legally as a limitation or denial of a *free appropriate public education (FAPE)* or as *disability-based harassment*, which could lead to denial of educational opportunity for students with disabilities. Clearly, these are issues that have direct applicability to the provisions and protections of the aforementioned laws (Learning Disabilities Association of America, 2014a).

The Office of Civil Rights (OCR) at the US Department of Education and the Office of Special Education and Rehabilitative Services (OSERS) have distributed documents over the past several years addressing the issue of bullying and students with disabilities (Council for Exceptional Children, 2014; Learning Disabilities Association of America, 2014a). This anti-bullying guidance includes:

- A 2013 "Dear colleague" letter and enclosure by OSERS, clarifying that when bullying of a student with a disability results in the student not receiving meaningful educational benefit under IDEA, the school must remedy the problem, regardless of whether the bullying was based on the student's disability.
- A 2010 "Dear colleague" letter by OCR, which elaborated on potential violations when bullying and harassment is based on race, color, national origin, sex, or disability.

- A 2000 "Dear colleague" letter by the OCR and OSERS, which explained that bullying based on disability may violate civil rights laws enforced by OCR as well as interfere with a student's receipt of special education under the Individuals with Disabilities Education Act (IDEA) (Council for Exceptional Children, 2014, para. 2).

The OCR also issued information to guide schools regarding the bullying of students with disabilities in October, 2014 (Lhamon, 2014). This guidance was disseminated through a letter to educators discussing the responsibilities of public schools in regard to bullying activities as they relate to students with disabilities, according to the Rehabilitation Act, Section 504, and Title II of the ADA. This letter of guidance makes clear that the protections for students with disabilities who may be the victims of bullying, regardless of the basis, extend to the students who may not be eligible for services according to IDEA 2004 standards, but who are entitled to specialized services through the Rehabilitation Act of 1973, Section 504. The overall message is that if students with disabilities are victims of being bullied, the federal law mandates schools to respond appropriately and immediately in the investigation of the issue, and resolve the concern by stopping the bullying and the possibility of this behavior being repeated (Council for Exceptional Children, 2014).

According to Catherine E. Lhamon, the assistant secretary for civil rights and the author of the 2014 letter of guidance, "bullying of a student on the basis of his or her disability may result in a disability-based harassment violation under Section 504 and Title II" (Lhamon, 2014, para. 7). If the bullying results in a hostile environment and interferes or limits a student's participation or benefit from school services, opportunities, or activities, remedies and resolutions must be enacted (Lhamon, 2014). From the legal perspective of non-discrimination of students with disabilities according to Section 504 and Title II of ADA, it is clear that schools must be concerned that disability-based harassment may lead to a denial of educational opportunity for students with disabilities (Learning Disabilities Association of America, 2014a).

Working toward Resolution

According to the Council for Exceptional Children, in its "CEC's policy on safe and positive school climate":

> Available research confirms that students feel safer and learn better when schools have clear policies prohibiting harassment and discrimination and when all members of the school community (students, parents, educators, administrators, and other school personnel) actively uphold the right of every student to a safe learning environment.
> (Council for Exceptional Children, 2008, p. 1)

While most people would no doubt support this contention, ensuring a safe and positive learning environment requires consistent attention.

To work toward this objective, numerous practices have been recommended, some of which will be discussed briefly here to provide examples. Perhaps a logical place to begin this conversation is with the schools and educational agencies, in that they have the responsibility for providing an environment conducive to learning and the students' personal

Figure 12.1 School counselors can play a critical role in advocating for students against bullying and supporting all students to be educated in safe and accepting environments.
Source: ©iStockphoto.com, www.istockphoto.com/photo/elementary-school-37979234.

safety. Schools must have anti-bullying policies in place and enforce them justly and con- sistently (Ali, 2010; Cantu & Heumann, 2000; Council for Exceptional Children, 2008; Shore, 2011). The policy must be clear and notify students and personnel that harassment of an individual with a disability is not only unacceptable but violates federal law (Cantu & Heumann, 2000). The policy should be reviewed not only with students and school staff members, but should also be shared with the parents of the students (Shore, 2011).

In addition to the existence and consistent implementation of a clear and compre- hensive school policy, it is important for school personnel to always attend to the afore- mentioned possibility that bullying may be having a detrimental effect on the students receiving a free appropriate public education according to their individualized educa- tion programs (IEPs). Consequently, as Musgrove and Yudin recommend in their letter of guidance from the US Department of Education, Office of Special Education and Rehabilitative Services:

> The school should, as part of its appropriate response to the bullying, convene the IEP Team to determine whether, as a result of the effects of the bullying, the student's needs have changed such that the IEP is no longer designed to provide meaningful educational benefit. If the IEP is no longer designed to provide a meaningful educational benefit to the student, the IEP Team must then determine to what extent additional or different special education or related services are needed to address the student's individual needs; and revise the IEP accordingly.
> (Musgrove and Yudin, 2013, p. 3)

As the Stopbullying.gov website (Bullying and Children, n.d.a.) also recommends, Section 504 teams should meet to ensure that the student's needs are being met through a review of the plan.

The previously mentioned 2013 guidance letter from OSERS (Musgrove & Yudin, 2013) also provided an enclosure entitled, *Effective Evidence-based Practices for Preventing and Addressing Bullying* (2013), which discussed several evidence-based practices for schools to consider for addressing the problem of bullying. Among the practices discussed were: (a) the implementation of a behavioral framework that is both comprehensive and multi-tiered; (b) the assurance of the provision of adult supervision; (c) the provision of ongoing support and professional development in the application of evidence-based techniques for responding to bullying and inappropriate behavior; and (d) the maintenance of the practices and policies related to bullying prevention over time to ensure that they become an integral part of the school's environment.

Adding to this list, the National Center on Birth Defects and Developmental Disabilities, Centers for Disease Control and Prevention (2014) also recommends that school personnel and other pertinent adults be certain that students with disabilities are aware of the meaning and practices of bullying, as some students with disabilities may not fully appreciate or recognize that they are being bullied, or they are uncertain how to discuss what is transpiring, or how to respond appropriately to it. The National Center for Learning Disabilities (n.d.b) notes the importance of determining safe ways for students to engage in the reporting of bullying and implementing anti-bullying awareness programming on a school-wide basis. As Raskauskas and Modell (2011) note, however, school personnel should be aware that modifications to existing programs may be required for students with disabilities if anti-bullying programs are to include *all* the students of the school.

All of the practices and recommendations discussed thus far certainly have relevance to the role of the school counselor in regard to the problem of bullying and students with disabilities. In their guidance letter, Cantu and Heumann (2000, para. 10) also propose some practices to preclude or eliminate harassment, some of which are even more directly related to the functions of a school counselor, such as "counseling both person(s) who have been harmed by harassment and person(s) who have been responsible for the harassment of others [and] implementing monitoring programs to follow up on resolved issues of disability harassment." Other activities in which school counselors may directly participate and that have a close association with their role functions include: (a) group counseling meetings or activities to discuss various aspects of bullying; (b) engaging the students in role-playing social situations; (c) presenting lessons associated with the theme of bullying or collaborating with other educational personnel in the presentation of these activities; and (d) supporting the students who are bullied and work to assist them with the acquisition and practice of coping skills (Shore, 2011).

Many times throughout this text, there has been mention of the importance of advocacy in regard to working with students with disabilities. This is again an applicable topic in the discussion of bullying and students with disabilities. Clearly, based on the discussion thus far, the school counselor may play a critical role in acting as an advocate for students with disabilities in numerous ways, including instances of bullying and harassment. Moreover, school counselors may also assist in the development of peer advocacy options. "Peer advocacy—speaking out on the behalf of others—is a unique approach that empowers students to protect those targeted by bullying" (PACER's

National Bullying Prevention Center, n.d., para. 1). For additional information in regard to the possibility of peer advocacy, please refer to the *Peer Advocacy Guide* (Hertzog, 2012) from PACER's National Bullying Prevention Center at www.pacer.org/bullying/resources/toolkits/pdf/PeerAdvocacyGuide.pdf.

The critical skill of self-advocacy has also been discussed throughout this text in regard to students with disabilities, and again school counselors can be a vital resource for enabling the students to acquire these skills. PACER's National Bullying Prevention Center (2014) provides an example of a self-advocacy resource in the form of a *Student Action Plan*, which invites the student, with or without assistance, to complete three steps: (a) describe the bullying situation and reflect on your reactions to it; (b) consider how that situation could have turned out differently, including what changes could be made; and (c) determine what would have to be accomplished for the changes to be achieved. Please refer to PACER's National Bullying Prevention Center (2014) at www.pacer.org/bullying/pdf/StudentActionPlan.pdf for additional information regarding this approach. Working with students with disabilities on such a plan and assisting them to complete the steps could have many benefits in the situation at the time, as well as the added advantage of having a tool from which to work in potential future situations.

Conceptual Application Activity 12.2

Interview Professionals about the Problem of Bullying Students with Disabilities

Directions: Interview two school counselors to relate their experiences with the issue of students with disabilities being bullied. What resolutions would they recommend for alleviating the problem? What insights have you gained from your interviews about this issue? Discuss your findings in small or large group formats.

With the potential for such high-stakes results for students with disabilities who are victims of bullying, it is clear why educators must be concerned with this issue. School counselors can play a critical role in ensuring that students with disabilities are not prevented from benefitting from an appropriate education and specialized services due to bullying behaviors, whether in person or through electronic media. By virtue of their educational preparation and expertise, school counselors will not only be a source of advocacy and support for the students, but also for parents and families of the students who are experiencing bullying, and a resource for other educational personnel who are working to ensure that all students have a safe environment in which to learn and grow.

Graduation Rates and Students with Disabilities

This text has had a major purpose of expanding the knowledge base and practice of school counselors to assist them as they become instrumental partners and engaged participants in providing an appropriate education and services to students with disabilities. Special education is an ever-evolving field and, like all aspects of educational services, requires reflection and critique and change in response to current and future

Figure 12.2 Assisting all students in reaching the goal of graduation from high school falls within the professional domain of school counselors.

Source: ©iStockphoto.com, www.istockphoto.com/photo/students-on-computers-37433292.

concerns. As a school counselor, your input into areas that are still of concern can prove to be invaluable, as you will be adding your special expertise and perception to the conversation.

One of the persisting areas of concern regarding the education of students with disabilities is the graduation rate of the students. This is an area of interest to all educators and school counselors, with particular relevance to those at the secondary level. As school counselors are actively involved in the guidance of students to meet their goals and requirements for completing their educational programs, they should be aware that there is still a lag in graduation rates for students with disabilities.

Examples of recent documentation have verified that the average graduation rate for students with disabilities is lower than that of the overall national average rate. A report entitled, *Building a GradNation: Progress and Challenge in Ending the High School Dropout Epidemic* (Balfanz et al., 2014) was issued by Civic Enterprises, Everyone Graduates Center at the School of Education at Johns Hopkins University, America's Promise Alliance, and Alliance for Excellent Education. The report is related to the GradNation campaign to increase the national graduation rate to 90 percent by 2020 (Learning Disabilities Association of America, 2014b). The report certainly provided some promising outcomes, noting that the national graduation rate had exceeded 80 percent for the first time in history, but it also recounted that in regard to students with disabilities, the national average graduation rate was 20 percentage points lower than the overall average graduation rate on a national level. Moreover, the report discussed the point that the rates of graduation for students with disabilities varied widely by state (Balfanz et al., 2014; Learning Disabilities Association of America, 2014b).

A second document was issued through the National Center for Learning Disabilities and is entitled, *Diplomas at Risk: A Critical Look at the Graduation Rate of Students with Learning Disabilities* (Cortiella, 2013). Although this report was more focused on the specific area of learning disabilities, it again exhibits an issue related to graduation with regular diplomas. Students with specific learning disabilities (SLD) comprise the largest group of students who are eligible for services through special education in the public schools, but only 68 percent of them left school in the 2010–2011 academic year with a regular diploma. Thus, although there have been improvements in the rates of graduation and dropout for students with SLD, the rate at which they secure high school diplomas is still low (Cortiella, 2013).

As assisting students in reaching their goal of graduating from high school falls naturally within the domain of school counselors, it is important that they are not only aware of issues of disparity, but work toward their elimination. Some of the options that may work toward a resolution may already be in place at the school and may require continued implementation or revision depending on the particular situation. For example, the authors of the aforementioned report *Building a GradNation: Progress and Challenge in Ending the High School Dropout Epidemic* (Balfanz et al., 2014) acknowledge that school practices such as multi-tiered support systems, team approaches for addressing academic and behavioral concerns, and increased options for inclusion in the general education environment may have an influence on improving the situation (Learning Disabilities Association of America, 2014b). In addition, the implementation of more effective transition programming, already an IEP-related requirement, should prove to be a method by which students complete their secondary requirements and move on to the next stage of their lives. The transition practices that have been discussed, particularly in Chapter 9, have the potential to positively impact the retention and graduation rates of students with disabilities.

Further, in their discussion of evidence-based practices related to dropout prevention, Pyle and Wexler (2012) note that the research indicates that schools can work toward prevention of the dropout problem by identifying students most at risk of dropping out of school, and providing them with instructional and behavioral support through access to an adult acting as their advocate, as well as through the provision of relevant and personal learning activities. "It is possible to identify, monitor, and intervene based on students' risk indicators to maximize student engagement, thereby increasing students' ability to progress in school, stay in school, and complete school" (Pyle and Wexler, 2012, p. 287).

Conclusion

The issues discussed in this chapter are not only current critical issues in the field of special education, but also have direct relevance to the role of school counselors as they work with students with disabilities. Continuing a commitment to lifelong learning and keeping current with the ever-evolving practices and concerns of school counseling and special education will not only encourage reflection on the positive and supportive relationship between the two fields, but will expand the school counselor's knowledge base and practices for working with the students with disabilities and the various stakeholders in their lives. Being aware of trends and issues of importance to students with disabilities and their families, and applying them to current situations, will enable school counselors to fulfill one of the major emphases of their roles, as noted on the position paper of the ASCA, *The Professional School Counselor and Students with Disabilities*: "Professional school counselors are committed to helping all students realize their potential and meet or exceed academic standards regardless of challenges resulting from disabilities and other special needs" (ASCA, 2013, para.1).

References

Ali, R. (2010). *Dear Colleague Letter (United States Department of Education, Office for Civil Rights)*. Retrieved from www2.ed.gov/about/offices/list/ocr/letters/colleague-201010.pdf.

ASCA (2013). *The Professional School Counselor and Students with Disabilities*. Retrieved from www.schoolcounselor.org/asca/media/asca/PositionStatements/PS_Disabilities.pdf.

Balfanz, R., Bridgeland, J. M., Fox, J. H., DePaoli, J. L., Ingram, E. S., & Maushard, M. (2014). *Building a GradNation: Progress and Challenge in Ending the High School Dropout Epidemic*. Retrieved from http://gradnation.org/sites/default/files/17548_BGN_Report_FinalFULL_5.2.14.pdf.

Blatchley, L. A. & Lau, M. Y. (2010). Culturally competent assessment of English language learners for special education services. *Communiqué Handout*, 38(7), 1–8. Retrieved from www.nasponline.org/publications/cq/pdf/V38N7_CulturallyCompetentAssessment.pdf.

Boztepel, E. (2003) Issues in code-switching: competing theories and models. In Teachers College, Columbia University, *Bullying and Children and Youth with Disabilities and Special Health Needs*. Retrieved from www.stopbullying.gov/at-risk/groups/special-needs/BullyingTipSheet.pdf.

Bullying definition (n.d.) Retrieved from www.stopbullying.gov/what-is-bullying/definition/index.html.

Cantu, N. V. & Heumann, J. E. (2000). *Dear Colleague Letter: Prohibited Disability Harassment (United States Department of Education)*. Retrieved from www2.ed.gov/about/offices/list/ocr/docs/disabharassltr.html.

Cortiella, C. (2013). *Diplomas at Risk: A Critical Look at the Graduation Rate of Students with Learning Disabilities*. New York: National Center for Learning Disabilities, Inc. Retrieved from www.ncld.org/images/content/files/diplomas-at-risk/DiplomasatRisk.pdf.

Council for Exceptional Children (2008). CEC's policy on safe and positive school climate. In *Council for Exceptional Children 2008 Policy Manual*. Retrieved from www.cec.sped.org/~/media/Files/Policy/CEC%20Professional%20Policies%20and%20Positions/safe%20and%20positive.pdf.

Council for Exceptional Children (2014). US Department of Education announces guidance on bullying of students with disabilities. *Policy Insider*, October 22. Retrieved from www.policyinsider.org/2014/10/us-department-of-education-announces-guidance-on-bullying-of-students-with-disabilities.html?utm_source=Copy+of+Policy+Insider+-+October+22%2C+2014&utm_campaign=PI+July+9&utm_medium=email.

Duarte, B. A., Greybeck, B., & Simpson, C. G. (2013). Evaluating bilingual students for learning disabilities. *Advances in Special Education*, 24, 129–139.

Echevarria, J. (2006). *Helping English Language Learners Succeed*. Retrieved from www.nassp.org/portals/0/content/53392.pdf.

Eckes, S. & Gibbs, J. (2012). The legal aspects of bullying and harassment of students with disabilities: school leaders' legal obligations. *Journal of School Leadership*, 22, 1065–1086.

Enclosure: Effective Evidence-based Practices for Preventing and Addressing Bullying (2013). Retrieved from www2.ed.gov/policy/speced/guid/idea/memosdcltrs/bullyingdcl-enclosure-8-20-13.pdf.

Gargiulo, R. M. (2015). *Special Education in Contemporary Society: An Introduction to Exceptionality*, 5th edn. Thousand Oaks, CA: Sage.

Gerena, L. & Keiler, L. (2012). Effective intervention with urban secondary English language learners: how peer instructors support learning. *Bilingual Research Journal*, 35(1), 76–97.

Goswami, U. (2004). Neuroscience, education, and special education. *British Journal of Special Education*, 31(4), 175–183.

Goswami, U. (2008). Principles of learning, implications for teaching: a cognitive neuroscience perspective. *Journal of Philosophy of Special Education*, 42(3–4), 381–399.

Hardman, M. L., Drew, C. J., & Egan, M. W. (2008). *Human Exceptionality: School, Community and Family*, 9th edn. Boston, MA: Houghton Mifflin Company.

Hertzog, J. (2012). *The Peer Advocacy Guide*. Minneapolis, MN: PACER Center. Retrieved from www.pacer.org/bullying/resources/toolkits/pdf/PeerAdvocacyGuide.pdf.

Hook, C. J. & Farah, M. J. (2013). Neuroscience for educators: what are they seeking, and what are they finding? *Neuroethics*, 6(2), 331–341.

Jensen, E. P. (2008). A fresh look at brain-based education. *Phi Delta Kappan*, 89(6), 408–417.

Kapantzoglou, M., Restrepo, M. A., & Thompson, M. S. (2012). Dynamic assessment of word learning skills: identifying language impairment in bilingual children. *Language, Speech and Hearing Services in Schools*, 43(1), 81–96.

Katzir, T. & Paré-Blagoev, J. (2006). Applying cognitive neuroscience research to education: the case of literacy. *Educational Psychologist*, 41(1), 53–74.

Klingner, J. K. & Harry, B. (2006). The special education referral and decision-making process for English language learners: child study team meetings and placement conferences. *Teachers College Record*, 108(11), 2247–2281.

Learning Disabilities Association of America (2014a). Bullying guidance focuses on students with disabilities. *LDA Legislative News*, October. Retrieved from http://ldaamerica.org/lda-legislative-news-october-2014/#bully?utm_source=LDA+Legislative+News+-+October+2014&utm_campaign=Legislative+News&utm_medium=email.

Learning Disabilities Association of America (2014b). Grad rate for student with disabilities continues to lag. *LDA Legislative News*, May. Retrieved from http://ldaamerica.org/lda-legislative-n ews-may-2014/#charterschools?utm_source=LDA+Legislative+News+-+May+2014&utm_campaign=Legislative+News&utm_medium=email.

Lerner, J. W. & Johns, B. H. (2012). *Learning Disabilities and Related Mild Disabilities: Teaching Strategies and New Directions*, 12th edn. Belmont, CA: Wadsworth, Cengage Learning.

Lhamon, C. E. (2014). *Dear Colleague Letter (United States Department of Education, Office for Civil Rights)*. Retrieved from www2.ed.gov/about/offices/list/ocr/letters/colleague-bullying-201410.pdf.

Limber, S. P. (2007). *Bullying among Children and Youth with Disabilities and Special Needs*. Retrieved from www.ldonline.org/article/20001.

Little, L. (2002). Middle-class mothers' perceptions of peer and sibling victimization among children with Asperger's Syndrome and nonverbal learning disorders. *Issues in Comprehensive Pediatric Nursing*, 25, 43–57.

Lyon, G. R., Shaywitz, S. E., & Shaywitz, B. A. (2003). Part I: Defining dyslexia, comorbidity, teachers' knowledge of language and reading a definition of dyslexia. *Annals of Dyslexia*, 53, 1–14.

Montgomery, W. (2001). Creating culturally responsive, inclusive classrooms. *Teaching Exceptional Children*, 33(4), 4–9.

Müller, E. (2011). Neuroscience and special education. *In Forum, Brief Policy Analysis*, July, 1–11. Retrieved from http://nasdse.org/DesktopModules/DNNspot-Store/ProductFiles/72_f2f7f9b7-ff92-4cda-a843-c817497e81e4.pdf.

Musgrove, M. & Yudin, M. K. (2013). *Dear Colleague Letter (United States Department of Education, Office of Special Education and Rehabilitative Services)*. Retrieved from www.policyinsider.org/2014/10/us-department-of-education-announces-guidance-on-bullying-of-students-with-disabilities.html?utm_source=Copy+of+Policy+Insider+-+October+22%2C+2014&utm_campaign=PI+July+9&utm_medium=email.

National Center for Learning Disabilities (n.d.a). *Seven Resources for Stopping Cyberbullying.* Retrieved from http://ncld.org/parents-child-disabilities/bullying/seven-resources-stopping-cyberbullying.

National Center for Learning Disabilities (n.d.b). *The Truth about Bullying and LD.* Retrieved from http://ncld.org/parents-child-disabilities/bullying/truth-about-bullying-ld.

National Center on Birth Defects and Developmental Disabilities, Centers for Disease Control and Prevention (2014). *Bullying.* Retrieved from www.cdc.gov/ncbddd/disabilityandsafety/bullying.html.

PACER's National Bullying Prevention Center (n.d.). *Peer Advocacy: A Unique Bullying Prevention Model for Students with Disabilities.* Retrieved from www.pacer.org/bullying/resources/students-with-disabilities/peer-advocacy.asp.

PACER's National Bullying Prevention Center (2014). *Student Action Plan Against Bullying!* Retrieved from www.pacer.org/bullying/pdf/StudentActionPlan.pdf.

Pyle, N. & Wexler, J. (2012). Preventing students with disabilities from dropping out. *Intervention in School and Clinic,* 47(5), 283–289.

Raskauskas, J. & Modell, S. (2011). Modifying anti-bullying programs to include students with disabilities. *Teaching Exceptional Children,* 44(1), 60–67.

Rose, C. A., Swearer, S. M., & Espelage, D. L. (2012). Bullying and students with disabilities: the untold narrative. *Focus on Exceptional Children,* 45(2), 1–10.

Rosenberg. M. S., Westling, D. L., & McLeskey, J. (2011). *Special Education for Today's Teachers: An Introduction,* 2nd edn. Upper Saddle River, NJ: Pearson Education, Inc.

Salend, S. J. & Salinas, A. (2003). Language differences or learning difficulties, the work of the multidisciplinary team. *Teaching Exceptional Children,* 35(4), 36–43.

Shore, K. (2011). *An Educator's Guide to Bullying Prevention.* Port Chester, NY: National Professional Resources, Inc.

Smith, D. D., Tyler, N. C. and Smith, S. (2014). *Introduction to Contemporary Special Education: New Horizons.* Upper Saddle River, NJ: Pearson Education, Inc.

Tommerdahl, J. (2010). A model for bridging the gap between neuroscience and education. *Oxford Review of Education,* 36(1), 97–109.

Turnbull, A., Turnbull, R., Wehmeyer, M. L., & Shogren, K. A. (2013). *Exceptional Lives: Special Education in Today's Schools,* 7th edn. Upper Saddle River, NJ: Pearson Education, Inc.

Unnever, J. D. & Cornell, D. G. (2003). Bullying, self-control, and ADHD. *Journal of Interpersonal Violence,* 18(2), 129–147.

Wiener, J. & Mak, M. (2009). Peer victimization in children with attention-deficit/hyperactivity disorder. *Psychology in the Schools,* 46(2), 116–131.

Willis, J. (2008). Building a bridge from neuroscience to the classroom. *Phi Delta Kappan,* 89(6), 424–427.

Young, J., Ne'eman, A., & Gelser, S. (2011). *Bullying and Students with Disabilities: A Briefing Paper from the National Council on Disability.* Retrieved from http://www.ncd.gov/publications/2011/March92011.

Appendix: Resources for Working with Students with Disabilities

The ASCA National Model and the Role of the School Counselor in Working with Students with Disabilities

- American School Counselor Association (ASCA)
  http://schoolcounselor.org
- ASCA Mindsets and Behaviors for Student Success
  http://schoolcounselor.org/school-counselors-members/about-asca/mindsets-behaviors
- ASCA Position Statement on the Professional School Counselor and Students with Disabilities
  http://schoolcounselor.org/asca/media/asca/PositionStatements/PS_Disabilities.pdf
- ASCA School Counselor Competencies
  http://schoolcounselor.org/asca/media/asca/home/SCCompetencies.pdf
- Council for Accreditation of Counseling & Relate Educational Programs
  www.cacrep.org

General Information in Regard to Students with Disabilities and Special Education

- Council for Exceptional Children (CEC)
  www.cec.sped.org
- Easter Seals
  www.easterseals.com
- IDEA Partnership
  www.ideapartnership.org
- The IRIS Center, Peabody College, Vanderbilt University and Claremont Graduate University
  http://iris.peabody.vanderbilt.edu
- National Center for Special Education Research (Institute of Education Sciences)
  www.dol.gov/odep
- Special Education Resources
  www.specialednet.com/resources.htm
- Special Education Resources on the Internet (SERI)
  www.seriweb.com

Information Related to Legislative, Procedural, and Educational Issues Focused on Students with Disabilities and Special Education

- American Speech-Hearing-Language Association (ASHA), Individualized Education Program (IEP) Guidance
  www.asha.org/SLP/schools/IEPs
- Center on Response to Intervention at American Institutes for Research
  www.rti4success.org
- Council for Exceptional Children, *A Primer on the IDEA 2004 Regulations*
  www.cec.sped.org/Policy-and-Advocacy/Current-Sped-Gifted-Issues/
  Individuals-with-Disabilities-Education-Act/A-Primer-on-the-IDEA-2004
  -RegulationsIDEA
- R. Heitin, *Writing IEP Goals*, LD Online
  www.ldonline.org/article/42058
- Individuals with Disabilities Education Improvement Act, Public Law 108–446, 108th Congress, An Act (2004)
  www.copyright.gov/legislation/pl108-446.pdf
- Massachusetts Department of Education (2001). *IEP Process Guide.*
  www.doe.mass.edu/sped/iep/proguide.pdf
  This is an example of a State Department of Education's website in regard to the IEP process. The reader is invited to locate his/her particular State Department of Education.
- Massachusetts Department of Elementary and Secondary Education, Special Education
  www.doe.mass.edu/sped/parents.html
  This is an example of a State Department of Education's website in regard to students with disabilities and special education. The reader is invited to locate his/her particular State Department of Education.
- OSEP Technical Assistance Center, PBIS Positive Behavioral Interventions and Supports
  www.pbis.org
- PACER Center
  www.pacer.org
- RTI Action Network, A Program of the National Center for Learning Disabilities (Response to Intervention)
  www.rtinetwork.org
- US Department of Education, Office for Civil Rights (2010). *Guidelines for Educators and Administrators for Implementing Section 504 of the Rehabilitation Act of 1973: Subpart D*
  http://doe.sd.gov/oess/documents/sped_section504_Guidelines.pdf
- US Department of Education, Office of Special Education and Rehabilitative Services (OSERS), *Welcome to OSEP, OSERS' Office of Special Education Programs*
  www2.ed.gov/about/offices/list/osers/osep/index.html
- US Department of Education, the Rehabilitation Act
  http://www2.ed.gov/policy/speced/reg/narrative.html
- Wrightslaw
  www.wrightslaw.com

Information Related to Issues Focused on Specific Classifications of Disabilities

- American Association on Intellectual and Developmental Disabilities (AAIDD)
  www.aamr.org
- American Speech-Language-Hearing Association (ASHA)
  www.asha.org/default.aspx
- Autism Society
  www.autism-society.org
- Children and Adults with Attention Deficit/Hyperactivity Disorder
  www.chadd.org
- Children's Mental Health and Emotional or Behavioral Disorders Project
  www.pacer.org/cmh
- Council for Children with Behavioral Disorders (CCBD), Council for Exceptional Children
  www.ccbd.net/home
- Council for Learning Disabilities
  www.cldinternational.org
- Division for Communicative Disabilities and Deafness, Council for Exceptional Children
  http://community.cec.sped.org/DCDD/home
- Division for Physical, Health, and Multiple Disabilities, Council for Exceptional Children
  http://community.cec.sped.org/DPHMD/Home
- Division on Autism and Developmental Disabilities, Council for Exceptional Children
  http://daddcec.org/Home.aspx
- Division on Visual Impairments and Deaf-Blindness, Council for Exceptional Children
  http://community.cec.sped.org/DVI/Home
- Easter Seals Autism Spectrum Disorder Services
  www.easterseals.com/our-programs/autism-services
- International Dyslexia Association
  http://eida.org
- Learning Disabilities Association of America
  http://ldaamerica.org
- National Center on Deaf-Blindness
  https://nationaldb.org
- National Center on Learning Disabilities
  www.ncld.org
- National Down Syndrome Congress
  www.ndsccenter.org
- National Down Syndrome Society
  www.ndss.org
- National Federation of the Blind (NFB)
  https://nfb.org
- National Library Service for the Blind and Physically Handicapped (NLS), Library of Congress
  www.loc.gov/nls

- TASH (formerly referred to as the Association for Persons with Severe Handicaps)
  http://tash.org
- The Arc, for people with intellectual and developmental disabilities
  www.thearc.org
- The National Institute on Deafness and Other Communication Disorders (NIDCD)
  www.nidcd.nih.gov/Pages/default.aspx
- United Cerebral Palsy
  http://ucp.org

Counseling Theories and Students with Disabilities

- Characteristics of Students with Attention Deficit Hyperactivity Disorder
  www.naset.org/2739.0.html
- Characteristics of Students with Autism Spectrum Disorder
  www.child-autism-parent-cafe.com/characteristics-for-autism.html
- Characteristics of Students with Emotional and Behavioral Disorders
  www.education.com/reference/article/children-emotional-behavioral -disorders
- Characteristics of Students with Intellectual Disabilities
  www.education.com/reference/article/characteristics-intellectual-disabilities
- Characteristics of Students with Learning Disabilities
  www.pepperdine.edu/disabilityservices/students/ldcharacter.htm
- Cognitive Therapy for Students with Emotional and Behavioral Disorders
  www.kidsmentalhealth.org/cognitive-therapy-for-children-with-behavioral-
  and-emotional-disorders
- Motivational Interviewing
  www.nova.edu/gsc/forms/mi_rationale_techniques.pdf
- Person-Centered Counseling with Students with Disabilities
  www.socialworktoday.com/archive/exc_011909.shtml
- Rational Emotive Behavior Therapy and Students with Disabilities
  www.academia.edu/7361167/Rational_Emotive_Behavior_Therapy_with_Diverse_
  Student_Populations_Meeting_the_Mental_Health_Needs_of_All_Students

Creative Counseling Strategies

- A Guide to Literature for Students with Disabilities
  www.kidsource.com/NICHCY/literature.html
- Social Stories
  www.kidsource.com/NICHCY/literature.html
- Using Art to Work with Students with Disabilities
  www.incredibleart.org/files/special.htm

Groups and Students with Disabilities

- www.brighthubeducation.com/special-ed-inclusion-strategies/74903-group-
  therapy-and-intervention-for-emotionally-disabled-students
- http://learningdisabilities.about.com/od/collegevocationalschool/ht/how2study-
  group.htm

Information Related to Transition Issues Focused on Students with Disabilities

- College and Career Readiness and Success Center at American Institutes for Research
  www.ccrscenter.org
- Division on Career Development and Transition, Council for Exceptional Children
  http://community.cec.sped.org/dcdt/home
- Easter Seals, Employment and Training
  www.easterseals.com/our-programs/employment-training
- Internet Special Education Resources: Gap Programs and Young Adult Transition Programs
  www.iser.com/young-adult-transitions.html
- National Post-School Outcomes Center (University of Oregon)
  http://psocenter.org
- National Postsecondary Education Programs Network (PEPNET2)
  www.pepnet.org
- National Secondary Transition Technical Assistance Center (NSTTAC)
  www.nsttac.org
- PACER's National Parent Center on Transition and Employment
  www.pacer.org/transition
- Transition Coalition, University of Kansas
  www.transitioncoalition.org/transition
- United States Department of Labor. Office of Disability Employment Policy
  www.dol.gov/odep

Providing Support for Educators who Work with Students with Disabilities

- www.educationworld.com/a_admin/admin/admin407.shtml
- www.pbis.org
- www.rti4success.org/essential-components-rti
- http://schoolclimate.org/climate
- www.washingtonpost.com/blogs/answer-sheet/wp/2013/05/02/why-collaboration-is-vital-to-creating-effective-schools

Information Related to Current and Evolving Issues in Special Education

- Center on Technology and Disability
  www.ctdinstitute.org
- Division for Culturally and Linguistically Diverse Exceptional Learners, Council for Exceptional Children
  http://community.cec.sped.org/DDEL/homepage
- Division for Research, Council for Exceptional Children
  www.cecdr.org
- National Center on Accessible Educational Materials
  http://aem.cast.org

- National Center on Educational Outcomes
  www.cehd.umn.edu/nceo/default.html
- National Dropout Prevention Center for Students with Disabilities (NDPC-SD)
  www.ndpc-sd.org
- PACER Center Multicultural Services
  www.pacer.org/multicultural
- PACER's National Bullying Prevention Center
  www.pacer.org/bullying
- Special Education Resources for General Educators
  http://serge.ccsso.org
- K. Stanberry & M. H. Raskind (2009). *Assistive Technology for Kids with Learning Disabilities: An Overview*, LD Online
  www.ldonline.org/article/33074

Index

accommodations 28, 41, 46, 81, 91, 93, 120, 170–3; collaboration 16; environmental supports 41, 168
advocacy 15, 167, 223–4
Adler, Alfred 110–12
American Association on Intellectual and Developmental Disabilities (AAIDD) 48
American Psychiatric Association (APA) 38
American School Counselor Association (ASCA) 10, 181, 227, 230
American Speech–Language-Hearing Association (ASHA) 42
Americans with Disabilities Act (ADA) of 2008 (P.L. 110–325) 5, 26, 29, 169, 172, 220
Americans with Disabilities Act Amendments (ADAA) 26, 29, 169
applied behavior analysis (ABA) 41–2
art, in counseling; materials 130–1, 141
ASCA Mindsets and Behaviors for Student Success 10, 12, 17
ASCA National Model: components and themes 3, 9–11, 13–16
ASCA School Counselor Competencies 6, 12
Asperger's disorder 38, 132, 221
assessments *see* evaluation
assistive technology: Alternative and Augmentative Communication (AAC) 51, 58
Attention Deficit Hyperactivity Disorder (ADHD) 52–3, 150, 219
autism spectrum disorder (ASD) 21, 37–9, 151, 232–3

behavior: adaptive 47; *externalizing* 43; functional behavioral and intervention plan 44, 86–7; *internalizing, 43 see also* assessment
Behavioral Theory 112–16
Berg, Insoo Kim 117
bibliocounseling 126–7
bullying 106, 141, 189, 217–24, 234; cyber 217, 219

Character Education 59, 190
child find 22, 157–200
classical conditioning 112
collaboration 16, 181, 183, 196–206
community asset mapping 199–200
consultation 97, 138, 179, 196–200
Council for Accreditation of Counseling and Related Educational Programs (CACREP) 6
Council for Exceptional Children 38, 157, 230–5
creative counseling approaches *see* specific theories

dance and movement, in counseling 126, 132
deaf-blindness 39, 57–8, 232–3
deafness 23, 37, 39, 54–5, 232
de Shazer, Steve 117
differential reinforcement of behavior 113
differentiated instruction 46
due process *see* procedural safeguards
dyslexia 40, 45, 213, 232

Education for all Handicapped Children Act (P.L. 94-142) 5, 20, 22
Education of the Handicapped Amendments (P.L. 99-457; P.L. 101-476) 21
Elementary and Secondary Education Act (ESEA) *see* Every Student Succeeds Act
emotional disturbance (ED) 37, 39–40, 42–4, 117
English language learners (ELLs) 214, 217
Epstein Typology of Collaboration 200, 205, 207
evaluation: accountability component 14; counseling 107; groups 149–50; multifactored 68, 78; nondiscriminatory 20, 22, 214
Every Student Succeeds Act 29–30

Family Rights and Privacy Act (FERPA) 30
Ferguson's Developmental Model of Community Involvement 200, 205–7
First Step to Success 187

free appropriate public education (FAPE) 5, 22, 220
functional behavioral assessment (FBA) 44, 51, 86

Glasser, William 116–17
goal: annual 80–1, 84; behavior 87, 115; career 156, 158; counseling 83, 112; educational 78; program 11–12; individual 106; performance 30; program 13; setting 145, 165–6
graduation 88, 163, 169; rates of students with disabilities 212, 224, 226

hearing impairment 37, 39–40, 53–5, 68, 121, 232
HELPING model 106

independent living 81, 159, 163, 174–5
Individual Education Program (IEP) 21–3, 27–9, 31, 78–98
Individual Psychology Theory 110–12
Individualized Family Service Plan (IFSP) 21, 73, 157
Individuals with Disabilities Education Act (IDEA) of 1997 (P.L. 105-17) 21
Individuals with Disabilities Education Improvement Act (IDEIA) of 2004 (P.L. 108-446) 20, 156, 160, 186 *see also* Individuals with Disabilities Education Act (IDEA) of 1997 (P.L. 105-17)
intellectual disability 39, 47–9, 118–19, 232–3
intervention: academic 86; ASD 41, 192; environmental supports 41, 86; pre-referral 65; social skill 192 *see* applied behavior analysis

leadership 15
learning goals *see* educational goal
least restrictive environment 20, 22, 88, 90
legal mandates *see* specific
literature, in counseling 126–7, 233

motivational interviewing (MI) 105, 233
multicultural 129, 212–13, 235
multiple disabilities (MD) 39, 50, 233
multifactored evaluation (MFE) 65, 68, 70, 78
music, in counseling 133–4

narrative counseling 121–3
neuroscience 133, 212–13
No Child Left Behind (NCLB) 4–5, 29–30

operant conditioning 112
other health impairment 37, 40, 51, 164
orthopedic impairment (OI) *see* physical disabilities

parental participation 20, 23
peer-mediated instructional approaches 46
person centered counseling 108–10
pervasive developmental disorder *see* autism spectrum disorder
physical disabilities 37, 39–40, 51
play, in counseling 132, 134
Positive Behavioral Interventions and Supports (PBIS) 44, 66, 189–91
procedural safeguards 23, 68
Project Achieve 190
Project Pathe 190

Rational-Emotive Behavioral Therapy 119–21
Reality Therapy 116–17
referral activities *see* multifactored evaluation
Rehabilitation Act of 1973 24, 94, 170–1, 221, 231
Response to Intervention (RTI) 24, 65–6, 186–8
Rogers, Carl 108

SAMIC acronym 116
school: administrator 30–2, 92, 182, 184; climate 180–1, 221; culture 180, 189, 216; nurse 9, 82, 182; psychologist 69, 92, 112, 182; resource officer 182; social worker 182
scriptotherapy *see* literature, in counseling
Second Step 187
Section 24–9, 52, 71–5, 91–8, 220–1
self: *actualization* 108; advocacy 86, 151–3, 162; affirmation 110; assessment 12; concept 45, 55, 86, 108–9; determination 51; efficacy 106; management 53; monitoring 51, 53, 86
social stories 127–8, 130, 193, 233
Solution-focused Brief Counseling 117–19
specific learning disability (SLD) 40, 65–7, 152
speech or language impairment 23, 40, 58–9, 82, 231–2
students who are twice-exceptional 59–60
summary of performance 24
systemic change 11, 15–16

theories, counseling *see* specific models
transition 87–8, 156, 169; early childhood 157–8; groups 152; post-secondary 158–65, 171, 234
traumatic brain injury (TBI) 23, 37, 40, 49

visual impairments including blindness 37, 39–40, 55–6, 232

WDEP system 116

zero rejection 20, 22

Taylor & Francis eBooks

Helping you to choose the right eBooks for your Library

Add Routledge titles to your library's digital collection today. Taylor and Francis ebooks contains over 50,000 titles in the Humanities, Social Sciences, Behavioural Sciences, Built Environment and Law.

Choose from a range of subject packages or create your own!

Benefits for you

» Free MARC records
» COUNTER-compliant usage statistics
» Flexible purchase and pricing options
» All titles DRM-free.

Benefits for your user

» Off-site, anytime access via Athens or referring URL
» Print or copy pages or chapters
» Full content search
» Bookmark, highlight and annotate text
» Access to thousands of pages of quality research at the click of a button.

 Free Trials Available
We offer free trials to qualifying academic, corporate and government customers.

eCollections – Choose from over 30 subject eCollections, including:

Archaeology	Language Learning
Architecture	Law
Asian Studies	Literature
Business & Management	Media & Communication
Classical Studies	Middle East Studies
Construction	Music
Creative & Media Arts	Philosophy
Criminology & Criminal Justice	Planning
Economics	Politics
Education	Psychology & Mental Health
Energy	Religion
Engineering	Security
English Language & Linguistics	Social Work
Environment & Sustainability	Sociology
Geography	Sport
Health Studies	Theatre & Performance
History	Tourism, Hospitality & Events

For more information, pricing enquiries or to order a free trial, please contact your local sales team:
www.tandfebooks.com/page/sales

 Routledge
Taylor & Francis Group

The home of
Routledge books

www.tandfebooks.com